Business in the Humane Society

John J. Corson

McGraw-Hill Book Company

NEW YORK   ST. LOUIS   SAN FRANCISCO   DÜSSELDORF   LONDON
MEXICO   PANAMA   SYDNEY   TORONTO

To Ellen, Laney, John Jay, and Cathy—
May they understand the change that will envelop them

HD
3616
446
C 64

BUSINESS IN THE HUMANE SOCIETY

Library of Congress Catalog Card Number 75-126171

07-013185-6

1234567890 VBVB 754321

Sponsoring Editor M. Joseph Dooher / Dale L. Dutton
Director of Production Stephen J. Boldish
Editing Supervisor Linda B. Hander
Designer Naomi Auerbach
Editing and Production Staff Gretlyn Blau, Teresa F. Leaden, George E. Oechsner

Preface

Business in the Humane Society is distilled from a lifetime spent in each of the three principal sectors of the American society—in academia, in business, and in public service. I have been privileged to serve almost equal thirds of my adult life in each sector and perhaps especially privileged to have been able to move back and forth a succession of times. In each of the past four decades, I have served in each sector.

The yeast that prompts the distillation found between the covers of this book is the change—substantial and rapid— that confronts scholars, businessmen, and government officials alike with irritating questions as to whether established concepts and notions still hold. To challenge the verities of systems of economic thought and political theory, the essentiality of profit as the guiding objective of all enterprise, and the logic of the axiom that public functions shall only be performed by public servants is disturbing indeed. But change—induced by population growth, by urbanization, by technological advance, by the collapse of space (physical and cultural alike), by organizational growth, and by the substantial increase of national and personal wealth—has posed these and other challenges.

It has been said that nothing is so invisible as the obvious. The truth of this assertion is suggested by the descriptions offered in this volume of the arrangements developed in this country for the performance of an expanding variety of social objectives. Well before the campus and ghetto riots of the late 1960s, there was an awareness—among scholars, if not among businessmen and government officials—that this country's citizens were demanding the fulfillment of unmet needs. But there was, and there is, little awareness of the extent to which traditional institutions —business, government, the universities, and others—have been adapted and knit together in a politico-economic system which differs conspicuously from the venerated pattern of our past.

What I have tried to do in this book is to point up how the changing values of the American people have established new objectives for their society, and how our institutions and the ways in which they are interrelated have been adapted in order to achieve these objectives. Even those readers of this volume who are familiar with the Washington scene, I venture, will be impressed with the magnitude and scope of the subsidy, contract, grant, and regulatory processes as they have evolved in recent decades. What I hope all readers will find fresh and revealing is the depiction of the extension of these and other processes into a modified and strengthened politico-economic system by which a society satisfies not only an expanding but also a changed variety of human wants.

I have been helped to see the nature of this evolution in the American politico-economic system by a stimulating group of approximately fifty business and governmental leaders that has met monthly for five years to examine and discuss the adaptations as they have become apparent. I was aided in forming this group in 1963 by Elmer Staats, then Deputy Director of the U.S. Bureau of the Budget and now Comptroller General of the United States, and by Charles E. Wampler, then vice-president and secretary of the American Telephone and Telegraph Company and now retired. Throughout the ensuing years not only Messrs. Staats and Wampler but also other busy executives traveled regularly from New York, Pittsburgh, Detroit, and elsewhere to meet and exchange views on the developments that add up to the modified and strengthened politico-economic system that I shall describe. I cannot claim that any one of my colleagues in what we have come to call the Business-Government Relations Seminar shares my conception of the whole; I know that my thinking has been greatly helped by the penetrating questions and views they have expressed.

The utility of this seminar and of the research that I undertook in 1963 and completed in 1969 was fortunately—but not surprisingly—recognized by those three perceptive and enterprising minds that have led the Carnegie Corporation during the decade of the 1960s: John W. Gardner, James A. Perkins, and Alan Pifer. Since 1963, they have provided not only the financial support required but also the encouragement that stimulated the investment of as many as 5,000 evening and weekend hours in the inquiry that underlies this volume.

I am also indebted to that other patron of would-be scholars, the Rockefeller Foundation, for the privilege of putting in perhaps 200 vacation hours at work on this volume while a guest at the Foundation's Villa Serbelloni on Lake Como during the summer of 1965.

That support made possible the assistance of Professor Charles T. Goodsell, now associate professor of political science at the University of Southern Illinois, during the academic years 1963–1964 and 1964–1965. Professor Goodsell contributed substantially and capably to the formulation of the early framework of this volume, to the organization and nurturing of the Business-Government Relations Seminar, and to the research that supports substantial sections of this volume. Only the pursuit of his academic career and our geographical separation prevented the continuation of a fruitful collaboration.

During the subsequent years I have been aided by Mrs. Ruth Crow and Mrs. Marta Erdman who, in turn, have assisted me as research and editorial assistants. During the past two years, as each chapter has been taking final shape, Mrs. Erdman has rendered invaluable, meticulous, and patient assistance. I am greatly indebted to her. And I am indebted to three friends and scholars—Mrs. Elizabeth S. May, former dean, Wheaton College (Massachusetts) and former member of the Export-Import Bank Board; Leonard S. Silk, former editor of *Business Week* and now senior staff member of The Brookings Institution, Washington, D.C.; and Dexter Keezer, economic advisor, McGraw-Hill, Inc., whose reading and criticism of each chapter have led to many changes for the better. The richness of their experience has contributed meaningfully to such insights as this volume offers.

Finally, I owe a large debt to my wife who, with unfailing generosity, not only shared my time with "the book" but shielded me from a thousand interruptions while I read and wrote.

John J. Corson

Contents

PART 1
Expanding Wants and Roles

CHAPTER 1

Changes in
the American Politico-economy

O_N the eighteenth day of April, 1906, a cow was standing somewhere between the main barn and the milking shed on the old Shafter Ranch in California, minding her own business. Suddenly, the earth shook, the skies trembled, and when it was all over, there was nothing showing of the cow above the ground but a bit of her tail.

The Shafter cow had stood thinking such gentle thoughts as cows may have, while huge forces outside her ken built up all around her and within a minute changed the configuration of the earth, destroyed a city, and swallowed her up.[1]

Analogously, a number of forces outside the customary concern of businessmen have been changing the configuration of the envi-

[1] Adapted from "The Dynamics of Change," *Kaiser Aluminum News,* vol. 24, no. 1, 1966.

ronment within which businessmen operate. Blind to these forces, many businessmen have attributed the change that has been taking place in the roles of business and government to the fact that the Democrats have been in power throughout most of the 40 years preceding 1970 or to the bureaucrats' distrust of the profit system. Few recognize that "behind institutions, behind constitutional forms and modifications," as one historian has written, "lie the vital forces that call these organs to life and shape them to meet changing conditions." [2]

CHANGING COMPOSITION OF POPULATION

During the postwar years this country's population has grown nearly 40 percent. But the population under 25 years of age and 65 and over has increased approximately 75 percent. By 1969 more than half of the total population was made up of individuals 25 years of age and less, and more than one-eighth of the population was over 65. This substantial growth of the population, and particularly of the younger age groups, means that the labor force of this country—i.e., that part of the population old enough (and not too old), able, and willing to work—will grow more in the decade of the 1970s than in any previous 10 years in our history.

These changes in the composition of this nation's population constitute the first of the vital forces shaping history. This force has propelled government into the job of educating and training more young people than ever before; of finding work for them; of ensuring housing for more new families each year; of providing supplementary income for more aged people when they can no longer work; and of providing the aged poor with health care.

URBANIZATION

Between 1946 and 1970 the proportion of this nation's population living in metropolitan areas has grown from approxi-

[2] F. J. Turner, "The Frontier in American History," in Jacob W. Landynski (ed.), "The Making of Constitutional Law," *Social Research*, vol. 31, pp. 23–43, 1964. Thomas Jefferson similarly said a century and a half earlier (July 12, 1815), "With the change of circumstances, institutions must advance also to keep pace with the times. . . ."

mately 56 percent to more than 66 percent. By the year 2000 it is estimated that it will have reached 78 percent!

Urbanization (and the accompanying trend, suburbanization) has brought with it problems of unemployment, inner-city transportation, pollution, waste disposal, housing, and education, all of which are aggravated by serious racial problems.

These problems stem from the simple fact that the pattern of life of millions living in metropolitan areas in 1970 differs markedly from the life their counterparts led a quarter of a century ago. The changes that have taken place as a consequence of the vast growth of big cities—changes in their jobs, homes, travel, recreation, and in their family relationships—have given rise to governmental activities that affect businessmen in various ways.

A single, homely illustration makes clear the kind of change and its implication. In my grandmother's home of eight bedrooms, on the edge of a small town, twelve members of the family, representing three generations, regularly met for lunch. Grandmother wouldn't have it otherwise! At lunchtime the whole family knew of any adventure, misfortune, or success experienced by each. Among that family was Cousin Fanny, an aged widow left penniless at her husband's death, whom grandmother *naturally* had taken in. In my son's three-bedroom home in the suburbs of a large city, no lunch is served, no aunts and uncles live, and there is no room in which Cousin Fanny could be tucked away. In the half century between my childhood and my grandchildren's, the pattern of family life has changed as much as has the physical character of the typical home.

TECHNOLOGICAL ADVANCE

A vast increase in new knowledge in every field, from abattoir management to zoology—technological advance, we call it—has created a new relationship between, on the one hand, study and research in basic science—traditionally the task of the university scholars—and, on the other hand, the creation of new products, new production processes, new services, and new weapons— traditionally the task of businessmen.

Old methods of invention are uncommon.[3] Watt's invention of

[3] Hendrik W. Bode in "Reflections on the Relation between Science and Technology" (in *Basic Research and National Goals,* a report by the National Academy of Sciences, 1965) points out that it has become increasingly apparent that basic research in science must precede further technological

the steam engine, Marconi's invention of the radio, and the Wright Brothers' development of the airplane were the result of intuition. But the transistor, Dacron, the polio vaccine, instant photography, the computer, and Corfam were the result of step-by-step advance from basic scientific knowledge. In short, basic research now precedes each subsequent step in technological advance.

This vast increase in knowledge, and recognition of what rich benefits it yields, have prompted a massive effort on the part of government to develop this country's scientific capability. The most apparent portion of this effort is the basic research contracted for by government as a means of developing new weapons and new space exploration gadgetry. But this effort also includes large expenditures for the support of education, for basic research in the universities (in many fields in addition to aerospace and electronics), and for the training of scientists and engineers.

That massive effort has been warmly supported because Americans generally believe that research will meet almost any need—an artificial heart; a cure for cancer; new methods of instruction or new methods of destruction; devices for the diagnosis of illness, the control of weather, and whatnot. It has been supported also by increasing recognition that a great and advancing scientific and technological capability is essential for military strength and for economic growth.

Two significant consequences for businessmen flow out of this new development.

First, the university, with government support, is assuming much of the creative function that heretofore has been, in large part, within the domain of business; e.g., a government contract with scholars at the Massachusetts Institute of Technology resulted in the development of a new curriculum for the study of

advance. Nelson, Peck, and Kalachek [in *Technology, Economic Growth and Public Policy* (Washington: The Brookings Institution, 1967), pp. 39–40] claim that "The growing relevance of science to invention has had four major consequences." First, it "has greatly raised the importance of formal education as a factor in invention. . . . Second, invention has become more of a separate activity, rather than one carried out on the shop floor as a joint product with current production. . . . Third, inventive efforts have significantly increased in those fields and on those problems which most fruitfully could exploit scientific knowledge. . . . Finally, by providing a context of knowledge for existing technology, advances in sciences have led to a succession of radical technological advances."

physics in secondary schools and the displacement of a textbook created and distributed by a private publishing firm. Some predict that within the next quarter century most of the new processes and new products will have their origins in university laboratories rather than in business firms.

Second, government has assumed risk taking which once was borne by business. Government assumes responsibility for the invention of new products, new processes, and new services through contracts for research that underwrite business expenditures and via grants to the universities for research and development.

ORGANIZATIONAL GROWTH

Since the close of World War II, big corporations, big government, big unions, big trade associations, big universities, big hospitals, and big churches have proliferated in the United States and in other advanced countries. Indeed, every segment of our life is organized. From the corporation that produces breakfast food, the national church organization that syndicates a daily sermon to radio stations, the commercial club that sells us the use of a swimming pool and tennis courts, the antismoking organization that will, in return for our contributions, wage a holy war against cigarettes, to the company that manufactures eyeshades to wear while sleeping—we rely on organizations for many goods and services the individual once provided.

The power and strategic importance of large organizations in our economic, political, and social affairs have become increasingly apparent. In our economic life, it is apparent in the products we buy, in the source of our wages and salaries, and in the welfare of our cities. In our political life, it is apparent in the activities of such organizations as the American Medical Association, the AFL-CIO, the Teamsters, the U.S. Chamber of Commerce, the National Education Association. the U.S. Conference of Mayors, the NAACP, and many others which endeavor to influence legislative actions, the election of candidates, and local decisions as to tax rates, the building of bridges and freeways, the development of schools, or the level of welfare payments. In our social life, it is apparent in the status a man holds in a big corporation, in big government, or in a big union. That status determines, in principal part, the social position his family enjoys, the clubs in which he will be accepted, and often influences even the kind of clothes he wears. And surely the growth of large organization can be seen in the size and activities of big government.

A key consequence of the development of large business organization and large government organization is the evolution of a series of interlocking partnerships between the two. Much has been written on the military-industrial complex. Similar "complexes" obtain in the fields of highway construction, health, housing, and education. And analogous complexes have grown up between government and the universities and government and the hospitals. The implications of this development are as yet little explored. Are we observing the evolution of a fundamentally new economic system which resembles both traditional free enterprise and a fascistic corporate state? Or are we seeing the establishment of a pluralism that distributes power among a multiplicity of organizations and limits its concentration either in big government or big business?

PERSISTING WAR AND COLD WAR

Wars have been looked upon traditionally as an aberration. Peace is, we have thought, the normal condition; war, we have reasoned, is an abnormal, painful condition to be done with as quickly as possible. But, since World War II, facts have belied this prevailing belief. The United States has been at war, or involved in a cold war, continuously for three decades. That involvement has necessitated the maintenance of the largest standing military force this country has ever known. It has claimed the facilities of a substantial proportion of this country's manufacturing facilities for the production of war matériel—lessening the amount they could produce for the civilian economy, even while technological advance was spurred on. It has fanned the flames of a devouring inflation. It has created the military-industrial complex against which President Dwight D. Eisenhower warned in 1960, suggesting that military leaders and industrialists found it mutually advantageous to perpetuate war.

The fear of this complex and its consequences in terms of an authoritarian and repressive government reached unprecedented proportions in 1969 when a variety of public leaders—a retired commander of the Marine Corps among them—warned the American people against the "threat of militarism." [4]

The five forces that have been depicted—population growth, urbanization, technological advance, organizational growth, and chronic war—lie at the root of changes that have taken place in government-business relations. To understand the impact of these forces on this relationship, however, let us look next at two secondary forces that flow directly from these primary forces: the collapse of space and the growth of national wealth.

COLLAPSE OF SPACE

Advances in the technologies of transportation and communication, population growth and shifts, and the growth of larger and larger organizations have created a society in which we live infinitely closer together than ever before.

■ *An international society.*   The jet plane and the communications satellite have shrunk this world. These inventions have not only enabled us to visit, to communicate, to trade, and to fight with peoples on every continent, but have also involved us in their economic, social, and political affairs. What happens in the Middle East, in Biafra, and in Vietnam now affects the taxes Americans pay, the profitability of business enterprises, the thoughts Americans think, and the ways they vote.

■ *A national society.*   We live closer together; we live physically closer together in the cities where most of us reside—note the massive urban apartment centers, the congestion of commuters on the freeways morning and afternoon, the lines to the supermarket checker or to the first tee of the public golf course. And the telephone, the telegraph, radio, television, and the printing press bind us closer to relatives, friends, suppliers, customers, and debtors who reside even the width of a continent away.

■ *A national economy.*   We live economically closer together;

[4] See, for example, a speech before the National War College by Senator J. W. Fulbright, May 19, 1969; a speech before the Jewish Center in Kansas City, Mo., by Senator Stuart W. Symington, May 16, 1969; an article by Marine General David M. Shoup, "The New American Militarism," *The Atlantic,* April, 1969; an article by J. K. Galbraith, "How to Control the Military," *Harper's,* June, 1969.

we live in what is truly a national economy—not a series of regional or local economies. Most families are vitally affected by the quality of the products made, the prices charged, the wages paid, and the subcontracting of no more than 100 national enterprises such as General Dynamics, General Electric, General Foods, General Mills, General Motors, General Tire and Rubber, and, let us add, AT&T.

■ *A national polity.* National magazines, radio, and TV confront citizens in every nook and cranny of this land with the political issues of the day—civil rights, Vietnam, the Middle East, Medicare, corruption in Congress, or the latest space flight. These media involve all of us more fully in the political life of the country. They have brought about a significant shift from "organization politics" to "participation politics"; they have created a situation in which a candidate for national office, or the spokesman for an issue, can go over the heads of organizations and delegates and appeal directly to the citizenry and lead them.[5]

None of us can know all the consequences of this collapse of space. But it seems clear that Daniel Bell is correct when he writes that "with the formulation of a national society the Federal government has gained a greater awareness of social needs, of the importance of anticipating and directing social change, and it has obtained a centralization of power unique to the American society."[6]

THE GROWTH OF WEALTH

The gross national product has more than doubled, in real terms, since 1946. Personal disposable income has substantially increased; that is, while more than 77 percent of the average family's budget went for food, clothing, and shelter in the 1920s, about 55 percent was required to meet these expenditures in the late 1960s.

As our national and our personal wealth have grown, our wants as individuals—and as a people—have expanded. As individuals, we have expanded our wants for food, clothing, and

[5] Tom Wicker, "In the Nation: The New Politics," *New York Times*, Mar. 21, 1968.

[6] *The Reforming of General Education* (New York: Columbia University Press, 1966), p. 73.

shelter in many ways; a higher standard of living offers more and better food, clothing, and shelter. In addition, more Americans —many more in 1969 than in 1946—can and do satisfy luxury wants for vacations, sailboats, the second or third car, the swimming pool in the backyard, or membership in golf clubs. As a people, we want more and better education at all levels and for all citizens. We want more medical and hospital services [7] and safe and cheap drugs. We want more and better housing for low-income families. We want—for the least fortunate in the richest society the world has ever seen—rehabilitative services, financial aid, and special education, health, and recreational services. We want pure air and pure rivers and streams. We want more in the way of recreation facilities and more access to the arts—the libraries, the theater, the opera, and the orchestra.[8]

THE EMERGING HUMANE SOCIETY

With the aid of science, technology, and effective industrial organization, the Industrial Society of the first five decades of the twentieth century in the United States enabled many Americans to satisfy an increasing variety of individual wants. Manufacturing was the principal source of employment. Progress was dependent upon the idol of the times, the production executive, i.e., the plant or works manager who harnessed men, materials, and machines in an effective effort to produce more and more. Productivity grew apace. The processes of industrialization—engineered work standards, the assembly line, and the increasing specialization of labor—were developed, and more recently automation was extensively introduced and the computer assigned a growing variety of tasks.

[7] The then president of the American Medical Association provoked a vigorous debate in 1967, when he asserted that medical care must be recognized by Americans as a privilege they can earn, not a right to which all are entitled. See "Is Health Care a Right or a Privilege?" *New York Times,* July 2, 1967.

[8] John W. Gardner has pointed out [*Excellence* (New York: Harper & Row, Publishers, Incorporated, 1961), p. 149] that the question "What's in it for me?" reflects an attitude "born of deep habituation to the marketing of one's energies in return for the necessities of life." In an affluent society in which we strive to provide a better quality of life for all citizens, do different motivations prevail for the individual?

Business enterprise occupied the center of the stage. As it progressed, it created and satisfied an ever-broadening range of material wants. Until the Depression of the 1930s, the role of government was limited to the satisfaction of a narrow range of social (as distinguished from individual) wants—national defense, the delivery of the mails, the provision of education, the construction of roads, and the maintenance of order. Government was repeatedly admonished not to interfere with or to burden the generator of progress—business enterprise.

The Post-Industrial Society was ushered in by the end of World War II. It was founded on a service economy. For the first time in history, the majority of all working people were engaged in the provision of services: in selling, banking and insurance (and, increasingly, small loan banking), selling and managing real estate, teaching, research, carrying on governmental activities, the rental of automobiles, the preparation of "convenience foods," hair dressing, podiatry, the provision of health care, and particularly the provision of rapidly developing transport and communications services. The entrepreneur of these times— the 1950s and the 1960s—created a chain of restaurants (Howard Johnson's or Marriott's, for example) or a chain of nursing homes, supermarkets, laundromats, slenderizing parlors, small loan companies, an automobile rental service (Avis, for example), a television station, or labor supply offices (the "Kelly girls," for example). Government's role expanded markedly; its expenditures for defense grew precipitously, but (fortunately) its expenditures for the satisfaction of social wants—i.e., for education, health care, the welfare of the least fortunate, and the support of scientific advance—grew just as rapidly.

The Post-Industrial Society was increasingly a professional and technical society. While the total labor force grew about one-third from the war's end to 1970, the number of professional and technical workers grew twice as fast, and the number of scientific and engineering workers grew even more rapidly. This latter growth reflected an even more fundamental characteristic. The Post-Industrial Society increasingly depended on the discovery, generation, and application of new knowledge. The developing industries of the 1960s bespeak the point. The chemical, computer, cryogenics, electronic, fluoritics, and plastics industries grew out of an expanding theoretical knowledge and an ever more fertile basic science.

NATURE OF NEXT SOCIAL STAGE

The character of the next social stage this country will experience is suggested by the insistent demands of the poor, the Negroes, and the students for a stop to the waste of war and a reordering of national priorities. These demands are rooted in the extensive communications system that has come into being: millions of people have moved into cities where they see and learn much in everyday contacts; television brings into the homes of nine out of every ten families a continuing picture of "how the other half lives." It is one thing to be poor and not know how much better off others are; it is another thing to be made aware recurrently of the better fortune of others. An obvious result has been that the needs of people in Harlem, in Watts, in Fayette, Mississippi, in South Side Chicago, or on the Indian reservations have been made widely known.

But the Humane Society that is gradually emerging is not to be an elaboration of the Welfare State against which businessmen railed in the 1940s and 1950s. Indeed, in contrast, the Welfare State will be viewed in retrospect as a pinchpenny conception of what the society is obligated to do for all its members, not merely for those who are poor.[9] The Humane Society is being shaped by the forces of change that have been depicted, by the demands of those who want to share more fully in the richness of this land, and by the sympathy with which such demands are viewed by political, business, and civic leaders. And thus, one can see emerging—if he is not blinded by dislike of the prospect —a social structure in which five additional concepts are firmly established.

■ *The concept of an expanding "national minimum."* The idea that every family shall be provided a decent minimum income originated with enactment of the Social Security Act in

[9] Arnold Toynbee has said that we stand on the threshold of an age which will be remembered as "the first since the dawn of history in which mankind dared to believe it practical to make the benefits of civilization available to the whole human race." Paul McCracken, chairman of the Council of Economic Advisers under President Nixon, in less extensive terms pointed to "a rapid, even accelerating advance toward a more egalitarian social and economic system" in remarks before the Economic and Political Forum of the U.S. Chamber of Commerce, Santa Barbara, Calif., Dec. 5, 1967.

1935. That idea has been expanded by each succeeding national administration, Republican as forthrightly as Democratic. The idea as expanded has leapt over such traditional precepts as "any able-bodied man or woman should not be given relief, but should work for a living" and "the society should not support the mother of illegitimate children and her bastard progeny." Gradually, it also has been extended to provide not just the indigent but all low-income families with needed health care through Medicaid, with publicly subsidized housing through other provisions, and with higher education for all those capable of benefiting from it.

■ *A modernized concept of human equality.* The innate worth of the individual was recognized in the American Constitution, but that recognition meant little for many citizens throughout the next century and a half. The civil rights revolution of the 1960s won for the Negroes and other minorities the right to vote in many states and improved education and job opportunities. But dignity in the sense of truly equal status in the eyes of his fellowman is not yet a reality for many Americans—Negroes, Mexicans, Indians, Jews, the young, and others. The pressure for equal status obviously will continue. It will bring greater equality of access to housing, education, and jobs, greater opportunity for promotion and, as these rights are wrested, greater social equality.

■ *A concept of self-fulfillment.* A true recognition of the worth of each individual will be accompanied by growing emphasis on the obligation of the individual to achieve his full potential (be it to become the best bricklayer or best biologist) and on the obligation of the society to eliminate all obstacles to that achievement.

A start at the elimination of such obstacles is manifest in the expansion of educational opportunity, for adults as well as youth, and in the expansion of training in the work establishment—in the emergence of the idea that routine repetitive work be replaced by assignments that offer opportunity to grow and advance on the job. Eliminating obstacles to achievement is apparent, too, in the reduction of racial discrimination and in the granting to many individuals of a larger voice in decisions that affect them.

But in an urban, computerized society of large organizations, fulfillment requires in addition that the individual be given scope, not be dwarfed and made anonymous; that he be encouraged, in the vernacular of the times, "to do his thing." The pressures to eliminate the obstacles to fulfillment in this sense are increasingly apparent.

The development of this concept of self-fulfillment will comprehend an extensive effort to help many Americans see that as they are granted a greater voice, they assume an obligation not "just to stand there" but to pitch in and improve their neighborhoods, schools, and homes and make the cities more responsive to the needs of the people who reside there. It will involve simultaneously the assumption by government of responsibility for enlarging the educational, cultural (art, music, and drama), and recreational facilities.[10]

■ *The concept of a livable environment.* The blue skies; clear, pure streams and lakes; fresh air; and lovely views that the poets made synonymous with America have been lost or impaired by the growth of population and the rush of people to the cities. The gross inadequacy of our cities for human habitation was recognized by a few in the first third of this century, but general recognition came like a bombshell in the 1960s.

That recognition bred a multiple demand which will gradually bring about more and better homes for a growing population, almost half of which cannot pay from their limited incomes the costs of decent housing. It will bring about simultaneously the redesign and reconstruction of the center city of every metropolis. It will bring about the elimination of air and water pollution. And that recognition will give birth to a new emphasis on the physical beauty of our cities and of the roadsides connecting one city with another.

The evolution of this concept was forecast by the contention made by the American Civil Liberties Union when it sued to

[10] A study by McKinsey & Company, Inc., of the financial condition of five major United States symphony orchestras in May, 1969, revealed that, despite the fact that most concerts were sold out, each orchestra faced "a severe economic crisis" and recommended that these orchestras seek essential additional grants from corporations and from the federal government.

Alvin Toffler poses the following questions in his article, "The Art of Measuring the Arts," *The Annals*, September, 1967: Should the Department of Labor, in determining for its own statistical purposes the minimally decent family budget, allow some amount in it for music lessons or art supplies? Can family life be truly "decent" if there is no allowance for music or art in it?

shut down the oil drills that polluted the Santa Barbara channel. The ACLU contended that the Constitution, when interpreted in light of conditions as they were in 1969, guarantees each individual "the right to live in and enjoy an environment free from improvident destruction or pollution."

■ *An expanded concept of consumer protection.* Belief in the doctrine "let the buyer beware" was made obsolete as the range of products and services the individual family buys was markedly broadened. In fact, the individual cannot effectively judge the quality, safety, utility, or real worth of the articles—new foods, drugs, appliances, clothing (Fortrel or Dacron, for example), automobile, lawn mower, snow thrower, or house—he must buy, or of the installment loan agreement or insurance policies he must sign from time to time.

To aid the consumer, a large body of legislation has been enacted,[11] and federal, state, and local governments have accepted in varying degrees the obligation of assuring the safety, purity, quality, and efficacy of many products and services and the reliability of statements made in advertising about them. These efforts by government enable the consumer to buy with assurance an ever-increasing range of complex items. These efforts also place on the producer the burden of abiding by steadily rising standards imposed by governmental regulators.

The Humane Society will be, in summary, increasingly people-oriented; it will rely less (yet predominantly) on goods and services produced for the market and more on publicly provided services, many of which are not yet envisioned. It will require, and will develop, a new body of professional educators, health workers, social workers, environmentalists, recreationists, consumers' counsel, and public inspectors. And it will be dependent upon the gradual expansion, refinement, and application of knowledge of economics, history, psychology, physiology, sociology, and process of governance. What the hard sciences did for the Post-Industrial Society, the soft sciences will be called upon to do for the Humane Society.

---

[11] The Consumer Credit Protection Act of 1968, popularly known as the Truth-in-Lending Act, illustrates such legislation. The prospect for still more extensive governmental action was forecast by President Nixon's recommendations to the Congress on Oct. 30, 1969, which he described as a "buyer's bill of rights."

RESHAPING THE POLITICAL ECONOMY

Historians in the twenty-first century, with the benefit of hindsight, will write that the composite impact of the seven elemental forces enumerated in this chapter gave rise to three persistent and related movements that markedly reshaped the nature of this country's political economy.

The first is the progressive expansion of the public interest. The public interest is an ill-defined or undefinable term. But the pragmatic processes of representative government have determined during the twentieth century that the provision of income to needy children and aged, disabled, and other persons is as much an element of the public interest as is the provision of roads for all to ride on; that the prices of drugs as well as water, gas, and electricity are affected as a result of the public interest; that the pollution of the air and the water or the hazards of the highways are threats to the public interest as great as the communication of typhoid fever.

In short, Americans laid the groundwork for the Humane Society by redefining what they regard as the responsibility of all the people, as distinguished from what is the responsibility of the individual and his family. Gilbert Fitzhugh, chairman of the board of the Metropolitan Life Insurance Company, has explained why. "It is," he said, "the demands of the American people that pushed government into assuming an ever increasing role."[12]

The second movement is a gradual blurring of the dividing line between "private" and "public." The expansion of the public interest has meant that a larger proportion of all goods, and especially services, are not bought by the individual or the family to suit his (or its) needs and tastes, but are provided by government or an agency (e.g., the Public Housing Authority) sanctioned and supported by government. Increasingly, government,

[12] "Business-Government Relationships in a Changing World," an address before the New York Chamber of Commerce, Dec. 7, 1967. See also James Tobin, "Frontier between Business and Government," *National Economic Policy* (New Haven, Conn.: Yale University Press, 1966), chap. 2, and J. M. Clark, "The Interpenetration of Politics and Economics," *Economic Institutions and Human Welfare* (New York: Alfred A. Knopf, Inc., 1961), chap. 10, pp. 226–244.

not the market, has decided in such areas as health care, education, transportation, housing, and urban development what facilities and services shall be provided.

As Americans "pushed government into assuming an ever-increasing role," they were confronted with the choice between steadily enlarging the machinery of government or finding ways to entrust to nongovernmental agencies (business firms and others) responsibility for carrying out public functions—from the building of aircraft and missiles to the operation of Job Corps camps and the direct employment of the "hard-core unemployed." They chose the latter course.

As a consequence, in 1969 a number of federal agencies (NASA, for example) performed more of their work through contracts with private business firms than they performed with their own employees. Each of a dozen private business firms (North American Aviation, for example) spent more federal tax dollars than any of a dozen of such federal agencies as the Department of Labor or the Federal Power Commission. Hundreds of nonprofit agencies, many of them created by the federal government, were contracted with to perform a wide range of public services.

And, commencing in the late 1960s, government encouraged business to perform at its own expense an increasing variety of tasks that had been regarded as governmental responsibilities. Among these are: providing jobs for the hard-core unemployed, including establishing plants in the ghettos; aiding in establishing new businesses to be managed by minority group members; building new housing in the ghettos or rebuilding the ghettos; [13] providing increased health care, education, and, in some instances, transportation to and from work for their employees; and curbing air and water pollution.

The dividing line between private and public has been still further blurred by a series of actions by the Congress and decisions of the Supreme Court. Mr. Winton Blount, then president of the U.S. Chamber of Commerce, asserted in mid-1968 that "property rights have been forgotten as a basic human right and have been lost in many places because of lack of government

---

[13] For example, on Aug. 12, 1969, the General Motors Corporation announced the lending of $1.1 million without interest to a nonprofit black housing corporation, Harambee, to construct more than 500 housing units to wipe out much of the slums in Pontiac, Mich.

protection." [14] Six years earlier Robert McCloskey, in a brilliant analysis of Supreme Court decisions, demonstrated that Congress (the representatives of the people) had enacted a series of statutes that limited the rights of the private property owner, the private employer, and the private marketer of goods (automobiles, drugs, shares of stock) and services wherever it deemed the choice to be property rights or personal rights, and that the Supreme Court (the interpreter of the Constitution) had upheld these statutes over the past two decades.[15]

The third movement has been a continual extension of governmental intervention into the functioning of the economy and the functioning of the individual enterprise. As government assumed responsibility for an increasing variety of functions, it sought and found ways (and expanded its use of old ways) to influence the allocation of national resources; that is, to direct national resources to purposes deemed by the Congress or governmental executives to deserve especial priority and away from those purposes to which the market would allocate these resources.

It made available massive amounts of credit to stimulate the construction of housing, to encourage small business enterprises, and to encourage the development of trade with underdeveloped countries. It provided tax credits to encourage the expansion and modernization of the machinery and equipment of productive enterprises. It made large payments to farmers to limit their production and made large grants for research to speed technological advance. It contracted with more than a thousand nonprofit agencies to involve the poor in the elimination of poverty in this country. And it developed and expanded its processes of economic planning to ensure that its activities as the nation's tax collector, as its largest employer, customer, and borrower, and as the regulator of money and credit were consistently related in an effort to speed national economic growth, limit unemployment, and constrain inflation.

Simultaneously, government expanded its regulation of indi-

---

[14] In a speech before the National Press Club, June 27, 1968.

[15] "Economic Due Process and the Supreme Court: An Exhumation and Reburial," *The Supreme Court Review,* University of Chicago Press, Chicago, 1962. For a more recent illustration see decision in *Amalgamated Food Employees, University Local 590 et al. v. Logan Valley Plaza, Inc. et al.,* May 20, 1968.

vidual enterprises in order to assure that their activities served the public interest. Its expanding concern with the health of individuals resulted in regulation of the industrial pollution of the atmosphere, the rivers, and the streams; of the efficacy of drugs; of the safety of automobiles and automobile tires; and of the advertising of cigarettes. Its expanding concern for the consumer has resulted in efforts to assure the quality and purity of products and to better inform the consumer; in some instances, government's desire to protect the consumer has involved the limiting of price increases. Its expanding concern with the welfare of employees is reflected in legislation and regulations as to minimum wages, hours of work, safety, and the income security of the worker. To protect investors, government has extended its regulation of securities to cover the sale of mutual funds and variable annuities and has tightened requirements governing the disclosure of information by corporations selling their securities to the public.

IMPACT ON BUSINESS

Some businessmen talk at times as though the Constitution of the United States prescribed that "this is the province of business and this is the province of government, and never shall one trespass on the other." This is far from the fact. Government has intervened in the functioning of the national economy and in the affairs of private business firms from the time of the writing of this country's Constitution. As the forces enumerated at the start of this chapter have changed both the environment in which these institutions—business and government—operate and the goals of the society, this intervention has been extended. To describe this trend is not to evaluate it as "good"; the purpose of this book is to consider why the trend persists and to suggest the consequences that ensue.

To what extent, as the goals of the society focus increasingly on the welfare of human beings, will the businessman's right to determine what products he will make or sell (e.g., cigarettes, pesticides) be delimited? To what extent will his freedom to set the prices at which he offers his goods or services for sale be abridged? To what extent will his freedom to hire and to determine, in negotiation with employees, the wages he will pay be circumscribed? To what extent will his decisions as to when and how much he will invest in additional plant and equipment or in research be influenced by government? What effect will prospective constraints have on the initiative and the motivation of businessmen? And will the businessman's influence on public policy decisions—the building of schools versus the building of antiballistic missile defenses, the revision of this country's welfare system versus the revision of its antitrust laws or the level of taxes—be lessened?

These questions cannot be answered in terms of such old chestnuts as: "That government governs best that governs least"; or "A dollar spent by government is a dollar wasted"; or "The clammy hand of socialism destroys the spirit of enterprise."

Such questions can only be answered in terms of the realities of a society fashioned by the forces described in this chapter. These forces challenge businessmen to think hard as to the environment in which free enterprise will operate in the future and to learn more about the functioning of government. Simultaneously, these forces require that government officials weigh advance toward new social goals in a realistic understanding of the functioning of business enterprise and learn more of the value systems that guide businessmen.

Despite the fact that the two parties in the evolving new government-business partnership are "obligated to walk an unfamiliar tightrope across a crevice whose dimensions and dangers have yet to be identified," [16] the new politico-economic system is not only in the offing but has actually come into being before our eyes. It needs refining and perfecting, because the values held by government officials and by businessmen differ as markedly as do the views of two men peering at the world through different ends of a long telescope. The legislator and the government executive look at current public problems (e.g., the conglomerate merger problem or proposals for a higher minimum wage) from the standpoint of the need of the whole society. The businessman sees in suggestions for the prohibition of mergers an unjustified restraint on the enterprise of the progressive business firm, and in the proposals for raising minimum wages an undue increase in costs for a firm that may find such costs sharply limit its profits.

There are business advisory groups available in Washington and in the state capitals in abundance. In Washington, for in-

[16] Richard J. Barber, *The American Corporation* (New York: E. P. Dutton & Co., Inc., 1970), p. 213.

stance, the Business Council, the U.S. Chamber of Commerce, the National Association of Manufacturers, trade associations such as the Manufacturing Chemists Association, and the Washington representatives of many corporations speak for business.[17] But the dialogue between these spokesmen and the government is generally a "dialogue of the deaf." Businessmen and government officials, guided by contrasting values, are often incapable of hearing and objectively considering each other's views. Such useful dialogue as does take place is focused almost exclusively on short-run problems—on what the administration will do about interest rates, wage-price guidelines, antitrust enforcement, a tax surcharge, or the limit on the public debt.

Little discussion of fundamental issues takes place. Neither business nor government has shown the inclination or the ability to view the evolution of the whole institutional apparatus of modern society—the corporation, the government bureau or commission, the university, the "authority," (e.g., the New York Port Authority or the Tennessee Valley Authority), the hospital, the "community development corporation," or Comsat—and the role each segment of that apparatus is expected to play.

A PREVIEW

How to enlist businessmen and government officials in more effective, continuing consideration of how a free people shape and adapt the politico-economic system to satisfy a broadening variety of individual and of social wants, as underlying forces change the kind of world in which we live, is the central concern of this book.

The next chapter describes the progressive extension of the public interest and business' reactions to pressures that it assume social, non-profit-making responsibilities and shows how and why this concept is altering the nature of the American politico-economy. Subsequently, in Part 2, Chapters 3 to 7 describe the "grants economy," i.e., the mechanisms which government has developed to get public objectives accomplished by nongovernmental agencies. In Part 3, Chapters 8 to 11, the extension of old

---

[17] John T. Connor, a leading businessman and twice a governmental official, pictured knowingly the roles of such groups and representatives in an address "The Shrinking Private Sector," before the Chemical Marketing Research Association, Sept. 18, 1967.

and the establishment of new forms of governmental regulation of business enterprise are pictured and weighed. In Part 4, the last two chapters sum up the consequences of persisting movements in terms of the relative roles and influence of business and government in achieving the goals of the American society of the 1970s.

CHAPTER *2*

The Expanding
Public Interest

PROVOKED by a description of increased intervention by government, the president of an electronics manufacturing firm in southern California asked: "Who determines—and on what grounds do they base their decision—that such governmental activity, that this or that new form of interference, is 'in the public interest'? [1] And what do you mean by 'the public interest'?"

If—as suggested in the preceding chapter—the expansion of what is deemed to be in the public interest is a key trend that has characterized the development of the Post-Industrial Society and forecasts the emergence of the Humane Society, this businessman's questions deserve full and considered answers, since understanding of the notion of public interest by businessmen is likely to be vital to the future development of their enterprises.

[1] See Chapter 1, page 17.

25

THE BUSINESSMAN AND THE
PUBLIC INTEREST

In general, the term "public interest" describes those actions or objectives which are in the best interests of all or most members of the society.[2] It suggests that there are simultaneously "particular interests" (those of the individual or the business firm) and "general interests" (those of all or most citizens), and it implies that the society, guided by certain generally accepted values (e.g., the dignity of man, the essentiality of freedom), is capable of determining what it regards to be in the public interest (e.g., such as the concepts I have indicated will characterize the Humane Society).

Thinking in terms of what is "in the best interests of all or most members of the society" is an uncommon exercise for many businessmen. Years of concern with the fortunes of a single enterprise have focused their thinking quite differently. And this focus leaves them not only unfamiliar with "the best interests of all or most members of the society" but in many instances opposed to the idea that there is an interest other than the welfare of the individual business concern.

Take, for example, the arguments that revolve around the minimum wage. Enactment of such legislation represents a determination that it is in the public interest to require that no individual shall receive a wage less than sufficient to maintain a conscionable standard of living.[3] But the businessman whose costs are raised by such legislation to the point that his profits are markedly reduced, the survival of his business is threatened, and he himself feels compelled to displace his least efficient workers sees such legislation as destroying what he regards as of prime

[2] For fuller definition and discussion of the meaning of public interest and the evolution of this notion see Carl J. Friedrich (ed.), *The Public Interest*, Nomos V (New York: Atherton Press, Inc., 1962), and particularly the essay in this volume by Harold D. Lasswell, "Public Interest: Proposing Principles of Content and Procedure," pp. 54–79. See also Richard E. Flathman, *The Public Interest* (New York: John Wiley & Sons, Inc., 1966), p. 82.

[3] This determination can and has been logically challenged (by businessmen among others) on the grounds that raising the minimum wage denies jobs to many unskilled workers (particularly, black teen-agers) and that this is not in the public interest. Obviously, it is not such a challenge that is being used here to illustrate a viewpoint voiced by many businessmen.

concern—the individual enterprise and those who earn their living as members of it.

Think also of the viewpoint voiced by some businessmen as to the relative value of service as a private executive and as a public official. A group of businessmen, for example, reflected some indignation when told that the head of this country's social security system had explained his refusal to accept the presidency of a private insurance company (at compensation more than twice as great as his present salary) with the statement, "It just isn't as important as what I am doing in the government." For the private executives this explanation was either unintelligible or unacceptable. Similarly, Robert McNamara's decision to accept the presidency of the World Bank when he left the Department of Defense was, for other businessmen, difficult to understand. By their values, this position was not as attractive an opportunity or as important a job as the presidency of the Ford Motor Company or a comparable job in an equally large private business enterprise. These opinions reflect either a lack of understanding of the nature of the public interest or the view that the public interest is necessarily of lesser consequence than the interest of the individual enterprise. This latter view is challenged by the substantial and progressive expansion of the public interest depicted in Chapter 1 as a cardinal characteristic of the society that has developed in the United States since the close of World War II.

Spokesmen for business, for labor, for farmers, or for doctors, however, will often contend, with myopic concentration on their own interests, that what they advocate is in the public interest. Businessmen are assuredly correct when they contend (as the U.S. Steel Corporation did in its 1965 Annual Report) that decisions as to the excellence of the product, as to pricing, as to conditions of employment, and as to the interest of their investors affect the public interest. In a society in which a vast majority of people use the products, pay the prices, work in the plants and offices, and increasingly invest in the securities of such corporations as U.S. Steel—their contention has merit. But this view of the public interest is, at the least, a narrow one. And while businessmen advance this viewpoint, simultaneously other particular interest groups argue loudly that, for example, public expenditures for the provision of medical services for the aged are *not* in the public interest (the organized doctors); that additional appropriations for the support of research are in the public interest (the organized universities); that additional expenditures for airports and air traffic control are in the public interest (the organized airlines, organized aircraft manufacturers, and organized cities); and that the establishment of rent supplements is in the public interest (organized cities and organized housing industry). In this welter of claims what, indeed, is in the public interest?

DEFINING THE PUBLIC INTEREST

In a democracy it is logical to hold that what is in the interest of all or most people should be determined by the people themselves or their representatives. But citizens, like the spokesmen for business, labor, farmers, or doctors, are guided by their individual and multiple interests; the citizen may simultaneously be a parent who wants the community to provide good schools and an employer who wants taxes to be kept down. The media of communications that influence their thinking are themselves influenced by their particular interests. Few elected representatives of the citizens can recognize, or are sufficiently independent to be able to represent, interests other than those of dominant segments of their constituencies (e.g., the organized rubber workers or a major military supplier). And the political institutions (e.g., the parties) are imperfect in determining what is in the interests of all or most citizens. Hence, public opinion, if it can be assessed, the expressed will of the citizens at the polls, or the decisions of a legislative body may not, in fact, define what is in the public interest.

Walter Lippmann has written that the public interest is "what men would choose if they saw clearly, thought rationally, acted disinterestedly and benevolently." [4] Essentially, he is saying that

[4] Walter Lippmann, *Essays in the Public Philosophy* (Boston: Atlantic Monthly Press, Little, Brown and Company, 1955), p. 42. McGeorge Bundy, *The Strength of Government* (Cambridge, Mass.: Harvard University Press, 1968), p. 58, illuminates the meaning of the public interest with this statement: "The public interest is what serves the freedom of all. But obviously the hard cases involve choices among freedoms. In this process of choice one can face questions of faith, questions of factual analysis, and questions of judgment on relative values. I hold it as a matter of faith, for example, that race prejudice is bad (I think I could prove it, but I believe it without proof). I hold it as a matter of factual analysis that there is no substitute for an open-occupancy law in combatting such prejudice, and I hold it as a matter of judgment that the freedom advanced by such a law far outweighs the

the public interest is what the reasoned judgments of intelligent men (journalists, for example) determine it to be. Plato among the ancients and Bertrand de Jouvenel among more recent writers voiced similar views. Alternatively, the economists (from John Stuart Mill to Richard Musgrave) had argued that the public interest is determined by the addition of all the private interests in the body politic. Still a third (and for me a more satisfying view) is that the public interest is what results from the workings of the pluralistic political power process, however imperfect that process is.

Thus the public interest *is* determined. Over time, as the forces of population growth, urbanization, technological advance, organizational growth, chronic war, the collapse of space, and affluence have confronted the American society with new problems and new hazards, responses have been initiated, and the machinery of democracy, creakingly and falteringly at times and with occasional false starts, has charted new courses which the citizenry has accepted as serving the public interest.

In a democracy it can be contended that in the long run what is in the public interest can be seen in what the citizenry has decided its government shall do. Later this chapter will test this contention in the light of significant actions that government has taken during the post-World War II years and the vigorous opposition that each expansion of governmental activity has provoked in two areas of expanding and controverted government activity—the maintenance of full employment and the protection of consumers.

DETERMINING THE PUBLIC INTEREST

What is determined to be "in the public interest" is a reflection of the values of contemporary society. These values are continually changing as has been illustrated by the evolution of the Industrial Society, the Post-Industrial Society, and the emerging Humane Society. The public interest is continually redefined, and new public policies are developed in an attempt to serve it.

unrestricted freedom in the sale and rental of real estate. To me, then, an open-occupancy law is in the public interest. And behind this sketch of a position is a whole series of opinions about what is wrong and what is right in our society, what will make it better or worse, and what is the relation between the individual and the society of which he is a part."

As Bailey has put it, "The American Democracy is built upon a number of unwritten propositions. One of the basic tenets is that political mechanisms are creatures of human intelligence and human will; that they are subject to change as human needs and expectations change." [5]

The expansion of what is recognized to be in the public interest is prompted by the values which a society develops and tries to make effective. These values are now being shaped by the vital forces identified in Chapter 1, pages 4–10.

If the society holds that no individual should have less than some minimum level of living (and that, the society has held, shall be a rising minimum), then the provision of better education or better health care, or drugs at lesser prices, may be in the public interest. But not all individual needs are a matter of public concern, for our society has always held that each individual should be self-reliant and that we should rely on the private enterprise system as fully as possible. Some means are required to determine what needs are common to large numbers within the population; that their satisfaction is essential to the good of society as a whole; and that the satisfaction of these needs should be undertaken by government rather than some other collective group (e.g., a community chest, a co-op, a university, or a nonprofit agency such as the YMCA or a community action agency).

In sorting out and assessing the vigorously pressed needs of different individuals and groups, and in determining that the satisfaction of certain needs is so important to the society as a whole as to warrant governmental action, there are some recognized principles. For example, it is generally agreed that:

■ The private economy is not capable of producing certain goods (e.g., national defense) or of providing certain services (e.g., the dispensing of justice or the exploration of space) and selling such goods and services at a profit; thus government should provide such goods and services.[6]

[5] Stephen K. Bailey, *Congress Makes a Law* (New York: Columbia University Press, 1950), p. 239.

[6] For excellent discussion of the factors determining what goods and services the private economy is motivated to provide and what goods and services the public wants, "is willing to pay for and expects government to assist it in achieving," see Peter O. Steiner, "The Public Sector and the Public Interest," in *The Analysis and Evaluation of Public Expenditures,* a compendium of papers submitted to the Subcommittee on Economy in Government of the Joint Economic Committee, Congress of the United States, 1969.

■ The private business firm operating in a competitive economy cannot afford to conserve some natural resources (e.g., the beauty of the landscape where strip mining is the only economic way of producing ores profitably), to overbuild its product to protect the consumers (e.g., to build safety belts, headrests, and other safety devices into automobiles), or to prevent certain unpleasant by-products (such as the smoke from furnaces or the stench from slaughterhouses) unless all competitors are required to do likewise; thus government is expected to regulate such activities.

■ The consumer, in many instances, does not have sufficient information or understanding to enable him to choose and evaluate many goods (e.g., the gasoline additive) and services (e.g., health insurance); hence government is expected to regulate such activities.

■ The market cannot be expected to induce business firms to respond promptly to the urgent but limited demand for certain goods and services (e.g., the production and operation of kidney dialysis machines, the production of artificial hearts, or the training of physicists); thus government must point the way and subsidize the needed production.

■ It is uneconomic to have business firms competing when scarce natural resources (e.g., the airwaves) are being utilized or when large investments are required (e.g., electric power); thus government grants and regulates monopoly rights.

■ Certain essential services are so relatively costly that many who need them cannot afford them (e.g., garbage collection and sewage disposal); thus government provides the service.

■ It is so desirable that all citizens should have access to certain facilities regardless of their ability to pay (e.g., parks and playgrounds, school buses, school lunches, higher education, and decent housing) that government should support in whole or in part the provision of such facilities.

■ The quality and nature of the goods and services made available (e.g., the quality of television programming, the range and quality of research, and the caliber of education) is of such general concern that government should see to it that these goods and services are produced and are of acceptable quality.

Because our traditions have tended to make it somehow seem disloyal for one to suggest that some goods and services may be better supplied and some resources better allocated in ways other than through profit-making firms operating in the market economy, expansion of the public interest has been slow. Yet the prevailing concept of what is in the public interest has been expanded. How?

Recognition of a need

The need for an extension of communal action to serve the public interest may stem from change—demographic change, geographical change, or technological change such as the advent of television or the discovery of a cure for poliomyelitis. It may stem from changing social attitudes toward a problem which has existed for a long time, such as the experiment with prohibition in the 1920s or the antipoverty and civil rights programs of the 1960s. Or it may stem from new knowledge (e.g., the effect of cigarette smoking on human health) or from increased power to deal with an existing problem, such as the greater capability given government to maintain economic stability and to promote economic growth by the New Economics.

In some cases a need apparent to only a few is suddenly and dramatically brought to public attention. The thalidomide tragedy brought into sudden focus the need for greater vigilance in the licensing of new drugs. The destruction of beach front property at Santa Barbara, California, by oil leaking from underwater wells created a demand for the control of such drilling. The stock market crash of 1929 and the ensuing depression made manifest the need for provision for the security of the unemployed, the widowed, and the aged. More often, a need experienced by the group most immediately affected—working women (day-care facilities), black teen-agers (jobs), retired persons (income to meet the overwhelming costs of medical care)—becomes recognized, after a torturously long period, by others.

That recognition is sometimes to be attributed to a persistent, socially minded individual who incurs the enmity of others as he insists upon recognition of such a need. Dr. Harvey Wiley incurred such enmity when he urged enactment of the original pure food and drug laws in 1906. Gifford Pinchot attracted such enmity when he argued that government should prevent the destruction of this country's national forests. Wilbur J. Cohen was the individual who persisted in directing the attention of this country to the needs of the aged for financial assistance in meeting the oppressive costs of hospital and medical care. Rachel Carson, through her book *The Silent Spring,* focused public attention on the effects of pesticides on human health. Ralph Nader publicized the need for improving the safety of automobiles and illustrated what could and should be done by requiring structural changes in automobiles and in automobile tires. In other instances business leaders have played an important role in promoting actions that were clearly in the public interest. Beardsley Ruml's role in promoting introduction of withholding of taxes is an illustration. The Committee for Economic Development, an association of national business leaders, has provided a succession of illustrations. And the Machinery and Allied Products Institute has advanced important proposals for the encouragement of capital expenditures that have been accepted as innovative contributions to the public interest.

Stimulation of concern

The need is recognized as a concern of the society, rather than of an individual or a group of individuals, only after such a persistent, socially minded individual or an interest group (e.g., organized labor) attracts the concern of allied interest groups, communications media, and eventually a (or the) political party (or parties). Thus the efforts of the advocate or of the interest group, like the pebble dropped in a pond, gain widening public concern which generates a change in public policy.[7]

The ability of powerful interest groups to thwart the efforts of the socially minded advocate or the minority whose need is urgent and to claim public attention for their own special interests is a constant threat to the American society. The post-World War II period is replete with illustrations of how such powerful interest groups as the organized physicians, organized manufacturers, or organized oil producers gained access to the media of communications and were successful in stimulating sufficiently widespread concern either to identify their own interests as the

---

[7] "Democratic government is subject to scrutiny to which no other human activity is subject in anything like equal degree. Interest groups, opposition party and press are the chief investigators. They are continually nominating issues or possible issues as candidates for public attention. . . . If any considerable number responds—and sometimes a very small number is sufficient—governmental adjustments follow. Yet issues of great popular potential . . . sometimes lie fallow for lack of adequate sponsors." Paul H. Appleby, *Policy and Administration* (University: University of Alabama Press, 1949), pp. 152–153.

public interest (e.g., tax allowances for the depletion of oil resources) or to delay the recognition of the public interest in the needs of minorities (e.g., the delay of the enactment of Medicare for more than a decade).

The stimulation of concern which precedes determination that the public interest warrants government's asssumption of responsibility for satisfying a particular need is an imperfect, sometimes exasperatingly long, and often unsure process. The process is made more uncertain by the limited ability of the media of communications to recognize what is in the public interest. In some instances, too, the press, television, and radio are rendered blind to the public interest by their own addiction to the status quo, the obfuscation spread by powerful pressure groups, or their own subservience to specific economic interests.

Enactment into law

Pressure-group activity and public opinion may indicate the existence of a new need or expectation without clearly indicating the way in which the need suggests the public interest should be served. Frequently, legislatures, when faced by a new demand claimed to be in the public interest, make irrational and inconsistent decisions.[8] Yet, in the final analysis it is the responsibility of the legislature to determine when the satisfaction of the needs of individuals will benefit the society as a whole.

The Chief Executive is simultaneously the active agent in most instances. It is he who is President (or governor, or mayor) of all the people and thus whose responsibility it is to discern what private purposes should be facilitated and what public concerns should be advanced.[9] If he measures up to this responsibility he

---

[8] Walter Lippmann (*op. cit.,* p. 45) has written, "It is easier to obtain votes for appropriations than it is for taxes, to facilitate consumption than to stimulate production, to protect a market than to open it, to inflate than to deflate, to borrow than to save, to demand than to compromise, to be intransigent than to negotiate, to threaten war than to prepare for it."

[9] McGeorge Bundy (*op. cit.,* pp. 59–60) has written this supporting statement: "I am far from asserting that the public interest is always and only what is opposed to some private or special interest. There is enormous value in the notion that the organized power of society exists to permit the realization of your private purposes and mine, and considerable force in the argument that society works well only when all its wheels know how to squeak and most of the squeaky wheels get greased. One of the reasons for confidence in the Executive Branch is that its elected chief is almost certain to have a lively sense of these proper private interests. If one were forced to

will be assailed by those whose individual interests are impinged upon (e.g., employers and the minimum wage), by those who fear innovative actions (e.g., organized business' opposition to the introduction of the New Economics), and by those who hold opposing views in such controversial areas as civil rights. Yet, recent history shows that in most, not all, instances, the Chief Executive rises to this responsibility, espouses those policies beneficial to the nation as a whole as he sees them—and concludes his term in office with the criticism of many who supported him for election earlier ringing in his ears.

The role of government—the executive and the legislature—as impartial determiner of the public interest is of growing importance in our complex industrialized society.[10] Population growth,

a choice between some absolute notion of Public Virtue and the practical process of balancing out all special interest, I think it would probably be better to choose the latter.

"But the balancing is not automatic, and a blind struggle among special interests is no prescription for the greatest happiness of the greatest number." The President, says Mr. Bundy, has both the opportunity and the duty to serve the public interest—a notion real to most Americans—while attending to various private concerns. In fact, "the quality of imaginative concern for what America ought to be is what Americans have valued most in their Presidents, next only to the evident capacity to govern." Ultimately, "we go beyond our belief in the public interest to a further act of faith by which we assert that questions about this interest are best resolved, directly or indirectly, by appeal to the electorate. We recognize the mix of public and private purposes which moves the individual voter, but we also suppose that the electorate can strike the balance—if not well, at least better than it can be struck in any other way. This assumption may well be larger and less provable than the prior assumption that such a public interest exists and that a President can play a unique role in defining it. But it is the necessary assumption of democracy, and we make it."

[10] This practical challenge to government's impartiality was expressed in a personal letter to the author by a thoughtful businessman:

"Government, through its bureaucracy and fortified to some extent by professional witnesses drawn from the academic world, has been proceeding on the assumption that the definition of the public interest is a special prerogative of government. It assumes this posture in dealing with persons and groups outside government so that in a substantial way the fundamentals are already decided in the government mind before it receives industry representations. This relegates the industry impact to details as distinguished from central issues.

"On the other hand, business and other elements of society, with the possible exception of leading members of the academe, have not faced up to the fact that they have abdicated a role in helping to define the public interest and in helping to develop and evaluate programs which are necessary to carry out soundly conceived public interest objectives."

urbanization, technological developments, organizational growth, chronic war, the collapse of space, and our growing affluence have simultaneously illuminated the needs of individuals, families, and groups; highlighted their significance to the society as a whole; and made possible the vast improvement in the quality of life. The determination of what actions shall be taken to advance the public interest is confused by the conflicting claims of selfish interest groups. But throughout the decades that have succeeded World War II, the process of determination has broadened the recognized public interest with the result that more and more needs are expected to be met through communal action.

Government has not achieved impartiality in arriving at such determinations. Government has not attained an optimal balance in the mix of programs it carries on to serve the public interest; illustrative inequities are obvious in the treatment of rich farmers versus low-income groups, in the support of public works versus poverty programs, and in the concern focused on defense versus the ills of the cities. This failure must be attributed to the continual clash of powerful economic interests; the quality of presidential leadership; the personal ambitions of officials and the administrative arrangements within the executive branch; the initiative, effort, and ambitions of individual legislators and their governmental and nongovernmental staffs; and the political commitment of political parties. Stephen Bailey summarized this situation when he wrote, "In the absence of a widely recognized crisis, legislative policy-making tends to be fought out at a level of largely irresponsible personal and group stratagems and compromises based upon temporary power coalitions of political, administrative, and non-governmental interests." [11]

The President, farthest removed from the clash of partisan interests, is frequently the single force capable of acting to protect the public interest. Hence, the growth of presidential power in the American society has been a significant element in the expansion of the public interest in the postwar years.

Public acceptance

While government is usually the positive force in determining the public interest, the public at large, through its power to accept or reject government policies in elections, is the final arbiter.

[11] Bailey, *op. cit.*, p. 236.

This ultimate public power, moreover, requires elected officials to give constant attention to opinion polls, letters from constituents, views expressed in public gatherings and newspapers, and other means of gauging popular acceptance or rejection of new and proposed public policies.

Many actions of government touching on technical matters or policies affecting only a small group—and this includes perhaps the majority of actions taken by government—attract little public attention. But, once undertaken, the general trends toward more intervention in business affairs, toward increased activity to promote social welfare, and toward the involvement of this nation in the political and economic affairs of the world do not persist unless they coincide with the needs and wishes of the American people.

CASE ILLUSTRATION I: FULL EMPLOYMENT

An example is offered by the gradual assumption during the post-World War II era, after Americans had held a contrary view for a century and a half, of the notion that government's assurance of a job for each individual is indeed required by the public interest.

Prior to the 1930s, the prevailing laissez-faire philosophy held that poverty and unemployment were the results of individual improvidence and laziness. Poverty and unemployment were believed to be problems of concern to the individual, to be resolved by him and his family, *not* by the government. Business recessions, it was believed, were inevitable temporary disruptions that did not warrant governmental action. In the long run, the prevailing view held, an unregulated private market brought about the most efficient use of manpower and capital and therefore acted automatically in the public interest.

The Depression of the 1930s brought an end to these views. With millions of people out of work, unemployment could no longer be ascribed to personal failings. The distress of millions of unemployed persons and their families was recognized to be of concern to the society as a whole. Moreover, the impact of the Depression demonstrated dramatically that free markets did not inevitably operate in the public interest.

The election of Franklin D. Roosevelt in 1932 marked the beginning of public policy to provide employment opportunities for those willing and able to work and to intervene extensively in the private market in order to promote the growth and stability of the national economy. However, most New Deal programs were designed to meet emergency needs; they were experimental in character and placed substantial but limited responsibilities upon the government. They sufficed to bring an end to the extensive unemployment of the mid-1930s only when supplemented (or replaced) by the military expenditures made as a consequence of World War II. It was the demand created by these expenditures that took up the slack in the nation's industrial capacity and provided jobs for most unemployed workers.

Passage of the Employment Act

The Employment Act of 1946 owed its passage to fear that with the ending of hostilities the nation would again experience depression and widespread unemployment. A *Fortune* magazine survey in 1944 showed that 68 percent of Americans felt that "the Federal Government should provide jobs for everyone able and willing to work, but who cannot get a job in private employment." Labor unions, some business leaders, and other groups were active in calling for government policies to prevent unemployment. Economists, influenced by the writings of John Maynard Keynes, felt that to promote economic growth and high employment government should take all necessary fiscal and monetary steps, should engage in massive public works, and should support such programs through deficit spending. Business groups, fearing recession, favored limited governmental action, chiefly in the form of incentives to business.

A proposed Full Employment Act was passed by the Senate in 1945. By the time the bill reached the more conservative House, public fear of widespread unemployment had declined. Opposition to the proposed act focused on the extent of government intervention in the market that would have been authorized. Many significant elements in the bill were altered or dropped.

As finally passed by both houses in 1946, the act authorized government to "foster and promote free competitive enterprise and the general welfare . . . and to promote maximum employment, production, and purchasing power." In addition, the law established the Council of Economic Advisers. In retrospect, this action was the most important provision. Reflected in the progressive action of the Council over successive years, the act has made explicit "the federal government's responsibility for using its resources to help avoid recessions and hence unemployment . . . [and transforming] the issue of conscious governmental intervention in the nation's economic welfare from 'whether' to 'how.' " [12] In short, the words of this legislation left the nature and extent of the responsibility government was to assume open to interpretation. But as the contextual circumstances within the American society changed over subsequent years, the values of the American people increasingly dictated that the public interest required that government assume unequivocally responsibility for minimizing unemployment.

The evolution of federal employment policies

The new law had relatively little direct impact on federal economic policy or on business functioning during the Truman administration. An unanticipated upsurge in private demand kept employment high even as military expenditures declined and men left military service for civilian jobs. Consequently, general public concern waned, while opposition to expanded government economic activity strengthened both in pressure groups and within the Congress. Military expenditures presented threats of inflation, and the need for control over wages and prices assumed more immediate importance than policies to maximize employment or economic growth.

The first dangers of recession and serious unemployment occurred during the Eisenhower administration, well after the conclusion of the Korean War. Eisenhower and his economic advisers, however, sought to avoid both budget deficits and intervention in the affairs of private business. Only a miniscule step to stimulate the aggregate demand of consumers was taken—luxury excise taxes were reduced.

During the Eisenhower administration, however, government grew and its power expanded. By 1956, military expenditures represented almost 10 percent of the gross national product. The expansion of housing to meet the needs of a growing population, deferred by the Korean conflict, was greatly spurred by the estab-

---

[12] Edward S. Flash, Jr., *Economic Advice and Presidential Leadership* (New York: Columbia University Press, 1965), p. 9.

lishment of loans and loan guarantees under the Federal Housing Administration and Veterans Administration.

These and other instances of expanded government power as purchaser, subsidizer, regulator, and guide of the private market became significant during the Kennedy administration,[13] when positive policies, deliberately designed to reduce unemployment and to stimulate economic growth, were initiated. President Johnson continued and expanded many of the Kennedy policies (e.g., the tax cut of 1964). And, between 1965 and 1968, rapidly rising military expenditures induced by the Vietnam War significantly reduced unemployment.

In summary, the policies established during these years provided, first and foremost, for the maximization of aggregate demand in order to reduce unemployment. This central effort was supplemented by a variety of programs which resulted in (1) training for increasing numbers, thus facilitating the employment of the least skilled; (2) the shifting of workers from areas of high unemployment to areas where jobs were available; (3) the improvement of the public employment service to facilitate the bringing of workers and jobs together; (4) the creation of a partnership between government and private industry to train and to hire the hard-core unemployed persons; and, finally, (5) the gradual acceptance of the idea that government should provide jobs for those for whom there remain no jobs in private employment. In total, these steps constituted a gigantic expansion of what was construed to be in the public interest only a third of a century earlier.

CASE ILLUSTRATION II: CONSUMER PROTECTION

In the words of President Kennedy, "If consumers are offered inferior products, if prices are exorbitant, if drugs are unsafe or worthless, if the consumer is unable to choose on an informal basis, then his dollar is wasted, his health and safety may be threatened, and the national interest suffers." [14] Government has long maintained authority to regulate certain aspects of business

---

[13] Walter W. Heller, *New Dimensions of Political Economy* (Cambridge, Mass.: Harvard University Press, 1966).

[14] *Special Message on Protecting the Consumer Interest,* Mar. 15, 1962.

activity to protect the consumer. But this area of governmental concern has been significantly expanded.

For the most part, government intervention has been concerned with four major needs:

1. *Safety*—assuring that drugs, foods, cosmetics, automobiles, toys, fabrics, etc., were not injurious to human health and life

2. *Honesty*—protecting the consumer against inaccurate weights and measures; unreliable or inaccurate advertising; overstatement of the efficacy of drugs; and misleading packaging, labeling, and guarantees

3. *Fair prices and varied products*—making the market work on behalf of the consumer through assurance of competition and the prevention of restrictive pricing practices

4. *Information*—aiding the consumer to evaluate what he seeks to buy by providing fuller, simpler, and more reliable information as to the contents of food products and other manufactured goods, the side effects of drugs, the health hazards of products, the cost of credit, and the provisions of sales contracts.

The origin of this concern with consumer protection can be traced to the Constitution, which authorized Congress to establish standard weights and measures. For the most part, however, during the nineteenth century, government followed the doctrine of *caveat emptor*—"let the buyer beware." The buyer was presumed to be responsible for and capable of protecting his own interests. While many abusive business practices undoubtedly took place, the relative simplicity of products, advertising, and sales practices and the decentralized nature of the market limited the need for protection.

By the end of the century, the ability of the consumer to evaluate the products he bought, to inform himself as to cost and value, and to detect hazards (e.g., in pesticides or inflammable clothing) had markedly diminished. Leaders and pressure groups inside and outside the government demanded reforms, and, as the effects of monopoly, unregulated food processing, and other problems were publicized, popular demand for protection grew. These developments led in the 1890s and 1900s to enactment of the first group of consumer protection laws: the Mail Frauds Statute, the Sherman Antitrust Act, establishment of the National Bureau of Standards, and the Pure Food and Drug Act.

A second major group of laws was passed about the time of World War I. This group included the Clayton Act, Federal

Trade Commission Act, Standard Container Act, and Transportation and Water Power Act. A third surge in regulatory activity took place in the 1930s. During that decade existing regulation of food and drugs, utilities, transportation, communication, trade practices, and advertising was vastly extended. A number of regulatory agencies were established, including the Civil Aeronautics Board, the refurbished Federal Power Commission, and the Securities and Exchange Commission. The Wool Labeling Act of 1939 was the first law requiring separate labeling provisions for particular types of products.

New forms of regulation, established since World War II, are clearly consistent with these earlier developments. The 1950s saw passage of the Celler-Kefauver Anti-merger Act, the food additive amendment to the Pure Food and Drug Act, and labeling laws for fur products, flammable fabrics, and textiles. In the 1960s, the regulatory agencies have been reorganized, and older legislation has been extended to cover new products and to meet new needs. The Kefauver-Harris amendments of 1962 extended drug regulation to the efficacy of drugs as well as their safety for human use. The Traffic Safety and Cigarette Labeling Acts extended regulation into two industries, while the Fair Packaging and Labeling Act and the Truth-in-Lending Act had an effect on business practices generally. The trend was highlighted when in October, 1969, President Nixon proclaimed a "buyer's bill of rights" and outlined a series of administrative actions and legislative proposals to protect consumers.

Changes in public understanding

Why has the public interest expanded to include these many new areas of government intervention and to require increased restriction of business freedom?

The multifaceted advance of technology has generated most of the new needs for consumer protection. For example, complex new drugs; pesticides and insecticides; radiation from electronic equipment; and pollution from automobile exhausts, paper factories, or electric generating plants have created numerous new hazards for human life. The complexity surrounding new technologies has markedly limited the consumers' ability to evaluate the advertising, labeling, packaging, and other marketing practices with which they are confronted. Conversely, this complexity and new media of communication endow business with greater ability to influence consumer behavior. Technology has greatly reduced the ability of the consumer to make an intelligent and informed choice, as the variety of products has greatly expanded and their complexity requires highly specialized knowledge. Technological changes have tended to centralize production and marketing, to separate and make increasingly impersonal the buyer-seller relationship, and to make it difficult for the consumer to judge and to register his views or complaints. Most government regulations have been concerned with new products and newly recognized hazards and with the limitations on the consumer in determining his own interests. Since 1962, government has also provided a number of channels whereby consumer views can be more strongly voiced.

In addition, the social concerns of government are apparent in increased efforts to protect the poor. The Truth-in-Lending Act is particularly directed at buying practices of low-income groups and the deceptive and exorbitant credit charges of some business firms serving these groups. Consideration is presently being given to greater regulation of door-to-door sales. Recent studies revealing that prices tend to be higher in the low-income areas of large cities than in wealthier areas and suburbs, while showing the reasons for such a state of affairs (e.g., greater risks, higher incidence of bad debts and thefts), also give promise that community values may call for government regulation of such prices.

In some cases, public protest has brought about the establishment of new regulatory powers. The thalidomide tragedy is an obvious example. It created an outcry which influenced passage of the Kefauver-Harris drug amendments. But in many instances government has had to lead in identifying threats to the public interest, with seemingly little popular support and over the substantial opposition of representatives of business.[15] In

[15] Enactment of the Truth-in-Lending Act stimulated the writing of a letter to the editor of the *Washington Post* by the chairman of the department of economics and business administration, Geneva College, Beaver Falls, Pa., that illustrates the divergence of views as to the extent to which the public interest requires governmental action to protect consumers. "I would hope," the letter writer wrote, "that the business community might evaluate the eight-year history and the struggle to get this bill passed. What has the business community gained by its foot-dragging tactics to keep adequate and necessary information from the consumers in as clear a fashion as possible? It would be hoped that the lesson learned here and the lessons learned in the passage of such other acts as the Wholesome Meat Act and the Fair Packaging and Labeling Act would make more and more businesses and associations reevaluate their whole attitude toward consumers' rights."

spite of a mounting body of scientific evidence as to the danger to human health caused by smoking, cigarette sales were little reduced before passage of the Cigarette Labeling and Advertising Act in 1965. Similarly, although evidence made increasingly clear that the hazards to human life caused by automobile accidents could be markedly reduced by the use of seat belts and the building of other safety features into automobiles, few consumers manifested any desire to purchase them until they were required by the government.

Consumer protection, like employment policy, is an area of public interest which may be expected to expand further in the future. Technological developments will continue to provide new and untested products, generate additional and unrevealed hazards to human life, and further reduce the ability of the consumer intelligently to determine what is in his own interest.

These developments promise the formulation of community values that call for government to extend its regulation to the products offered for sale, the marketing practices and, increasingly, the prices at which products or services are sold. A critical issue is: Can such standardization or even prohibition of products, control over advertising, labeling, packaging, and the limitation of profits be effected without limiting the innovation and motivation of business enterprise?

A SUMMARY ANSWER

What then is the public interest and who determines it? It is, as these quests for full employment and consumer protection illustrate, an act of faith, a manifestation of the conscience of the American society and of its traditional and continual desire to enhance the dignity of man.[16] It is a continuing reminder that "private rights are not exhaustive of the public interest and that private interests include much more than self-interests."[17]

It is determined by the society, with its various parts interacting as intricately as the finest and most complex Swiss watch. In that interaction the values of the society are shaped by

[16] For expansion of this viewpoint see in Friedrich, *op. cit.*, the following articles: Harold D. Lasswell, *op. cit.*, p. 78; Stephen K. Bailey, "The Public Interest: Some Operational Dilemmas," p. 106; and J. Roland Pennock, "The One and the Many: A Note on the Concept," pp. 177–82.

[17] Pennock, *ibid.*, p. 182.

the changing world in which the American people live and make their living.

The successive determinations of the post-World War II decades demonstrate that Americans have concluded that in an urbanized, compacted, organized society, if the dignity of each individual is to be enhanced to the extent to which advancing technology and growing wealth make this possible, government should assume substantially greater responsibility for the positive guidance and control of the national economy and of individual enterprise.

Yet, as the society has called upon government to assume substantially broader and greater responsibilities for the public interest, it has preserved its pluralistic character. Despite the increase of governmental power and activity, other sectors of the society have been called upon to perform new and added functions essential to fulfillment of the public interest. Legislation, financial support, and governmental administration alone cannot create opportunity in an industrialized, organized economy; combat the problems of poverty, civic unrest, and discrimination in an affluent society; or assure the innovative power to provide economic growth, new products, and advances in health or education.

In subsequent chapters we will picture the imaginative, even exciting, means that have been developed and invented to harness the capabilities and the zeal of business enterprises, the universities, the hospitals, and a myriad of nonprofit institutions and groups of concerned citizens in fulfilling the public interest.

PART 2

The Grants Economy

THE growth of the grants economy is, perhaps, the least heralded and the most significant structure change in the American political economy during the post-World War II decades. More apparent, and more discussed, are the decline in agriculture and the burgeoning expansion of the defense industry. Yet the former is, in 1970, substantially a historical incident, while the latter, though of dramatic importance, encompasses a lesser segment of the gross national income than does the grants economy. In the five succeeding chapters the growth of major segments of the grants economy (subsidies, contracts, grants), the forces impelling this growth, and its consequences will be examined.

CHAPTER 3

Subsidies— An Old Tool, New Uses

O_{UR} government has always subsidized private business.[1] The first tariff act was passed in 1789 to protect "infant industries" and to permit them to develop, i.e., in today's parlance, to encourage economic growth. The same law granted a 10 percent reduction in customs duties on goods imported in American vessels to encourage the development of a strong merchant marine as an aid to national security. In the nineteenth century, the government encouraged trade by providing land and cash

[1] "Government has subsidized private enterprise, both in industry and in agriculture, throughout the Nation's history. It has done so directly and indirectly. In some cases, acting directly, it has made outright gifts: grants of public lands or payments from the Treasury. More often, it has given aid in less open ways: by rendering services for which it makes no charge, by selling goods and services for less than they are worth, and by exempting some enterprises from taxes that others must pay." Clair Wilcox, *Public Policies Toward Business*, rev. ed. (Homewood, Ill.: Richard D. Irwin, Inc., 1960), p. 429.

grants for the development of privately owned transcontinental railroads. In the New Deal era, government greatly expanded the market for private housing by credit programs which made home loans available to many more people.[2]

Most subsidies provided by government today were established before World War II, but the forms in which subsidies are given and the purposes for which they are given have changed. Subsidies for the merchant marine and for railroads continue,[3] and even larger subsidies (initiated later) are provided for commercial airlines. The effort to induce private enterprise to construct housing still represents the public purpose for which the bulk of the governmental subsidy in the form of credit is provided. Cash grants have not increased significantly, but new and enlarged programs for the provision of credit, tax concessions, services, and preferential policies have provided greater benefits for business and have consumed more government revenue than ever before. The growing concern with the quality of life for all Americans and the need for continuing economic growth suggest that subsidies may become an even more significant tool of government in the future. Hence, the purpose of this chapter is to picture the ways in which government uses subsidies to promote particular activities that serve the public interest—those that provide needed transportation services, expand international trade, serve social needs (e.g., housing), ensure national security, and promote economic growth. We will depict the forms of subsidy used, indicate why they are needed, consider what alternative measures government could take, and appraise subsidies as a tool of public policy.

[2] The term "subsidy," as this paragraph indicates, is used to comprehend all benefits provided by government—cash grants, loans and credit guarantees, tax concessions, and services—which are provided to induce an institution or an individual to undertake an activity deemed to be in the public interest. The difficulty of defining the word subsidy is effectively illustrated in Warren G. Robinson, "What Is a Government Subsidy?" *National Tax Journal*, vol. 20, no. 1, pp. 86–92, 1967. See also Chapter 1 of *Subsidy and Subsidy-effect Programs of the United States Government,* a report prepared for the Joint Economic Committee, March, 1965.

[3] In late 1969, Senator Vance Hartke suggested a new form of subsidy to aid the rehabilitation of railroad passenger service—the purchase by the federal government of railroad rights-of-way and leasing them back to the railroads at an advantageous rental rate.

PURPOSES SOUGHT

Transportation

The economic growth of this nation, communication among all regions and all citizens, and national security are each dependent upon efficient transportation. Hence, the transportation industries have always been recognized as being "affected with the public interest," and throughout the nation's history subsidies to transportation have been more openly granted than in any other field.

To encourage private firms in the building of ships and the operation of an American-controlled merchant marine, the federal government provides direct cash subsidies to shipbuilders and ship operators.[4] A secondary objective is to compensate for higher building and operating costs in the United States than in other nations with which American firms compete in ship construction or operation. Direct payments, in the form of mail subsidies, are also made to domestic airlines. Loans and loan insurance are available to shipbuilders and operators and to railroads. In addition, government provides navigation aids, maintains inland waterways, and operates airports. Ever since the outset of air transportation, government has heavily subsidized the design and construction of new aircraft and, most recently, the development of a supersonic aircraft. In 1969, federal expenditures for these several subsidies for transportation approximated $2 billion.

In addition, the transportation industries benefit from the subsidylike effect of government expenditures for defense and for exploration in space. These expenditures have been concentrated in aerospace projects and have led not only to profits for the builders of aircraft but also to major innovations in commercial aircraft. Preferential policies benefit the shipping industry by restricting intercoastal trade and foreign trade carrying government cargo to United States flag vessels.

---

[4] "It is interesting to note that the only Federal statutes using the word 'subsidy' are those dealing with ship construction and ship operations. The term is also rarely used in Executive orders and regulations." *Subsidy and Subsidy-effect Programs of the United States Government, op. cit.,* p. 3.

The conspicuous failure of transportation to keep up with urban expansion has made it obvious that federal assistance is needed. In the face of a spectacular urban growth and spread, transit expansion was handicapped by charters, restraints, jurisdictional boundaries, and technological inertia. Routes tended to remain the same despite population shifts; the total national trackage of rail rapid transit grew by only 30 miles in two decades; average speeds remained the same, and so did the stations and the fare-collecting systems. Commuter railroads fared no better. Long a losing proposition, they seemed to become more moribund each year. Of the 41 metropolitan areas that had commuter services in 1935, only 20 had any service at all in 1961, and only 83 of an original 240 separate routes were in operation.

The automobile has become the primary mode of travel within urban areas. In 1970, two out of three people in metropolitan areas travel to work by car—by and large unmindful of air pollution or the annual total of 4 million injuries resulting from car accidents.

Yet, it has been estimated that "nearly one-third of the urban population—and particularly the poor who must depend on public transport—suffer from being served inadequately or not at all by the vast automobile-based systems on which we have come to depend." [5] The fiery explosion in Watts illuminated the crucial relationship between transportation and urban development. In part the riots there were triggered by "one of the least adequate networks of public transportation in any major city." The lack of transport barred residents of this slum from jobs and contributed to their frustration. Studies showed that to travel by public transport the 16-mile distance to Santa Monica (a center of jobs), the residents of Watts needed 1 hour and 50 minutes, 3 transfers, and a one-way fare of 83 cents. Subsequent demonstration projects in Watts showed that when direct transport to jobs was provided in Santa Monica and other parts of the metropolis, daily ridership more than tripled in three months.

The Urban Mass Transportation Act of 1964 authorized federal financial aid to assist public and private companies in planning more adequate mass transportation and in carrying out these plans. Under HUD's grant program, two-thirds of the cost of planning, engineering, and designing mass transportation proj-

[5] U.S. Department of Housing and Urban Development, Urban Transportation Administration, *Tomorrow's Transportation*, 1968, p. 17.

ects are federally funded. Federal grants through fiscal 1968 totaled almost $500 million, and another $32 million was spent on pertinent research and development. Projects range from such mammoth ventures as Chicago's $600 million program and the new rapid transit system for the San Francisco–Oakland area (involving 16 miles of subways and tunnels, 31 miles of aerial lines, 24 surface miles, and 4 miles under the Bay) to more modest projects for improving city congestion (e.g., a minibus in Washington), introducing public transportation to towns that had none (e.g., in Rome, New York), setting up fringe parking areas, or testing new transit systems (e.g., the monorail at the Seattle World's Fair) and component technology.

In an urbanized society, urban transportation is a needed social service. In an industrialized society, linked economically, politically, and culturally with every part of the world, all other forms of transport also serve essential ends of the society. If such transport of an adequate level of efficiency and safety is to be available, there is accumulating evidence that privately owned transport enterprises must either be subsidized or nationalized. Other democratic-capitalistic states—Great Britain, for example—have chosen the course of nationalization. But Americans have traditionally relied upon private enterprise for the provision of needed goods and services. The development of an efficient, progressive, and expanding national system of air transport indicates our ability to couple public support and regulation with private initiative and financing in the achievement of a public purpose. It foreshadows the further use of such mixed effort, particularly in the rehabilitation of the railroads and the development of intrametropolis transport.

Foreign trade

This country's federal government has always sought to induce private business firms to develop overseas markets for their goods and services. The expansion of foreign trade has promoted an international division of labor and exchange and thus increases total output and benefits consumers and producers in this and other countries. Simultaneously, this expansion of foreign trade has facilitated this country's relations with other nations and built up recognition of mutual dependence. During the post-World War II period, while expenditures for the waging of cold and hot wars have been large and persistent, the expansion of exports by American firms has tended to reduce our unfavorable balance of payments; the increasing investment of American capital in foreign lands has worked in the converse direction, although serving political ends as important as the expansion of trade in goods and services and providing the basis for a future backflow of earnings. Hence, while government has been utilizing subsidies to encourage foreign trade and foreign investment, by the mid-1960s it found it necessary to impose controls on investments in foreign lands.

The justification of subsidies to encourage foreign trade and investment lies in the particular problems which the businessman encounters as well as in the political ends government activities serve. A principal problem is that of obtaining credit. Financial institutions have been reluctant to extend credit for use in foreign markets because of the especial risks the borrower may encounter—expropriation of property by the foreign government; incontrovertibility of foreign funds; losses due to war, insurrection, or revolution. Since 1934, the Export-Import Bank of the United States has provided credit assistance for exporters, while during more recent years the Agency for International Development has also provided similar support for investors in the less developed countries. During the late 1960s, these agencies provided guarantees approximating $2 billion per annum for private overseas export and investment projects. Most of these guarantees covered only political risks, with private financial institutions covering normal credit risks. An additional $200 million in direct credit was provided.

A second problem facing the would-be exporter or overseas investor is lack of knowledge about commercial opportunities, tariff restrictions, and other factors affecting business operations overseas and the foreign businessmen's and consumers' lack of familiarity with, and hence demand for, American products.

The Agency for International Development and the Department of Commerce actively seek investment and trade opportunities abroad (AID only in the less-developed countries). Under a program begun in 1963, AID shares with private investors the costs of surveying specific investment opportunities. It is estimated that this program generates about $80 of new investment for each dollar spent by AID.[6]

[6] Agency for International Development, "The Foreign Assistance Program," *Annual Report to the Congress*, 1968, p. 15.

The Commerce Department, through its Bureau of International Commerce (BIC) and Business and Defense Services Administration (BDSA), provides more varied services. The Bureau collects from United States commercial attachés information regarding trade opportunities for American exporters and information pertaining to tax, regulation, and tariff problems. This and other information useful to exporters is distributed to businesses and trade associations through regular publications and through a computerized system that keys specific information to producers of appropriate commodities. The BIC also participates in trade promotion activities—establishes exhibits in international trade fairs, conducts trade missions in collaboration with United States companies, maintains centers and displays abroad for American products. The Commerce Department's field offices throughout the United States make BIC and BDSA information readily available to business firms in the areas they serve and strive to find solutions for the individual exporting problems and needs of particular firms.

A third form of subsidy—less direct but which clearly benefits American firms engaged in foreign trade—is the requirement that financial assistance to foreign governments be tied to purchases within the United States. Since 1959, AID has tied a growing proportion of its foreign commodity assistance to purchases within the United States. Before this provision was adopted, from 40 to 50 percent of such funds were spent in this country. In the late 1960s, more than 90 percent of AID commodity purchases were made in the United States. To this must be added long-term loans and foreign trade credits by the Eximbank to finance purchase of United States capital equipment and services. The greatest share of this market created by federal aid to foreign governments is enjoyed by producers of industrial and agricultural machinery, chemicals, motor vehicles, iron and steel, and fertilizers.[7]

Trade with developing nations has grown during the 1960s primarily because of United States economic assistance, particu-

[7] Between Jan. 1, and May 15, 1968, it was estimated that the following corporations derived export business in the following amounts (in millions) as a consequence of the foreign aid program: Allied Chemical—$2.3; Caterpillar Tractor—$5.4; Coastal Chemical—$2.3; Ford—$2.3; International Harvester—$3.2; International Minerals and Chemical—$2.1; Kaiser Jeep International—$2.1; Rohm and Haas—$2.4; United States Steel—$3.2. *Business Week*, Aug. 3, 1968.

larly foreign assistance tying policies. Indeed, the significance of United States procurement policies and the indirect subsidies they provide United States exporters "is most easily seen in the case of a number of U.S. commodities that are priced above world levels but which are nevertheless exported because AID funds are restricted for purposes of their purchase." [8]

The nation's balance-of-payments position is such that foreign assistance would have to be greatly reduced if such tying provisions were discontinued. The alternatives to other subsidies that promote foreign aid—direct trade by the government itself or the use of gunboat diplomacy in lieu of credit guarantees to protect our foreign commercial interests—are inconceivable or, at the least, uninviting. Yet the mercantilistic character of these tying provisions, contradicting a foreign policy that strives to liberalize trade, generally means that they negate other economic and political objectives while promoting the interests of some business enterprises.

Finally, since the end of World War II, government has increasingly striven to induce the universities and other institutions to assist the growth of the developing countries—to aid in building their schools, their health services, their agriculture, and other elements of these evolving societies. The objectives of this effort are the same as those that prompt subsidies for business in this field—to promote trade and international stability. Only the means of subsidy differ.

Housing

The provision of more adequate housing for the nearly 6 million families [9] that occupy substandard living quarters—the principal social welfare objective sought by subsidies—has also been fostered through direct government action: hiring architects, buying land, and engaging contractors to construct public housing projects. The provision of housing for millions was not envisaged when public housing agencies were established in the late 1930s. As the magnitude of the problem became clearer, the government looked for means of involving business enterprise in the solution of this social problem. Thus, it turned to the exten-

---

[8] Charles D. Hyson and Alan M. Strout, "Impact of Foreign Aid on U.S. Exports," *Harvard Business Review*, vol. 46, no. 1, pp. 63–67, 1968.

[9] U.S. Bureau of the Census, *Statistical Abstract of the United States: 1968*, p. 709.

sion of credit by the federal government to induce adequate private investment in housing, chiefly in single-family dwellings for middle-income families.

Some direct home loans (e.g., in designated "housing credit shortage areas") are made to individuals, but the major form through which government subsidizes home construction is the insuring of loans by the Federal Housing Administration (FHA) and the Veterans Administration (VA). This means of subsidy and the assurance of a secondary market on which mortgages insured by the FHA and VA can be purchased by the Federal National Mortgage Association (FNMA) substantially reduce the risk of the private financial institution. Roughly half of all new government commitments for guarantees and insurance of private loans each year are for housing loans insured by the FHA, and about one-sixth of all private housing units constructed each year are financed with the aid of the FHA or VA program.

Federal credit programs have expanded the home loan market not only directly but also by influencing private credit practices. Innovations begun by FHA and VA, including longer maturity of loans and increased loan-to-value ratios, have been adopted elsewhere and have made it easier to obtain conventional financing. Eligible low-income and moderate-income families can get FHA insurance on loans of up to 100 percent of home cost. Other provisions have further expanded the housing market by assuring the availability of credit to groups with special needs.

Still another form of subsidy was launched in the late 1960s to attract private investment to the provision of housing for the poor. Under the rent supplement programs, eligible low-income families and individuals are permitted to occupy approved, privately owned housing and pay less than the prevailing rent. The government makes supplementary payments directly to the project owner. In effect, the government subsidizes private enterprises to construct and operate public housing projects. Contracts and tax incentives have been suggested as other means of encouraging large-scale business involvement in housing for the poor.

In retrospect it is clear that the federal government has gradually developed various forms of subsidy to achieve expanding housing objectives. New means introduced during the 1960s —national housing partnerships, turn-key contracts for public housing construction, interest subsidies for moderate-income home buyers, and neighborhood development corporations—

indicate the continuing effort to utilize private enterprise in achieving national goals in this field.[10]

Unemployment

Hard-core unemployment is another social problem with which government has been unable to cope without the use of subsidies. In the depressed areas (i.e., those having more than 6 percent unemployment), the Department of Agriculture, the Bureau of Indian Affairs, and other federal agencies have long sought to provide assistance to the jobless. More recently, the Economic Development Administration has provided training for disadvantaged persons in these regions to equip them for permanent jobs in industry in other sections of the country. But these programs have reached only a small proportion of the hard-core unemployed and have had limited success. Despite a long period of unprecedented prosperity during the 1960s, there were still about 1.5 million hard-core unemployed in the country in 1969, about half a million of them in the 50 largest cities.

Civil rights regulations help to alleviate the situation, but cannot help those who lack skill. Public works projects may—like welfare assistance—meet immediate needs, but do not provide a permanent solution that would integrate the poor and the unqualified into society. Training constitutes a constructive step when realistically matched with the needs for workers in the labor market. But business has traditionally and logically employed the best trained and the most experienced workers available. Such hiring procedures are slanted against the poor (who are poor, in many instances, because they are undereducated, untrained, and inexperienced). After the problem had persisted for more than three decades, it was suggested that a subsidy be provided to compensate private employers for training, counseling, and for meeting the additional costs of hiring inexperienced, undereducated individuals. This suggestion resulted in creation of the federal JOBS (Job Opportunities in the Business Sector) program. This program, spearheaded by the National Alliance of Businessmen, authorizes the Department of Labor to contract with business enterprises to reimburse them for the special costs

[10] Morton J. Schussheim, *Toward A New Housing Policy: The Legacy of the Sixties*, Supplementary Paper no. 29, Committee for Economic Development, 1969, offers a succinct and stimulating description and analysis of developments in the field of housing during the 1960s.

involved in providing the extensive education and training required by unemployed persons with little or no skill and experience. Employers assume responsibility for equipping those workers and motivating them sufficiently to offset the lower reliability and higher turnover rate often experienced in the employment of disadvantaged personnel. The original goal set in 1968 was to provide 500,000 jobs by 1971, at an average cost per trainee of $2,900. By the beginning of 1970, some 380,000 disadvantaged workers had been hired under the JOBS program, and some 200,000 of them still remained on the job.[11] As the JOBS effort proceeded, the National Alliance of Businessmen continued to stimulate business participation. The aggregate number put to work, when compared with the number of unemployed, is not large, but the feasibility of using this new form of subsidy has been demonstrated. This JOBS program constitutes a significant involvement of business enterprise in meeting a social problem and is an additional step in the evolution of the mixed economy in a society increasingly concerned with the quality of life for all Americans.

National security

The strength of our national defenses is as much dependent on the efficiency and advancing technology of those enterprises to which government entrusts the development, manufacture, and management of weapons systems as it is upon the recruitment, learning, and caliber of the Armed Forces. The private enterprises which perform much of the research and development, produce weapons and equipment, and provide supportive services for the Department of Defense (as well as those that serve the Atomic Energy Commission and the National Aeronautics and Space Administration) are obviously "affected with the public interest." Thus they are provided substantial subsidies in the form of direct loans and loan guarantees; in the form of government-owned plants, machine tools, and other forms of capital equipment; in the form of tax deductions for capital investment and for research and development expenditures; and in the form of reimbursements for research undertaken without immediate relationship to the items being produced or developed for the government. The combined effect of these subsidies may enable a de-

---

[11] *Manpower Report of the President,* A Report on Manpower Requirements, Resources, Utilization, and Training, prepared by the United States Department of Labor; transmitted to the Congress March, 1970, p. 62.

fense contractor, using government funds, plant, and equipment, to carry out his responsibilities under a government contract while utilizing and risking a limited amount of private resources. The profits derived from contracts, the commercial gains relating to government-sponsored research and skills developed under government contracts, and the many subsidy benefits have all contributed to the development of a huge defense and aerospace industry heavily dependent on government and also wielding substantial influence in government.

Such subsidies supplement the basic opportunities that these defense contractors derive from the contracts they obtain for research, development, or production. They are extended (along with other forms of aid which promote innovation and growth throughout the business community) for the very simple reason that national security is heavily dependent upon the capabilities, vitality, and economic strength of these business enterprises.

The need for that strength forms the roots of what has become known as the "military-industrial complex." That term is used to criticize an "unholy alliance" between military leaders who allegedly strive to enhance their power and strength and the industrial executives whose prosperity depends on defense contracts. There is little doubt that a military-industrial complex exists. (Assuredly "construction-housing," "publishers-education," and "road builders-public roads" complexes also exist.) The venal character of its objective—i.e., to build an unnecessarily large military establishment—may be debatable. But the only clear alternative to contracting with private defense contractors and supplementing the contract with subsidy benefits would be massive research and production efforts by government agencies themselves; in short, the nationalization of defense industries. The alternative of nationalization is, at the least, inconsistent with this nation's traditions and would tend to magnify even more the power and influence of the military in national affairs. The alternative that has been developed—a government-private business collaboration—is controllable and constitutes a more efficient use of this nation's organizational resources.

Economic growth

Since private enterprise is the source of employment for most of this country's workers and produces the goods and services upon which our society depends, government has always striven to ensure business growth and prosperity. The many government subsidies and subsidylike activities promoting business growth include the services of the Patent Office and the Post Office, and favorable tax provisions (e.g., the lower taxation of capital gains). Other forms of subsidy have been used to encourage business investment, to promote innovation, to expand and protect markets, to develop natural resources, and to aid small business. What chiefly distinguishes subsidies established since World War II is that they reflect a more sophisticated understanding of the national economy and an intent to manipulate it, while aiding the individual enterprise.

To encourage investment, business enterprises have always been permitted to deduct the depreciation of capital equipment from the income on which taxes were paid. Since 1954, in order to further encourage investment in new equipment—and thus expedite economic growth—accelerated depreciation has been allowed in the earlier years of an asset. In 1962, a more significant step was taken to encourage business expansion—a credit against taxes of up to 7 percent of the cost of investment was allowed and depreciation allowances were further liberalized. These provisions substantially reduced the cost of new capital equipment and facilities and raised the consequent rate of earnings on investments, with the result that firms were prompted to increase their capital investments. The granting of these tax subsidies was timed to coincide with other government efforts to achieve full employment and speed the nation's rate of economic growth. They provided an effective subsidy of about $2 billion.[12] By the end of 1966, as inflationary pressures grew in the economy, the investment credit and accelerated depreciation deductions were temporarily suspended, to be reenacted in 1967 and finally repealed in 1969 as a part of a general reform of taxes and as a further effort to curb inflation.

To encourage innovation, businesses have been permitted since 1954 to deduct as expenses for income tax calculation all outlays for research and development in the year they are made or, at their option, over a period of five years. In addition, the government itself has invested more and more heavily in research, largely through contracts with business enterprises. This research is undertaken to achieve defense, space, health, and other pur-

[12] Joseph A. Pechman, *Federal Tax Policy* (Washington: The Brookings Institution, 1966), p. 121.

poses, but it is a subsidy to the business sector per se. The extent of government support of research and development is discussed at greater length in Chapters 5 and 6.

To expand and to protect the markets served by this country's business enterprises, the federal government has persisted during the postwar years in bargaining for reciprocal tariffs and in 1962 effected a major adjustment of American tariffs. In the past, the primary purpose of tariffs was to permit infant industries to develop. In the last third of the twentieth century, different issues are at stake. The standard of living enjoyed by American workers brings with it production costs that are higher than those in competing industrial nations. Hence, government has kept tariff barriers up in order to maintain a high level of employment in particular industries. Government also acts to protect certain industries in the interest of national security (e.g., maintenance of production facilities for such essential materials as oil and steel). These actions are taken in the knowledge that higher tariffs lead to retaliatory actions by foreign governments, hamper the growth of some developing nations whose political association we strive to maintain, and limit United States sales abroad. Moreover, these actions are taken despite recognition that tariff protection weakens incentives for innovation and efficiency.

To develop this country's natural resources, tax provisions granting sizable (and controversial) benefits to minerals producers have been enacted. Oil and gas producers are granted a depletion allowance (amounting to 27.5 percent of sales until 1969, when it was reduced to 22 percent) as a deduction from income taxes. The producers of other minerals are granted similar though lesser allowances (e.g., 15 percent for copper, silver, and gold; 10 percent for coal). These allowances are estimated to cost the government about $1.3 billion in annual revenues. In addition, unlimited immediate write-offs are permitted for capital costs incurred in exploring and developing oil and gas resources, and deductions of up to $400,000 are granted those who explore and develop other mineral resources. These tax subsidies are advocated on the grounds that the development of this nation's mineral resources is of great importance to the economy and to the national security; opponents argue that these resources are not of such great importance to the national security and that the profits earned offer an adequate incentive to assure exploration by the private developer, even if he had to assume its risk.

Encouraging small business

Federal subsidies are provided for small enterprises in recognition of the fact that they encounter risks and difficulties that are more easily weathered by larger firms and on the assumption that small enterprises contribute innovation and competition vital to the health of the economy. Some 5 million business firms are considered "small" by the Small Business Administration standards. The provision of direct loans and loan insurance for small, independent enterprises and corporations formed by small business concerns to make joint purchases constitutes the major subsidy for small business firms. Credit is provided by the Small Business Administration and by Small Business Investment Companies, which are privately owned and licensed by the SBA. In 1969, direct loans and loans through the SBIC totaled close to $1 billion. The SBA administers special programs designed to help small businessmen out of temporary binds or dire emergencies: the displaced business loan program helps to resettle businesses uprooted by federally aided construction projects; disaster loans offer assistance in areas stricken by natural disasters; the economic opportunity loan program reaches out to those "outside the economic mainstream"—the economically and socially disadvantaged people in very low income brackets. In an effort to stimulate the growth of small entrepreneurship and the development of Negro-owned enterprises, the SBA has made or guaranteed more than 12,000 soft loans since 1965 to aspiring businessmen without even a shoestring to start on. Initially unsuccessful (because of a large number of business failures), the program has rallied; a new, more realistic approach has won the support of dozens of major banks and has a better chance for future success.

To improve their abilities to manage business firms, small businessmen are provided advice on various aspects of business management through a series of publications and through the services of individuals from SBA field offices capable of counseling on management problems. They benefit from tax provisions which set a lower rate of taxation on the first $25,000 of corporate income and exempt investments of up to $25,000 in calculating the investment credit allowed under the 1966 amendment to the corporate income tax.

To assure small business enterprises a substantial share of federal contracts, they are informed of opportunities for sales to the government, and a proportion of contracts must be allotted to them. Increasingly, however, the military and aerospace contracts (which make up the bulk of government purchases) involve products and services which can only be provided by large corporations. In fiscal year 1967, small business obtained 21 percent of prime contract awards in military procurement, representing $8.3 billion. Less than 5 percent of prime contracts, however, consisted of small business set-asides,[13] i.e., contracts that are "set aside" for award to small businesses.

But are subsidies for small business obsolete in a political economy made up in increasing part of large organizations? In the modern, large-scale, technological economy, is small business, by and large, efficient in the production of today's goods and services? Should small business units be encouraged and preserved to ensure the "openness" of the American society?

HOW EFFECTIVE ARE SUBSIDIES?

In a democratic, free-enterprise society, is there a satisfactory alternative to government subsidization of business activities which serve public objectives?

Before attempting to answer this central question, consider these more immediate questions. How effective are subsidies in accomplishing the purposes for which they are used, e.g., to provide housing for low-income families, to put the hard-core unemployed back to work, etc.? To what extent do they actually influence the businessman and encourage him to engage in activities that do contribute to the public interest? What are the costs, direct and indirect, of the various forms of subsidy? What advantages and difficulties do they present for government and for the business enterprise?

Cash payments

Each year the federal government pays over $400 million in cash subsidies to ship operators and builders and to the constructors of commercial aircraft. In addition, it makes payments under the JOBS program and other payments related to stockpiling and contracting. The aggregate of these direct cash payments is relatively small when compared to the billions of dollars made avail-

[13] U.S. Senate, Select Committee on Small Business, *Eighteenth Annual Report,* 1968, pp. 14 and 20.

able as subsidies in other forms. Yet cash payments offer some obvious advantages over other forms of subsidy. Their cost is easily determined and easily controlled; they are readily administered; i.e., the recipients can be clearly identified and the specific requirements to be exacted of them can be enforced.

Cash payments are generally confined to business activities on which there is general agreement as to their contribution to the public interest. Agreement on these subsidies has been hammered out as the responsible government agencies have justified their payments in seeking annual appropriations from Congress and in meeting public criticisms. Cash payments are the only form of subsidy which is identified explicitly in the budget and therefore subject to the discipline of the appropriation process. This exposure to public appraisal tends to make businessmen less willing to lobby for and to seek direct cash payments and tends to make more rigorous the requirements and controls to which recipients must conform.

Direct credit and credit guarantees

Direct loans outstanding to the business sector as of 1967 amounted to about $13 billion in federal funds.[14] Of this total, nearly $11 billion represented housing loans; $1.5 billion was for small business loans; nearly $1 billion was devoted to economic development loans; and the remainder was made up of loans to shipbuilders and operators, exporters, railroads, and the defense industries.

Federal credit is extended primarily to meet those needs "affected with the public interest" which entail risk that limits the availability of private credit. For example, a sizable part of all housing loans are made to finance the construction of housing in slum areas, where high economic and other risks discourage financing by private banks, insurance companies, and other lending agencies. Export loans, similarly, serve a public purpose and involve relatively greater risks. Economic development loans are made to enterprises which must succeed in areas where there are few financial resources, presumably limited markets, and, consequently, large risks.

Interest rates for federal credit for such public purposes are deliberately held below private credit charges. SBA disaster loans

[14] U.S. Treasury Department, Fiscal Service, Bureau of Accounts, *Federal Credit Programs of the United States Government,* June 30, 1968.

and economic opportunity loans, for example, involve interest charges lower than other types of small business loans. FHA credit for low-income housing is extended at a lower interest rate than obtains for housing loans made by private lenders. Federal educational loans, which have benefited more than 2 million students over the decade since their inception, are now being increasingly provided through private loans which are guaranteed by state or private nonprofit agencies or insured by the federal government; such private loans totaled $687 million in 1968–1969, nearly nine times the figure recorded at the inception of the program in 1966. The President's Commission on Budget Concepts noted that "most Federal loan programs contain at least some element of subsidy. . . . if this were not true, a serious question could be raised about the appropriateness of such activities being conducted by the Federal Government rather than by private financial institutions." [15] The Commission recommended that the full cost of interest subsidies be disclosed in the expenditure accounts of the budget and that effective measures be developed to reflect the element of risk involved, larger in federal loans than in Treasury borrowing.

Credit guarantees extend government's ability to accomplish public objectives by drawing large sums of private funds into the financing of public needs. Despite their scope and variety, direct government loans and guarantees of private loans to domestic private borrowers constitute only a small part of the total volume of credit (about 10 percent of the estimated gross private debt of $1,031 billion outstanding on June 30, 1966).[16] In terms of purpose and direction, this is a highly significant 10 percent. Both through the direct extension of credit and through the guarantee of the private extension of credit, government intervenes substantially and increasingly in the functioning of the economy. In return, it does require conformity with standards and practices that limit the freedom of individual enterprises. But this intervention has not deterred business from using those forms of subsidy. Indeed, credit programs have proven highly effective in inducing business firms to engage in the satisfaction of a variety of public

[15] *Report of the President's Commission on Budget Concepts,* 1967, p. 51.

[16] Bureau of the Budget, *Special Analyses, Budget of the United States, Fiscal Year 1968,* p. 64. See also, *Federal Credit Programs,* A Report by the Secretary of the Treasury to the Congress, Jan. 21, 1967, p. 4, printed for the use of the Committee on Banking and Currency, U.S. Senate.

wants. The success of this form of subsidy in inducing business enterprise to aid in meeting public purposes foretells its greater use in the future.

Services

All private enterprises in this country benefit to some degree from services which the government provides to business without charge or below cost (of course, they do pay taxes!). Most firms send out their mailings at charges which do not cover the costs incurred by the Post Office; many rely upon information provided by government agencies; some receive management or technical assistance from government experts; a few depend upon complex government operations and facilities designed specifically to meet their needs. The diversity of such services makes difficult the reaching of judgments as to the utility or cost of this form of subsidy.

In terms of the number of business firms served and the cost to the government, the major service-subsidy is the postal service. A deficit operation for all but very few years throughout its history, the Post Office Department reached a landmark of sorts in 1967: a billion-dollar deficit.[17] Of every postal dollar spent, 19 cents represents a subsidy from the Treasury. This subsidy—nearly half of which pays for carrying at a loss the second class mail, consisting mainly of newspapers and periodicals—is justified on the grounds that by facilitating the distribution of publications it contributes to the spread of knowledge and information essential in a democracy. With the advent of radio and television, this benefit has become less essential, but it is still significant. The low cost of distribution enjoyed by newspapers and magazines constitutes, however, a substantial subsidy for both those who publish them and those who advertise in them. Other enterprises also benefit from the low-cost distribution of their advertising material, much of which is generally (and often appropriately!) referred to as "junk mail." [18]

[17] U.S. Post Office Department, *1967 Annual Report of the Postmaster General,* Financial Supplement, pp. 5 and 82.

[18] In 1969, a proposal was considered by the Congress that an independent corporation be established to operate the postal services. This proposal further provided that each category of mail should bear its demonstrably related cost, plus an allocation of institutional costs determined with regard to market factors (e.g., elasticity of demand, financial impact on user, value of service). In addition, the Congress might (if this proposal were adopted) vote

"User studies" are periodically conducted to assess the value of government publications and some other government services; the results of such studies enable the executive and legislative branches to determine whether such services should be continued. But the diversity of subsidized services provided by the government makes it difficult to reach judgments as to the utility or cost of this form of subsidy, and the utility of many subsidized services (with the notable exception of the postal service) in inducing business to engage in activities that serve a public end is even less apparent.

Tax benefits

The principal tax benefits used to subsidize and thus to induce business enterprises to follow courses of action deemed to be in the public interest are the investment tax credit, depreciation allowances, depletion and capital costs deductions for mineral producers, deductions for research and development expenditures, and the lower taxation of the first $25,000 of corporate income.[19]

Powerful inducements can be offered business enterprises through the use of tax benefits (or "tax expenditures" as the opponents of such measures dub them!). Those in government find it tempting to use such tax provisions to promote public objectives, because they *appear* less costly than other forms of subsidy. Businessmen favor aid in this form because it appears less like a subsidy and is not accompanied by as much control over their activities. The tax benefits, however, are perhaps the most difficult form of subsidy to use effectively.

"A large proportion of the Federal tax receipts given up in the form of a tax credit are very often wasted in the sense that they do not result in any *increase* in expenditures for the desired pur-

appropriations to the independent corporation from time to time to subsidize the mailing privilege of particular groups (e.g., the blind) for which a direct public subsidy is intended.

[19] In 1969, the Nixon administration proposed abandonment of the investment tax credit and the granting of tax benefits to business firms that hire hard-core unemployed. Other industrial countries, in contrast, offer a greater range of tax benefits, including special deductions or lower tax rates for enterprises in underdeveloped areas and industries which are considered particularly important to economic growth. See *Foreign Tax Policies and Economic Growth,* Conference Report of the National Bureau of Economic Research and The Brookings Institution (New York: Columbia University Press, 1966).

pose," warns Congressman Wilbur D. Mills, chairman of the House Ways and Means Committee; he believes that "the increase in expenditures for the particular purpose that results from a tax credit could be achieved at a much lower cost in terms of the impact on the budget deficit if the additional investment were financed through direct expenditures." [20]

The relative effectiveness of this form of subsidy in relation to its costs is not clear. "Tax expenditures," as former Assistant Secretary of the Treasury Stanley S. Surrey has noted, "are imbedded in the revenue side of the Budget and their cost is not disclosed. . . . Their efficiency . . . is thus not compelled to meet the rigid tests [being developed for] direct Budget expenditures." [21] Surrey particularly opposes the use of subsidies to draw business into activities which are attractive only in terms of after-tax profit; he suggests that when tax provisions are used to achieve social welfare ends, the greatest benefits flow not to the poor, but to the private investors.

Even stronger opposition to the use of tax benefits has been voiced by Joseph Pechman, an eminent tax scholar of the Brookings Institution:

> . . . the best contribution a tax system can make to growth is to maintain as much neutrality as possible among different incomes and expenditure. Only in this way will the market allocate economic resources efficiently among alternative uses. Departures from neutrality are justified when the market mechanism is imperfect and the tax system is the most efficient method of correcting the deficiency. . . . Experience in practically every country indicates that there is no logical place to stop once erosion of the tax base has set in. Instead of promoting growth, tax privileges put a premium on earning and disposing of incomes in tax-sheltered form and distort economic activity. Such violations of horizontal equity contribute to taxpayer dissatisfaction and create pressure for the enactment of additional benefits.[22]

[20] "Back Door Spending," extension of remarks of Hon. Wilbur D. Mills of Arkansas in the House of Representatives, Dec. 13, 1967.

[21] In a speech, "The Federal Tax System—Current Activities and Future Possibilities," given before the Boston Economic Club on May 15, 1968.

[22] Joseph A. Pechman, *Report of the Canadian Royal Commission on Taxation: A Summing Up*, Studies of Government Finance, Reprint 134 (Washington: The Brookings Institution, 1967), p. 4.

Indirect benefits

The provision of subsidies in the form of indirect benefits poses especially difficult problems of appraisal. Examples of such indirect, and difficult to evaluate, subsidies are tariffs, the tying of foreign aid to purchases in the United States, government contract provisions for the support of incidental research or development, the reservation of intercoastal trade to American-flag vessels, the stockpiling of strategic materials, and the disposal of surplus government property. Such subsidies impose cost elsewhere in the economy while benefiting particular business interests. Their net value to the society is difficult to calculate and questionable.

A PUBLIC POLICY TOOL

Let us return to the central question posed earlier: In a democratic free-enterprise society, is there a satisfactory alternative to government subsidization of business activities to encourage the development of transportation and the expansion of foreign trade, to improve the welfare of people, to strengthen our national defenses, and to spur economic growth?

An obvious alternative is direct performance by government, similar to government operation of the postal system. That alternative would involve government ownership and operation of predominantly commuter carrying railroads; it would include governmental construction and operation of housing projects; it would include government's employment of unemployed workers; it would include the production in government's own arsenals and plants of the armament, matériel, missiles, and planes now produced by private enterprise. It might imply still other government activities, for example, the ownership and mining of vital mineral resources.

This alternative of direct performance by government has been rejected. Rather, subsidies—direct and indirect—have been firmly established as an important tool of public policy. Their use is frequently criticized as inequitable, as unduly favoring particular interests. Mrs. Martin Luther King, for example, has said that "our Congress passes laws which subsidize corporations, farms, oil companies, airlines and houses for suburbia, but when it turns its attention to the poor, it suddenly becomes concerned about balancing the budget."[23] Such criticism has been warranted in specific instances and at particular times; tariffs and the oil depletion allowances offer examples. But criticism of such instances should not obscure the central fact that subsidies now are utilized to serve a function they did not serve in the early history of this country. In the 1800s, subsidies to business were utilized to stimulate the growth of particular industries (e.g., the merchant marine and railroads) and, indirectly, to serve broad social objectives. During the decades from 1930 to 1970, subsidies have increasingly been utilized to achieve an expanding variety of public objectives; they are one of several devices (contracts and grants being others) that provide the cement that holds a mixed economy together.

If, as seems certain, subsidies will be utilized even more extensively in the decades ahead, it is high time that the effectiveness of various forms of subsidy—cash payments, credit, purchases, tax benefits, and the provision of services—be appraised. The degree to which each induces the desired action by business enterprise, stimulates economic growth while serving social needs, and achieves its ends at minimal and apparent—not hidden—public costs, differs markedly.

Despite the need for refinement, subsidies are a proven and useful tool for implementing public policy. They have been vulnerable to the manipulation of powerful interests that benefited from subsidies and have been especially vulnerable to such manipulation when provided in indirect forms, e.g., as a tax benefit as distinguished from a cash grant. Nevertheless, subsidies have been established as one of the important mechanisms this society can and does use to galvanize its various institutions—business prominently among them—into pursuit of the goals its members have set. Subsidies are, indeed, an essential tool which government—as "the central institution in the society of organizations"[24]—uses to accomplish its ends.

[23] *Business Week,* May 19, 1968, p. 168.

[24] Peter F. Drucker, *The Age of Discontinuity* (New York: Harper & Row, Publishers, Incorporated, 1969), p. 225.

CHAPTER 4

The Contract— A Mechanism for Involving the Private Sector

SINCE the early days of this republic, the federal government has contracted with business firms, individuals, and other agencies to get part of the public business done. The government has contracted for the building of roads, canals, and dams; for the delivery of the mail; for the inspection of steamships; and for many other purposes. The vast and immediate spurt in federal activities following our entry into World War II forced a large increase in contracting for goods and services from nongovernmental agencies. Since that time, government's dependence on nongovernmental agencies, and on the contract as a mechanism for drawing on their services, has persisted and grown.

This change has been described as "the greatest desocialization that this country has experienced." It has established "a new form of Federalism," i.e., a "federation" through which the federal government gets work done in association with private enterprise. This chapter pictures the extent to which government has gone in using nongovernmental institutions to perform public functions (in whole or in part) and assesses the significance of this development to the American economy and to the freedom of the individual enterprise.

THE GROWTH IN GOVERNMENT PURCHASES

Since 1946 the purchases [1] of goods and services from private enterprises by all levels of government have increased seventeen-fold. The value of purchases by the federal government has increased more than twentyfold since 1946, and more than a hundredfold since 1929; state and local government purchases have risen more than tenfold since 1946. The growth of government purchases is stated more precisely in Table 4.1.

If the influence of price inflation is eliminated, the growth in

TABLE 4.1 *Government Purchases of Goods and Services, Excluding Compensation of Government Employees, Selected Years* (*billions of dollars*)

Year	Total	Level of government		Type of purchase	
		Federal	*State and local*	*Structures*	*Other*
1929	$ 4.2	$ 0.4	$ 3.8	$ 2.5	$ 1.7
1939	5.7 *	1.7	4.0	2.7	3.1
1946	6.2 *	2.6	3.6	1.6	4.7
1950	17.0 *	7.6	9.4	6.8	10.3
1955	40.0	25.7	14.3	11.4	28.6
1960	52.2	31.7	20.5	15.9	36.3
1964	65.5	38.1	27.4	20.0	45.5
1968	105.1 *	60.1	45.0	27.6	77.4

* Totals differ because of rounding to billions of dollars.
SOURCE: Department of Commerce, Office of Business Economics, *Survey of Current Business,* August, 1965, pp. 36–39 and July, 1969, pp. 29 and 30.

[1] The term "purchases" comprehends all goods and services bought by the government from private enterprise. The term "contracts" comprehends particularly, although not exclusively, the purchase of "nonshelf" goods and services, i.e., those goods and services developed, produced, or provided to meet particular, and often exclusive, needs of the government.

the volume of purchases still indicates a striking expansion, at least sixfold between 1929 and 1969.

As the population grows and the variety of services rendered by government to the citizenry expands, government's purchases —from pencils, paper, desks, trucks, machinery, equipment, and buildings to missiles, reactors, artificial hearts, and the services of those who design and develop such materials—inevitably increase. Hence, the federal government purchased more goods and services in 1969 than in 1946 to meet the needs of public employees in carrying out new and expanded government functions, e.g., space exploration, social security, the control of environmental pollution, airport and freeway construction, and postal service. Federal government grants for the construction of highways, hospitals, and schools resulted in substantially increased purchases by state and local governments.

The vastly enlarged defense and space programs have been principally responsible for the increase in federal purchases since World War II. Defense purchases represented approximately three-fourths of the aggregate value of all federal purchases, and aerospace purchases (much of which were for defense) represented about one-third in 1968; Table 4.2 reflects the growth of purchases in these fields. A large military establishment has been maintained for more than two decades of "semipeace." The technological character of the weapons required by the military has advanced in geometric terms and brought with it a consequent

TABLE 4.2 *Military Procurement Actions and Aerospace Expenditures of Federal Government, Selected Years* (billions of dollars)

Year	Net value of military procurement actions	Expenditures for aerospace products and services	Aerospace expenditures as percent of total federal purchases *
1952	$43.6	$ 6.1	18.5%
1954	13.3	11.2	37.9
1957	21.5	12.5	41.8
1960	23.7	13.3	41.9
1964	28.8	17.9	47.1
1968	43.8	21.4	35.6

* Excluding employee compensation. See Table 4.1.
SOURCES: *Military Prime Contract Awards and Subcontract Payments of Commitments,* issued annually by the Office of the Secretary of Defense; *Aerospace Facts and Figures, 1969,* Aerospace Industries Association of America, Inc., p. 13.

increase in cost in scientific talent—in physicists, chemists, engineers, and astronomers—as well as in dollars. For example, development of the Polaris submarine missile system consumed for a period of years the efforts of thousands of scientists as well as the expenditure of billions of dollars. And this cost is multiplied by the rapid obsolescence of these weapons systems and the need for their replacement by even more devastating weapons within a few years.

The flight of the Russian Sputnik in late 1957 stimulated the undertaking of the federal space exploration program. This program has resulted in expenditures of $4 to $5 billion per annum for rockets, missiles, space vehicles, related equipment, and research covering a wide spectrum of knowledge (e.g., in aeromedicine and in the organization of very large enterprises). The flight of the Russian Sputnik prompted also a rigorous reassessment of the ability of the American educational system to produce the required stock of mathematicians, engineers, and scientists.

CONTRACTING OUT—SCOPE AND CAUSES

The scope

Two other items must be viewed to gain a full understanding of the increased dependence of government on "contracting out." The first is the proportion of the total administrative budget of the federal government that is expended for contracted services and supplies.

In 1946, approximately:

- 20 percent of the total was expended for contractual services and supplies.
- 30 percent was expended for personnel services and benefits.
- 25 percent was expended for grants and fixed charges.
- 20 percent was expended for the acquisition of capital assets.
- 5 percent was expended for miscellaneous other purposes.[2]

By 1966, these proportions of the total administrative budget of the federal government had been significantly changed:

[2] These proportions are approximated on the basis of less reliable data that are available for the years since 1960, yet are believed to be substantially accurate.

■ 34 percent of the total was expended for contractual services and supplies.[3]

■ 22 percent was expended for personnel services and benefits.

■ 22 percent was expended for grants and fixed charges.

■ 18 percent was expended for the acquisition of capital assets.

■ 3 percent was expended for miscellaneous.

The second is the broadening variety of services being contracted for. Consider these examples of the utilization of the contract by agencies and departments of the federal government other than the military departments and NASA:

■ The General Services Administration contracts each year for (1) the maintenance of real property and equipment, (2) architectural and engineering services, (3) defense materials handling, and (4) custodial and guarding services.

■ The Veterans Administration contracts for the services of civilian hospitals and physicians for the dependents of military personnel in some circumstances and contracts with private insurance companies for the carrying of life insurance on veterans.

■ The Atomic Energy Commission contracts for the operation of government-owned production plants.

■ The United States Information Agency contracts for the preparation of films, books, surveys, etc., for the conduct of this agency's functions overseas.

■ The Office of Education has established and contracts with 20 regional educational laboratories, each organized as a nonprofit corporation with its own board of directors. In addition, it contracts with 14 university-based educational research and development centers. A recent trend—contracts between public schools and the "learning industry"—experiments with using the profit motive to upgrade education.[4]

---

[3] By 1969, 29.3 percent of the total of the "unified budget" (a new budgetary concept which includes both the "administrative" and "cash" budgets) was expended for contracted-for services and supplies. The high level of spending for government procurement was a stated reason for the establishment in late 1969 of a Commission on Government Procurement to conduct a broad study of prevailing procurement statutes, regulations, policies, and procedures.

[4] The first federally funded "guaranteed performance" contract of this type was granted to Dorsett Educational Systems, an Oklahoma teaching machines maker, to teach remedial reading and mathematics to some 200 junior and senior high school underachievers in Texarkana, Ark. In February, 1970, the

■ The Agency for International Development contracts with universities and with profit-making enterprises for the provision of technical assistance.

■ The Department of Labor has contracted with Urban Leagues in 45 cities to find on-the-job training opportunities for 30,000 people in these communities and has contracted with the Institute of Industrial Launderers to develop training programs for mentally retarded persons.

■ The Social Security Administration is required by the Medicare legislation of 1965 to contract with the nonprofit Blue Cross Associations, profit-making insurance companies, or other enterprises to serve as agents for the federal government in receiving claims from and making payments to hospitals or doctors for services rendered to those covered by Medicare.

■ The Office of Economic Opportunity contracts with private enterprises, profit-making firms, universities, and nonprofit agencies for the conduct of training in the Job Corps camps and with more than 1,000 local nonprofit agencies for the planning and provision of services for the poor.[5]

In the light of this varied use through the contract of private enterprises—universities, various nonprofit agencies and, principally, business enterprise—the prediction by Peter Drucker that "The next major development in politics, and the one needed to make . . . our tired, overextended, flabby and impotent government effective again, might therefore be reprivatization of the 'doing,' the performance of society's tasks"[6] seems incongruous. Four years before Drucker offered this belated prophecy, a newspaper columnist wryly commented: "Some old New Dealers, who looked upon business as the enemy of the Federal government,

San Diego school board approved a $1.4 million, three-year contract with Educational Development Laboratories, Inc. (a division of McGraw-Hill Book Company) to boost the reading achievement and lagging language skills of nearly 10,000 minority children in southern California (*Washington Post*, Feb. 2, 1970).

[5] An official of the Office of Economic Opportunity has opined that the profit-making organizations generally have accomplished the tasks assigned to them more effectively than the universities and nonprofit community groups (Joseph Kershaw, then assistant administrator, Office of Economic Opportunity, at the Woodrow Wilson School, Princeton University, May 6, 1966).

[6] *The Age of Discontinuity* (New York: Harper & Row, Publishers, Incorporated, 1969), p. 235.

would turn over in their graves if they saw what is happening today. The Administration—fully aware of what it is doing—is enlisting the motive power of profit to generate social progress." [7]

The causes

The basic cause of increased contracting out by government is our turning to government to provide a vastly broadened range of services. As a people, we have determined—despite the misgivings of many—that we want government actively to provide more and more services (e.g., the operation of day-care centers, the promotion of educational television, the development of improved texts for the teaching of physics, and the putting of a man on the moon).

A second and elemental cause is government's need for men and women with the especial talents required to perform these new and expanding services. Vannevar Bush, a distinguished scientist and professor at the Massachusetts Institute of Technology, formulated during World War II (when he served as Administrator of the Office of Scientific Research and Development) the doctrine that to get its work done the government should seek out the men, women, and agencies, within or without the government, especially talented to perform the needed tasks. This central idea—wholly consistent with the increasing specialization experienced in the subsequent quarter of a century—has had much to do with the increased use of the contract to get the government's work done. A contributory influence was the simple fact that government pay scales (for professional and administrative personnel) being relatively low, it was often necessary to contract out to those institutions where qualified personnel were available. A further consequence of this influence was the creation of some nongovernmental agencies [8] where talented individuals could be employed at higher than governmental scales and put to work on increasingly complex tasks of government.

A third cause of the trend toward contracting out is the recurring effort, revived in the early 1950s and still quite lively, to "get the government out of business." This effort has the double rationale of lessening government competition with private enter-

[7] Roscoe Drummond, *Washington Post*, Mar. 21, 1965.

[8] For example, RAND, Institute for Defense Analyses, Research Analysis Corporation, and Logistics Management Institute.

prise and of pursuing an ideology pertaining to the role of government that has deep roots in the American society. An inventory of "commercial-type" activities being carried on by government agencies was compiled in 1955. It indicated that in some 20,000 installations the federal government was manufacturing such items as helium, rubber, electric power, ice cream, and false teeth. Such services were being rendered as trucking, blueprinting, warehousing, baking, and garbage collection. The succeeding efforts to turn these activities over to private industry had partial success. Most synthetic rubber plants erected in World War II, for example, were sold to private owners. The Department of Defense divested itself of several automobile repair shops, nurseries, and laundries. Bluebeard's Castle, a hotel and tourist attraction in the Virgin Islands, was sold. Yet other operations are still in government hands. They will likely remain so because they are integral to agency work, more expensive when contracted out, or have too much political pressure backing their continuation.[9]

A fourth cause of this trend has been the desire to limit the number of governmental employees. Criticism by members of the Congress as to the expansion of public payrolls has been met by the simple expedient of contracting for activities formerly performed within government. For example, in one federal department several hundred clerical employees were eliminated from the federal payroll by contracting with the former supervisor for the performance of the whole task—the punching of tabulating cards.

A fifth cause has been the vast magnitude of some government undertakings. Projects such as the construction of the DEW Line or the supersonic transport required such extensive staffs and such large facilities that government found it essential to enlist the collaborative efforts of two or more large private enterprises with the particular scientific and managerial competences needed. The Apollo program required a vast industrial effort involving 20,000 contractors (though of the $24 billion spent to put men on the moon, one-third went to the four largest prime contractors).

[9] See, for example, U.S. Senate, Committee on Government Operations, *Government Competition with Private Enterprise*, 88th Cong., 1st Sess., 1963.

DISTINCTIVE GOODS AND SERVICES

When buying such mass-produced goods as desks, automobiles, and paper clips and such common services as transportation, food service, and building maintenance, government can turn to the commercial market. These goods and services are available to anyone, and government is only one of many of the seller's customers. It can buy on the open market by soliciting competitive bids from several suppliers and awarding the contract to the qualified bidder offering the lowest price. The request for bids can specify precisely the goods or service wanted; the contractor can calculate his costs of supplying such known goods or services with exactness and base his price on such a calculation. Thus a firm price may be agreed upon in advance, and the government can contract with the knowledge that it is protected by (1) the right to reject the item if it does not meet specifications and (2) the competition of numerous suppliers.

But a large and increasing proportion of the goods and services bought by government cannot be procured by such conventional procedures.[10] Guided missiles, nuclear fuels, the development of a manned space laboratory, or the evaluation for the Office of Economic Opportunity of the effectiveness of the Job Corps—these are examples of purchases made only by government. Four characteristics of such goods and services, utilized only, or principally, by government, dictate the need for other than conventional procurement procedures.

The critical nature of the goods

First, such goods and services are often of vital importance to the national interest. The military security of the nation requires that a Polaris missile be extraordinarily accurate. A radar network must be as reliable as is conceivably possible. A space

[10] For a dissenting opinion see Robert B. Hall, "The Armed Services Procurement Act of 1947 Should Be Reformed," *The GAO Review*, Spring, 1969, pp. 10–19. See also the statement of Elmer B. Staats, Comptroller General of the United States, before the Subcommittee on Military Operations of the Committee on Government Operations, House of Representatives, Apr. 15, 1969, pp. 16–21; Mr. Staats strongly urged increased use of formal advertising in government procurement and improved methods of negotiation.

capsule—the Apollo, for example—or an artificial heart to be implanted in a human being must have very high safety factors built into it. The nation's morale and prestige, as well as ethical considerations, dictate the highest achievable standard of performance. The contractors involved must be fully competent to provide the high order of accuracy, reliability, and safety required.

The uncertainty of costs

Second, a new missile or rocket engine must undergo a long process of development during which the "state of the art" must be advanced. This requires technological breakthrough and the overcoming of some expected and many unexpected problems. The pace of accomplishment cannot be predicted; the problems to be met in development and production cannot be foretold.[11] Thus it is impossible for buyer and seller to discuss, estimate, and agree in advance on a given price which will cover the seller's costs and offer him the opportunity to earn an adequate profit. Hence, a contract that sets a firm, agreed-upon price (conventionally called "firm-fixed price," or FFP, contract), customary in the procurement of well-developed, mass production items, is not practicable.

Limited market for defense-space products

A third distinguishing feature of many goods and services contracted for by government is that they are not salable on the commercial market. Few, if any, private buyers would be found

[11] In September, 1968, the latest of a long series of studies of this characteristic of weapons system production, *Essential Technical Steps and Related Uncertainties in DOD Weapons System Development,* prepared for the Aircraft Industries Association, illuminated the extensiveness of the period during which a contractor wrestles with "anticipated unknowns" and "unanticipated unknowns" before production plans can be completed and costs estimated. Subsequently, in May, 1969, cancellation by the Department of the Army of a contract with the Lockheed Aircraft Corporation for production of the Cheyenne helicopter highlighted the uncertainty of costs. The costs under an $800 million contract far exceeded what had been anticipated, and the Army canceled this contract after more than $100 million had been expended because it had no "substantial assurance that satisfactory aircraft would be delivered." At the time of cancellation, Daniel J. Haughton, chairman of the board of Lockheed, protested that "The development problems —which are normal and to be expected in achieving a major technological step forward—can be solved. . . . [They do not] constitute justification for the drastic action taken by the Army." *Wall Street Journal,* May 20, 1969.

for an Explorer satellite or a nuclear warhead even if the national interest would permit a private party to purchase one or the other. Although there is some opportunity for contractors to adapt for commercial markets the goods and services originally provided for the government, still it remains a fact of life that for much that it buys the government is the sole buyer.

In economists' language, a "monopsony" obtains, i.e., the market is one in which there is a single buyer and more than one seller. In a monopsony the sellers are dependent on the buyer, as in a monopoly the buyers are dependent on the seller. In actuality, the situation is not classically monopsonistic for, in many instances, only a few (or one) sellers possess the capability required to produce the goods or service the government seeks. Nevertheless, a substantial dependency is created when a contractor commits a large or major part of his facilities to serve this specialized governmental market. Such contractors develop capabilities that are different from those required for successful operation in traditional commercial markets.

Throughout the private sector of the American economy, a substantial though indeterminable number of such government-oriented contractors have been created. The makers of aircraft, missiles, aerospace systems and related electronics equipment, and the builders of ships constitute the bulk of this segment of the private sector.[12] But a number of firms and private agencies (e.g., universities, nonprofit institutions such as RAND, the educational laboratories and twoscore like institutions, and hundreds of social agencies such as the National Urban League, the Family Service Association of America, and the African American Institute) have also developed a similar dependence upon the continuance of governmental contracts.

Few potential producers

Finally, we must take into consideration that as there is a limited market for many goods and services contracted for by government, so there is a limited number of suppliers that possess the

---

[12] Such firms as Avco, Collins Radio, General Dynamics, Ling-Temco-Vought, Lockheed, Martin Marietta, McDonnell Douglas, Newport News Shipbuilding, Northrop, and Raytheon sold more than 50 percent of their total output to the government for a succession of years during the 1950s and 1960s. Most of these companies strove vigorously during the mid-1960s to diversify and thus to reduce their dependence on government purchases.

talents and the capabilities required. The number of aerospace companies capable of developing the Gemini space capsule or of producing the supersonic transport is rigidly limited. The number of agencies qualified to conduct for the U.S. Office of Education a survey of the caliber of education in slum areas of the major cities or to develop for the U.S. Public Health Service an electronic pacemaker for ailing human hearts is similarly limited. In a highly advanced technological society in which specialization prevails, the talent equipped to perform tasks on the frontier of the society's interests is very, very scarce.

ADAPTING PROCUREMENT

These distinguishing characteristics of many of the goods and services that government buys have given rise to significant adaptations in procurement practices.

Facilities and finance are provided

For example, to make some government contracts more attractive, to encourage contractors to develop unique capabilities, and to lessen the risk assumed when contractors embark on complex, large projects, the government provides, in some instances, facilities and financial assistance.

The furnishing of government-owned plant and equipment lessens the capital investment and, hence, the risk taken by the contractor. It is thus regarded by some as a significant subsidy for those contractors that are provided with such plant and equipment. It must be recognized, however, that the provision of such facilities utilizes plant and equipment (especially machine tools) inherited in many instances from World War II. The guarantee of the contractor's credit to facilitate the obtaining of capital from private credit institutions similarly lessens the impact of the uncertainty involved in unprecedented tasks. The making of advance and progress payments on contracts reduces the working capital required by the contractor and lessens the amount of private capital put at risk.

In the mid-1950s, assistance provided in these forms was substantial and important. In succeeding years, both the absolute and the relative importance of these forms of assistance was significantly reduced. By 1962 the value of plant and equipment provided was only $2.7 billion, or nearly 10 percent of total awards;

the value of loans and payments provided was down to $2.6 billion, or slightly over 9 percent of awards.[13] Since 1965 the value of government-furnished plant and equipment made available to contractors has substantially increased and approximated a third of the value of military procurement awards.[14] Similarly, the balance outstanding of V-loans, advance payments, and progress payments approached $8 billion, or 19 percent of the total procurement value.[15]

Contracting methods

The distinctive character of much that government buys has dictated that the bulk of such procurement shall *not* be made on the basis of competing price bids from several sellers. Of the $431 billion of military procurement let between 1951 and 1967, only $60 billion (13.9 percent) was the result of formally advertised bidding. The remaining procurement was let by what is called "negotiated" bidding, an intricate process of inviting and discussing bids from firms with known capabilities. Such discussion involves the negotiation of price, but it comprehends in addition many other aspects of the work to be done and the ability of the contractor to do it. In 1969, awards on a price competitive basis constituted some 40 percent of the total Department of Defense purchasing.[16]

And the bulk of such procurement is *not* made in the form of

---

[13] Arthur D. Little, Inc., *How Sick Is the Defense Industry?* Cambridge, Mass., 1963, pp. 56–57.

[14] *Economy in Government Procurement and Property Management,* Report of the Subcommittee on Economy in Government of the Joint Economic Committee, April, 1968, p. 7.

A 1963 survey by the Stanford Research Institute (*The Industry Government Aerospace Relationship,* vol. II, p. 119) disclosed that the cost of government-supplied property exceeded the value of property reported on corporate balance sheets by 13 of the largest military contractors.

[15] The Armed Services Procurement Regulation (Section E503) provides that progress payments equal to 80 percent of the costs incurred in government contracts may be made available. In substantial part these payments are made necessary by the refusal of the federal government to consider interest as an allowable cost.

[16] U.S. Congress, Joint Economic Committee, *Economy in Government— 1967: Updated Background Material,* 90th Cong., 1st Sess., November, 1967, pp. 29, 52. Office of the Secretary of Defense, *Military Prime Contract Awards and Subcontract Payments or Commitments,* July, 1968–June, 1969, p. 38.

fixed price contracts. During World War II, the "cost-plus-fixed-fee" (CPFF) contract was used to procure much of the matériel and services bought. Under such contracts the government agrees to pay the contractor for all acceptable costs incurred to carry out the project and an additional flat fee. During and after the Korean War, CPFF contracting became increasingly common; from 1955 to 1960, the proportion of total Defense Department awards made in this form rose from 20 to 38 percent.

The CPFF contract meets the difficulty of uncertain costs, but it provides no motivation for the contractor to keep costs to a minimum. To remedy this, "cost-plus-incentive-fee" (CPIF) and "fixed-price-incentive" (FPI) contracts were utilized. Such contract forms set targets in advance—for costs in the case of CPIF and for price in the case of FPI. The extent to which the contractor is able to meet these targets provides the basis for the final calculation of his profit. During the McNamara regime at the Department of Defense (1961–1967), incentive contracts were increasingly used to reduce costs and to improve contractor performance. During this period use of the cost reimbursement type of contract dropped and use of the fixed-price type of contract increased from 57.9 to 78.9 percent of total awards.[17] The consequence of these trends is that the contractor is given greater motivation and assumes greater risk when carrying out a Defense contract.

Contract administration

Yet the freedom and motivation provided by these trends may be negated by extensive, and sometimes meticulous, surveillance of the contractor's performance during the course of the contract.[18] Any firm that enters into a contract with the government—not merely those business firms, universities, and nonprofit institutions that undertake contracts involving goods or services of critical

[17] *Office of the Secretary of Defense, Military Prime Contract Awards and Subcontract Payments or Commitments,* July, 1966–June, 1967, pp. 44, 47.

[18] Edward J. Morrison has concluded after a detailed analysis of Air Force procurement (a major segment of the total of Defense procurement) that "A new structural relationship has been created in which the Air Force, as a buyer, makes specific management decisions about policy and detailed procedures within aerospace companies." "Defense Systems Management: The 375 Series," *California Management Review,* Summer, 1967, p. 17.

importance—accepts the obligation of abiding by policies in significant respects similar to those of a government agency.[19]

The critical nature of the goods contracted for lends especial importance to the processes utilized by the contractor to control the quality of the product, whether a jet engine or a new drug. Because of the inherent uncertainty of development, as compared with manufacturing, almost continuous monitoring may be required. The advanced and sophisticated nature of the goods and of the technologies upon which they depend means that tolerances must be fantastically small, and the opportunities for malfunctioning are extraordinarily great. To work, the integration of all components of a complex weapons system must be near-perfect.[20] From the consequentially rigorous requirements imposed on the contractor's day-by-day operations, and from those additional requirements attributable to the nature of the contract and the simple fact that the contract is with the government, flow significant elements characteristic of the government-contractor relationship.

Government influences and controls the contractor's decision making as to the choice of products the firm produces and the nature of the research it carries on, the source of capital funds that it uses, the manner in which it conducts its internal operations, and the social policies that it accepts to guide its internal and external operations.[21] The influence is pervasive wherever the contracts (for research and development as well as for production of weapons systems, space systems, atomic energy projects, and, most recently, systems for oceanographic exploration) are governed by the procurement legislation and regulations of the

[19] Michael D. Reagan, *The Managed Economy* (New York: Oxford University Press, 1963), p. 193.

[20] The calamitous 1967 fire at Cape Kennedy resulted in NASA's TIE (technical integration and evaluation) contract with Boeing. Under its terms Boeing is charged with checking up on all major Apollo contractors and with coordinating, verifying, and managing Apollo on the ground; at the peak of the program 2,000 Boeing engineers worked on TIE. *Business Week,* May 24, 1969, p. 128.

[21] For development of this theme, see M. L. Weidenbaum, "Arms and the American Economy: A Domestic Convergence Hypothesis," *American Economic Review,* May, 1968, and M. L. Weidenbaum, "The Government Oriented Corporation," *The Modern Public Sector* (New York: Basic Books, Inc., Publishers, 1969), chap. 2, pp. 31–66.

Department of Defense. These regulations may specify, as a part of the contract, that the government agency shall have power to review and veto company decisions as to which activities shall be performed in-house and which contracted out; when contracting out, what preferences shall be given to small businesses or to businesses located in economically depressed areas; what kinds of advertising are permissible; which products shall be bought domestically rather than imported; what internal financial reporting systems shall be used; what type of industrial engineering and planning system shall be utilized; what safety rules shall be promulgated; what minimum as well as average wage rates shall be paid, how much overtime work may be authorized, and still other aspects of operations.[22]

More general in their application to business firms and private agencies undertaking contracts with the federal government are statutory and regulatory provisions that use governmental procurement to enforce a wide range of public policies. The goals sought by these provisions often are completely extraneous to the objective of a particular contract, and their enforcement may make the contractor's operations more costly and less efficient and reduce the opportunity for gain.

For example, the Buy American Act of 1933 was designed to promote American industry. It requires the government, and in many instances its contractors, to buy (with exceptions) raw materials or manufactured goods from United States firms when they are available, even though foreign materials and products may cost less by 25 percent or more.[23] Other statutory examples are provided by the Davis-Bacon Act of 1931, a minimum wage law which states that construction contractors must pay wages

[22] These illustrations apply particularly to contractors for the Defense Department and NASA, and are based on provisions of the Armed Services Procurement Regulation, for example, sec. 1–707, 1–800, 1–1700, 3–900, and 12–601.

[23] Asher Isaacs and Reuben E. Slesinger, *Business, Government and Public Policy* (Princeton, N.J.: D. Van Nostrand Company, Inc., 1964), p. 383, estimated that if the government had ignored the Buy American policy, it could have saved up to $100 million on purchases in the year 1954. In 1966, the Joint Economic Committee disclosed that the Department of Defense was permitting "a 50 percent differential in favor of American products (hand tools) while GSA [was] . . . allowed to use only a 6 percent differential." The DOD policy was designed to help the balance-of-payments problem. *Economic Impact of Federal Procurement—1966*, a Report of a Subcommittee of the Joint Economic Committee of the Congress of the United States, p. 9.

and fringe benefits comparable to those prevailing in the community in which the project is located, and the Walsh-Healy Act of 1936, which establishes labor standards for employees in production-connected jobs on all government contracts exceeding $10,000 in value. The practical impact of the Walsh-Healy Act is negligible because other labor legislation and a booming economy have raised wage levels, but the Davis-Bacon Act has had a significant influence in leveling wages up.[24]

Civilians on military bases overseas may be subject to the same off limits and curfew regulations as are military personnel. Atomic Energy Commission regulations prohibit "moonlighting" by contractor employees when outside work would interfere with their duties, create a conflict of interest, or "subject the AEC or the contractor to public criticism or embarrassment." [25] And, in still other instances, contractors are required to adopt the same safety regulations that are used by the Army Corps of Engineers.

IMPLEMENTING NEW OBJECTIVES

Implementation of the leading social objective of this generation—granting equal rights to Negroes—has become an important goal of government purchasing. President Eisenhower tried, through the Committee on Equal Employment Opportunity, to encourage nondiscriminatory hiring by government contractors. Little was accomplished, however, until the civil rights movement of the 1960s gathered momentum and an Executive Order was issued which called for termination of contracts if such a hiring policy were not adopted. Informal attempts were made at first to secure cooperation from contractors, but later the sanction of contract termination was employed. Other efforts against bias resulted in a campaign to sign nondiscriminatory agreements with contractors and a policy of requiring from contractors "pre-award" pledges to take affirmative action in this field. The Civil Rights Act of 1964 extended equal-employment-opportu-

---

[24] See Herbert C. Morton, *Public Contracts and Public Wages: Experience under the Walsh-Healy Act* (Washington: The Brookings Institution, 1965).

[25] Arthur S. Miller and W. Theodore Pierson, Jr., "Observations on the Consistency of Federal Procurement Policies with Other Governmental Policies," *Law and Contemporary Problems*, vol. 29, p. 289, Spring, 1964.

nity requirements to all businesses above a certain size (25 employees, eventually), but the hiring policies of contractors continue to be of particular governmental concern.

Two additional public policy objectives sought through government procurement bear less directly on the internal operations of the individual contractor: the encouragement of small business and the geographical distribution of contract awards.

The Small Business Administration has striven to assist smaller firms in obtaining contracts through a program of set asides. This program has permitted only small firms to bid on those contracts set aside. In other prime contracts, contractors are required to subcontract, where possible, with small firms. In the defense and space fields, the set-aside program has had little value for small firms, but the second program has resulted in small firms receiving about 40 percent of the subcontracts let. Yet throughout the 1960s, a large proportion of all defense and space business has been concentrated in as few as 100 relatively large firms.[26] In general, small firms have fared better with the procurement of civilian agencies of government, receiving up to half of the prime contracts awarded by the General Services Administration.[27]

A parallel attempt has been made to use government procurement to foster the economic development of depressed areas. A set-aside program was established, similar to that for small business. Like its counterpart, however, it has largely failed in achieving its objectives—more than a third of all military procurement goes to three of the wealthiest states: California, New York, and Texas.[28]

[26] Albert N. Schrieber, "Small Business and Government Procurement," *Law and Contemporary Problems*, vol. 29, pp. 390–417, Spring, 1964. See also "100 Companies and Their Subsidiary Corporations Listed According to Net Value of Military Prime Contract Awards," issued annually by the Office of the Secretary of Defense, Directorate for Statistical Services.

[27] Murray L. Weidenbaum, "The Military Space Market: The Intersection of the Public and Private Sectors," included in *Competition in Defense Procurement, Hearings before the Subcommittee on Antitrust and Monopoly of the Committee on the Judiciary*, U.S. Senate, June 17 and 21 and Sept. 10, 1968, p. 896.

[28] Roger E. Bolton, in perhaps the most authoritative study of the economic impact of defense purchases, *Defense Purchases and Regional Growth* (Washington: The Brookings Institution, 1966), concludes that the prevailing policy that dictates placing contracts with the "most efficient" firm or the

INDEPENDENCE AND ACCOUNTABILITY

The extensive use of the contract as a mechanism to involve private enterprises—profit-making business firms and non-profit-making universities, hospitals, and other institutions—and the comprehensive rules, regulations, and practices that have been developed to guide the carrying out of these contracts prompt us to reconsider why government has preferred to use private enterprise rather than to perform these tasks in-house. It is because government needs the talent, the capabilities, or the acceptance of a professional group [29] that it contracts with a private nongovernmental institution—a business firm, a university, a hospital, a nonprofit agency, or a social agency. The contractor cannot perform its task effectively, cannot put its full talent and capabilities to work for the government, and cannot contribute creatively to the end sought unless it has freedom to go about the task according to its own best judgment. At the same time the contracting government agency must assume ultimate responsibility for the activities performed under the contract.

Depressing the entrepreneurial function

The American society has benefited greatly from the contribution of its entrepreneurs. Within that category must be included —in addition to the individual who started a business, conceived

firm offering the "least cost" may not be the most desirable policy. His conclusion points to the economic significance of defense purchases when they constitute as substantial a proportion of the gross national product as has been the case during the 1960s. See also "Federal Expenditures to States and Regions: A Study of Their Distribution and Impact," prepared by the Subcommittee on Government Relations of the Committee on Government Operations, U.S. Senate, June 29, 1966.

[29] Illustrative of this reason for contracting out are (1) a contract between the Department of State and the Conference Board of Associated Research Councils for assistance in the selection of "Fulbright scholars" for assignment to fellowships overseas, and (2) a contract between the Department of Health, Education, and Welfare and the American Psychological Association for assistance in the accrediting of university graduate departments of psychology in connection with programs of the Department. In both instances the federal department entrusts to an external agency responsibility for making judgments of the peers in a profession, which the profession would be loath to have the government make.

a new product, or developed a new service—the teacher who developed a new private school to meet a particular need; the physician who carried on his research even while he carried on his practice and developed a new cure; those civic-minded women who, recognizing the pitiful plight of abandoned infants, gave their time, energy, and money to the establishment of an agency to find adoptive and foster homes. In each such venture, there was risk, the promise of reward, the social good. Is the contribution of the entrepreneur today being depressed or lost?

The substantial expansion of governmental activity can stimulate or depress that vital private entrepreneurial effort. Government assumes that function when it becomes the sole conceiver of new weapons systems, of new educational ventures, of new health research, and new social agencies.[30] It encourages the assumption of that function by the private sector when it makes resources available to support ideas in fields that promise some social good.

Let us examine what happens in the production of weapons systems. In many instances, military research people conceive of the weapon needed, let a contract for its development and, subsequently, its production; government is both entrepreneur and consumer. Alternatively, the defense contractor may, and often does, conceive of a new weapon, submit an unsolicited proposal to the government, and be awarded a contract for its development; in this case, the contractor has performed the entrepreneurial role.

These alternative examples oversimplify the real-life process; they imply too sharp a division between contractor and contractee. The scientists, engineers, and executives from the government and from the contracting firms work constantly together. In many instances it would be impossible to trace the origin of an idea to either a private or a public brain. The idea is the consequence of the interaction between thoughtful men in the firm and in the government.[31]

[30] This point of view was vigorously—and aptly—presented to the Congress in late 1969, in opposition to proposals for the taxation of philanthropic foundations on the grounds that such taxation would diminish funds available for private social agencies and further concentrate such activities in government.

[31] See Merton J. Peck and Frederic M. Scherer, *The Weapons Acquisition Process: An Economic Analysis* (Boston: Harvard Graduate School of Business Administration, 1962), pp. 236–238, for realistic depiction of this interaction between the private and the public sector.

Under prevailing contract practices the contractor assumes less risk (and has less opportunity for gain) than has been traditionally associated with entrepreneurship. Development of a weapon, a new drug, an educational curriculum, or a new design for low-income housing during the stage when it is uncertain whether the product will work is financed in full or in major part by the government. A market is substantially assured by a known need and government's prospective demand for the product.

Most weapons contracts include one or more of such risk-transferring features as the provision of plant, equipment, working capital, and the guarantee of credit. But the extent to which the risk is transferred varies greatly. When incentive-type contracts are negotiated, the contractor assumes greater risk and enjoys the prospect of greater profit. He may assume greater risk when government does not furnish the plant, equipment, and other resources he requires, although such additional risk may be offset by other contract terms. He is subject to the risk that advance in weapons technology may make his product obsolete before it is produced. This possibility highlights the fact that while the defense contractor may experience little or no price competition, he does face a form of rivalry that constitutes substantial risk. The defense contractor must keep technologically up with or ahead of his rivals if he is to succeed in this field; and, since many defense contractors rely largely on defense-space contracts, the prospect that a major government contract in the contractor's field of specialization will be lost to a rival is a substantial risk indeed.

Limiting managerial discretion

Effective performance by organizational enterprises—a business firm, a nonprofit research laboratory, or a community action agency—depends heavily, we have come to believe, on the capability of management; and the effectiveness of management depends, in significant part, on the exercise of discretion. Is managerial discretion limited under prevailing contractual arrangements? Must it be? Should it be?

Freedom in the choice of personnel is limited. Equal-employment-opportunity requirements in government contracts achieve a valid objective but may impose difficult adjustments on the contractor's work force. Security requirements similarly serve an essential end when "classified work" is performed, but create inflexibilities to which managements have to become accustomed. In some few instances government contracting officers stipulate that certain individuals must be assigned to work on the project, or a contractor may be required to substitute a particular individual for another whom government officials deem incapable. Managerial discretion is limited, in other instances, by requiring approval of "make-or-buy" decisions, i.e., decisions on whether to produce a component (or a service) or to purchase it from a vendor. When a contractor makes a decision to buy rather than to make a component, he must conform with regulations as to the method of selecting a subcontractor; for example, he may be expected to conform to the small business and depressed area set-aside programs earlier depicted, and he must subsequently monitor the subcontractor's performance just as his own is monitored by the government. Finally, managerial discretion may be still further limited by government contract administrators assigned full time to a contractor's establishment or by government auditors.

The full-time contract administrator oversees the contractor's operations to assure conformance with contract provisions and prevailing regulations (i.e., the Armed Services Procurement Regulation). His full-time presence may mean that the plant management is induced to do what the resident representative deems desirable rather than what the contractor's judgment dictates, although in practice the representative (usually a military officer) often becomes more a spokesman for the contractor than for the government.

Government auditors may limit managerial discretion by (1) offering judgments as to whether inventories are adequate or excessive and as to whether inventory items are adequately standardized,[32] and (2) extending the scope and detail of their audits to comprehend the *processes* by which the contractor manages as well as the *results* he achieves.[33]

With the nonprofit contractor, the tendency to limit managerial discretion is even more compelling. Lacking any measure of profit, government contractors tend to intervene even more, i.e., to express judgments as to *how* the contractee should carry out

[32] See Martin Ives, "Audit Techniques in Defense Contracting," *Journal of Accountancy*, Sept., 1963, pp. 58–63; see also *The Government Contractor and the General Accounting Office*, a report prepared by the Machinery and Allied Products Institute and the Council for Technological Advancement, 1966.

[33] Paul F. Hannah, "Government Buying Erodes Management," *Harvard Business Review*, vol. 42, pp. 55–56, May–June, 1964.

the work or to fix limits as to the maximum salaries that may be paid. Simultaneously, there is an apparent effort to develop new measures of cost effectiveness to appraise the value of what is done by a regional educational laboratory, a university medical school, or a federally funded research center.

In summary, the problem (for civilian government as well as for contractors in the defense and space fields from which most examples have been drawn) created by increasing use of the contract to get public work done is: How to develop the understandings and institutional arrangements that will enable both the executive and legislative branches of government to maintain a strong central policy direction over the contract apparatus while giving the contractors (profit-making and other) such freedom and independence as will maximize incentive and provide them with an opportunity to make a distinctive and creative contribution to the government. To date this has proven a difficult, indeed, an almost insuperable task!

OBLITERATING PUBLIC-PRIVATE DISTINCTIONS

As the scope of social wants broadens and the variety of responsibilities thrust on government increases, the American society is forced to find new ways of mixing public and private enterprise in the production of wanted goods and services. Timeworn dogma as to the inequities of socialism and the essentiality of keeping government out of business offers little help. The task is to find new and relevant ways of getting public work done, be it building a nuclear submarine, making payments under Medicare, developing an artificial heart, or involving the poor in raising the level of living in slum areas.

Alternative ways of accomplishing this task include:

■ The government corporation, such as the Commodity Credit Corporation, Panama Canal Company, or the proposed public corporation to operate the Post Office Department [34]

■ The public authority, such as the New York Port Authority and the Tennessee Valley Authority

■ The joint public-private corporation, such as Comsat (the

---

[34] *Toward Postal Excellence,* the Report of the President's Commission on Postal Organization, June, 1968.

Communications Satellite Corporation established in 1962) and the Public Television Corporation (established in 1968)

■ The nonprofit agency, such as the university, the hospital, or a variety of research and social agencies

■ The "semigovernmental" corporation, such as General Dynamics, Raytheon, Lockheed, McDonnell Douglas, and others

■ The private corporation which obtains substantial contracts from the government but does the bulk of its business with commercial customers, such as General Electric and IBM

In the evolution of these ways of accomplishing public tasks there has been a continuous effort to obtain, in varying degrees, four essential elements:

1. The specialized talents required for effective performance of tasks that were often new and unprecedented, and sometimes very large

2. A degree of independence for the management of the enterprise that would ensure efficient, creative, and economic performance

3. The supplementation of public financing by additional private financing of the enterprise (e.g., the Tennessee Valley Authority, Boeing's supersonic transport, and Comsat)

4. The maintenance of essential public control of public tasks, with simultaneous elimination or minimization of governmental involvement in the operational aspects limiting entrepreneurial zeal or managerial discretion

The result of these persistent efforts has been twofold. Over the decades since World War II, there has been established in the United States an extended governmental structure that involves a substantial segment of the private sector of this country's economy in the performance of public services. Stubborn timeworn concepts of the separate and exclusive provinces of business and government have been rendered meaningless.

CHAPTER 5

Nurturing Technological Advance

P_{RIOR} to World War II, this nation relied primarily upon private industry, universities, hospitals and other institutions, and individuals to advance the frontiers of knowledge, to develop new processes and products, to discover scientific truths—in economics and psychology as well as in chemistry, physics, and mathematics—to reveal the causes of disease and develop the cures.

ASSUMING A NEW RESPONSIBILITY

Throughout the nineteenth and early twentieth century, owing to the initiative of private enterprise—businessmen, professors, and physicians principally—the United States led other countries of the world in harnessing technology to the development of products, processes, and new concepts (e.g., the national income accounts as a tool of analysis in economics). But it relied heavily upon Europe for advances in basic research, for the training of many scientists, and for the models used by our universities in developing scientific education.

The first major proposal that government should stimulate and support scientific education, the development of new knowledge, and the widespread undertaking of research grew out of the experience government had had during World War II in the utilization of a variety of agencies to perform essential research, e.g., in the development of radar. This proposal was presented in a report entitled *Science, the Endless Frontier* by Vannevar Bush.[1] The report, submitted to President Truman in 1945, recommended that "Government should accept new responsibilities for promoting the flow of new scientific knowledge and the development of scientific talent in our youth." It proposed establishment of a National Research Foundation to provide support for basic research and for scientific education.

Bush's proposal effectively changed government's traditional role in relation to science. In substance, Bush proposed that government accept responsibility for a function this country had previously left to the private sector to perform. By the late 1960s the federal government had assumed responsibility for ensuring that this nation would enjoy the benefits of a rapidly and broadly advancing technology, even as a century earlier it had assumed a similar responsibility for the advance of agriculture.

In 1970, the federal government finances most of the basic research carried on in this country; serves as a prime source of financing for universities and other nonprofit research-performing institutions; and supports scientific education by loans, fellowships, and grants. It has also asserted its responsibility as the "balance wheel," to use George Kistiakowsky's descriptive phrase; it strives to ensure that academic research, "little science," and the social sciences are pursued even while major research in the hard sciences is carried on in large volume to underpin the defense and space programs. Government accepts responsibility for seeing to it that a well-proportioned pattern serves the national interest.[2] Important as science is, the public interest calls for science in its place, in perspective, in conjunction with all other disciplines.

[1] Washington: U.S. Government Printing Office, 1945.

[2] See National Academy of Sciences, *Basic Research and National Goals*, A Report to the Committee on Science and Astronautics, U.S. House of Representatives, Committee Print, March, 1965.

To discharge this expanding function the National Science Foundation was created in 1950, a Special Assistant to the President for Science and Technology was appointed in 1957 (a few weeks after Sputnik I flew), a Federal Council for Science and Technology was set up in 1959, and an Office of Science and Technology was established within the Executive Office of the President in 1962.

In the closing days of World War II, it was still possible to charge specific government agencies with responsibility for specific areas of science. By the 1960s, this was no longer possible. A conflict developed between the concept that an agency should be responsible for all research in a particular discipline and the concept that each scientific discipline will likely be used by two or more agencies and that the need is for horizontal communication within each discipline across agency lines. The government has responded (1) by creating interagency coordinating committees and (2) by creating in some instances a new agency to deal with a new technology (e.g., NASA, AEC); thus "an agency developed around a technological theme rather than a social mission." [3]

GROWTH AND TECHNOLOGY

Growth is essential—for an individual or a society. What makes growth occur in a society is still largely a mystery, but an advancing technology is clearly a major cause of growth.[4] What kind of environment and stimuli encourage growth is still not clear. But that growth is dependent upon the well-balanced and persistent increase in knowledge—economic and sociological knowledge, as well as knowledge of the more exact sciences—is quite clear. Our national security, the resolution of the problems that blight our domestic life—health care, urban transport, environmental pollution, crime, and unemployment—and long-term national economic growth are dependent, we have come to realize, on the speeding of technological advance.

[3] Harvey Brooks, "The Federal Establishment for Science and Technology: Contribution to New National Goals," in *Research in the Service of Man: Biomedical Knowledge, Development and Use,* a conference sponsored by the Subcommittee on Government Research and the Frontiers of Science Foundation of Oklahoma for the Committee on Government Operations, U.S. Senate, November, 1967.

[4] The mystery has lessened since the publication of Edward F. Denison's notable volume, *The Sources of Economic Growth in the United States and the Alternatives before Us* (Committee for Economic Development, 1962).

Hence, the federal government now finances two-thirds of all research conducted in universities and half the research carried on by industry. And the vast increase in this support (from $75 million in 1940 to close to $17 billion in 1970) has raised "serious questions regarding the resulting pattern of research effort and the role of government in the development of American technology . . . possible distortions in the allocation of scientific and technical resources" and "the even broader question of what effects the continuation of this situation might have over the long term on the structure of the American economy." [5]

Hence, this chapter examines the reasons for this vast increase in federal support and weighs its significance on the character of the developing political economy—on private innovation and on the structure of the national economy.

SUPPORT OF PRIVATE INNOVATION

Government can stimulate private research efforts (1) by establishing a legal framework and climate for research and (2) by providing active support through financial or other aid. Government has long provided the first kind of stimulus; since World War II, it has also provided large and steadily increasing financial aid to stimulate private research.

The Constitution provides two ways of stimulating private initiative to bring about technological advance—through the issuance of patents and through the establishment of standard weights and measures. From the early nineteenth century, the federal government has engaged in programs to disseminate scientific information. Over the intervening years, these several methods of assisting private innovators have been continued, expanded, and supplemented in order to spur the development of new knowledge and its applications in the private sector.

Government patent policy

The reservation of exclusive rights to an invention for a limited time, by the issuance of a patent, rewards the originator of new knowledge and encourages rapid introduction of new products and services into the market. Patenting obviates the need for se-

[5] Chamber of Commerce of the United States, Committee on Science and Technology, *Criteria for Federal Support of Research and Development*, 1965, p. 2.

crecy, and the disclosure of information required to obtain a patent makes available new knowledge which is the source of further innovation.

The expansion of government contracting with private enterprises during the post-World War II years has posed a new and complex problem. It is, in short, this: When a new product or method is developed in the course of carrying out research and development supported by government funds, should the patent be held by the government or by the private inventor?

The objectives of present government policy are these: "The use and practice of these inventions and discoveries [i.e., those developed in the course of carrying out government contracts] should stimulate inventors, meet the needs of government, recognize the equities of the contractor, and serve the public interest." [6] But the departments and agencies of Federal government strive to achieve these objectives in various ways.

Four different practices exist.[7] The Department of Defense customarily allows its contractors to keep government-financed patents for commercial development; it retains for the government the right to utilize the invention without charge and the right to revoke a license if the contractor does not make use of it. The Atomic Energy Commission, in contrast, takes title for the government to all patents developed under government-supported research and development. It may, but seldom does, waive its rights in favor of the contractor. When it takes title, it allows the invention to be used without charge by industry generally. The National Aeronautics and Space Administration takes title as does the AEC, but it waives it rights in favor of the contractor much more frequently than does the Atomic Energy Commission. The three national health agencies within HEW (particularly, the National Institutes of Health) require each recipient of a grant for research in medicinal chemistry to report all inventions arising out of grant-supported activities; they then determine the grantee's rights, if any, under the patent.[8]

[6] From *Memorandum and Statement of Government Patent Policy,* issued by President Kennedy in 1963.

[7] See *A Review of NASA's Patent Program,* March, 1967, for a full description of licensing policy, and W. Henry Lambright, "Government, Industry and the Research Partnership: The Case of Patent Policy," *Public Administration Review,* May–June, 1968, pp. 214–221.

[8] Reporting to the Congress in 1967 on "Problems Affecting Usefulness of Results of Government-sponsored Research in Medicinal Chemistry," the Comptroller General of the United States found this to be a serious handi-

Business contends that the government's objectives will be better achieved and "the government will generally get a better research job done under the license policy and . . . a property right in the form of a patent can usually be converted into a public benefit more quickly, more efficiently, and more cheaply when privately held than when public ownership separates that right from the propulsive force of the profit motive." [9] This view is sharply challenged however by some who argue that government should retain title to such patents and make them available to all comers on a royalty-free basis.[10]

Setting of standards

The establishment of standards and codes by the National Bureau of Standards and other government agencies is designed to accomplish three objectives: to encourage technological innovation, to facilitate commerce by assuring the uniformity of goods produced in different states, and to protect public health and safety.

But standards and codes can become barriers to innovation when they fail to keep pace with changes made possible by new developments. Then they discourage private producers from seeking or adopting new methods of production. To avoid this undesirable effect, the Bureau has departed from the practice of setting specific and detailed standards and in recent years has developed new criteria based upon performance.

Dissemination of information

Thomas Jefferson proposed in the early nineteenth century that government bring the aid of the sciences to the farmers. But it remained for the Agricultural Extension Service, a half century later, to provide for the continual dissemination of scientific information to farmers throughout the nation. From this early

cap "in bringing potential therapeutic agents to the point of practical application," since the drug companies have refused to carry on grant-supported research under such conditions and discontinued screening and testing services for compounds prepared under NIH-financed research.

[9] Statement of Charles I. Derr, Machinery & Allied Products Institute, in *Hearings before the Subcommittee on Patents, Trademarks and Copyrights, Committee on the Judiciary,* U.S. Senate, 89th Cong., June, 1965, part I, p. 241.

[10] See, for example, Leonard Baker, *The Guaranteed Society* (New York: The Macmillan Company, 1968), pp. 136, 139, and 143.

focus on agriculture, government has extended its efforts to disseminate scientific data. Most federal departments and agencies now make some forms of technical information available to the public.[11] In addition to distributing information stemming from government projects, they maintain information centers and assemble, in bibliographies and abstracts, information as to new scientific developments and new knowledge for dissemination in a wide variety of publications.

Federal efforts to disseminate technological information to the public have been increased and made more effective in recent years. However, they are hampered—particularly in the fields of defense, space, and atomic energy—by security-impelled administrative restrictions. One study has estimated that DOD restrictions keep about one-third of all federally controlled technology out of the conventional channels of information dissemination.[12]

The vital enrichment of the stock of scientific knowledge available to all private firms, and to all citizens, takes place through publication. The universities constitute the principal source of such new knowledge since the bulk of all basic research is performed there, and they are committed to the publication of results that they may be available to all. In addition, governmental agencies [13] and those few industrial firms that do carry on basic research publish valuable new knowledge.

Financial encouragement

Traditionally, this country's government has not granted subsidies to profit-making enterprises for the support of research, al-

[11] The Clearinghouse for Federal Scientific and Technical Information, administered by the Department of Commerce, is the major distributor of information. It assembles and categorizes nonclassified engineering and physical science data generated through government research and collects significant information from other national and international sources.

[12] Legislative Reference Service, Library of Congress, *Policy Planning for Technology Transfer*, 1967, p. 3.

[13] The National Aeronautics and Space Administration, the Atomic Energy Commission, the National Bureau of Standards, the agricultural experiment stations—all contribute a steady flow of new knowledge to the public domain. For example, the Aerospace Research Application Center (ARAC), established by NASA under contract with the Indiana University Foundation, receives machine-readable files and microfiche copies of all nonclassified information generated by the space program, the Atomic Energy Commission, and the Department of Defense. The ARAC information resources also include the machine-readable files of Engineering Index, Inc., and the Chemical Ab-

though in his *Report on Manufactures,* Alexander Hamilton proposed such aid.[14] Alternatively government has encouraged research by private enterprises by granting favorable tax treatment. The current costs of carrying on research, for example, are deductible against net corporate income. In recent years, this form of encouragement has been reaffirmed. The Internal Revenue Code of 1954 (Section 174) made clear that all current costs for research and development are deductible, thus removing uncertainty that earlier led to restrictive interpretations. In addition, certain capital outlays associated with the conduct of research were made deductible.[15]

The fact that gifts to nonprofit organizations engaged in scientific research are both deductible from income taxes and exempt from gift and estate taxes also constitutes a large stimulus to research. These tax concessions have resulted in the establishment or expansion of many institutes, foundations, and nonprofit corporations, supported by business firms and aimed at adding to

stracts CONDENSATES file. Firms may subscribe to a variety of information services and products based on these resources for as little as $150 per year. Typical fee for a medium-sized firm is approximately $2,000 per year for a complete package of services which allows the firm to subscribe to regular distribution of information relevant to their needs, to receive any material on file, and to obtain responses to inquiries concerning information available on a given subject.

[14] In Europe, government bounties for technological advances were early established as part of the mercantilist economic system. In modern times, European states have employed the device of a joint public-private research association to assist in advancing industrial technology. In Britain, for example, research associations have existed since 1918; about 50 such associations, concerned with the problems of particular industries ranging from baking to wool, are financed both by the contributions of industrial members and by government grants. Similar organizations exist in West Germany, Belgium, France, Sweden, and Japan. For further discussion, see Murray L. Weidenbaum, "Government Encouragement of Private Sector Research and Development," *Studies in Comparative International Development,* vol. I, no. 9 (St. Louis: Washington University, 1965), pp. 125–128.

[15] In other democratic-capitalistic countries, capital expenditures incurred as a basis for conducting research and development are usually written off only through depreciation allowances. In certain instances this is also true in the United States; for example, when the resultant property has a determinable useful life. For a comparative treatment of 24 countries, see J. Van Hoorn, Jr., *Tax Treatment of Research and Development,* Organisation for Economic Co-operation and Development, 1962.

man's knowledge and solving common problems, at what is, in effect, a reduced cost of investment.

In addition, under certain circumstances federal contracting agencies reimburse firms engaged in research for one-half of the costs of the research that the firm has undertaken and carried on at its own initiative. This financial support is available even though there is no assurance that the research undertaken will yield findings of direct value to the government; indeed, it is not even required that the results be made available to the scientific community generally.[16] Until 1970 the Department of Defense made approximately $1 billion available for the support of such independent research.

Direct promotion of industrial innovation

Two additional programs were launched in the 1960s to stimulate business to apply new technological knowledge.

The Office of State Technical Services, established within the Department of Commerce in 1965, supports state efforts to assist business, particularly small business, in obtaining and applying new technology. The programs are modeled on earlier activities of the land-grant universities, which aided farmers to identify their problems and to apply technological information or advice.

Similarly, the National Bureau of Standards launched the Textile and Apparel Technology program in 1963. Under this program the Bureau of Standards disseminated information on textile technology, conducted systems analysis of the industry, and joined with interested apparel firms in the support of research designed to solve problems common to the entire industry on a cooperative basis. The program was discontinued in January, 1968.

Projects similar to the apparel program were proposed in the

---

[16] Only contractors having government cost-reimbursement type contracts are eligible. DOD, the most liberal supporter of independent research and development, requires that projects be related to the product lines in which the government has contracts. The AEC requires that IR&D costs be provided for in advance in regular contracts and that projects must be shown to benefit those contracts. Similarly NASA will not reimburse unsolicited IR&D proposals. See Richard N. Flint, "Independent Research and Development Expenditures: A Study of the Government Contract as an Instrument of Public Policy," *Law and Contemporary Problems*, vol. 29, pp. 611–630, Spring, 1964.

machine tools and building industries as part of a Civilian Industrial Technology program. That program was opposed on the grounds that federal support might interfere with the functioning of the free market. Instead of the sizable and continuing program envisioned, modeled on European public-private research associations, only the short-lived textile program was funded. No attempts have since been made to promote innovation on an industry-by-industry basis.

THE NEWER ROLE
OF GOVERNMENT

Even while the relationship of an advancing technology to the rate and direction of national economic growth has become increasingly clear,[17] the persistence of the cold war—and intermittent hot wars—has been responsible for the bulk of governmental support for the discovery, development, and application of new knowledge. Throughout the postwar years, expenditures in support of military technology and related space technology have made up 80 percent of all government spending for research and development.

By the mid-1950s, leaders of this nation's scientific community were vigorously voicing three elemental facts. They contended that technological advance is dependent upon a substantial and prior investment in basic research; that the research required to expand fundamental knowledge should not be governed—and distorted—by the needs of the military; and that this country could no longer afford to rely on the uncoordinated activities of scientists in universities, in private research institutions, and in business enterprises pursuing their individual interests with limited resources. The new knowledge thus acquired and

[17] In his study, *The Sources of Economic Growth in the United States and the Alternatives before Us,* Edward F. Denison disclosed that 20 percent of the economic growth achieved between 1929 and 1957 was the direct consequence of advances in knowledge. A more recent study affirms and supplements this finding. Richard R. Nelson, Merton J. Peck, and Edward D. Kalachek (*Technology, Economic Growth, and Public Policy,* Washington: The Brookings Institution, 1967) identify technology as the catalyst in achieving economic growth and note that advances in technology contribute to growth by providing new and improved products and better methods of production and also by spurring the advance of education and the rate of capital investment, other direct sources of economic growth.

the balance maintained among various sciences simply would not suffice to serve the needs of an expanding population and to keep this nation competitive—economically and militarily—in an ever-more-compacted world.

Basic research

Their admonitions—supported by the continued threat of war —had effect. Federal expenditures for the support of basic research increased twentyfold between 1953 and 1969. This growth represented greatly increased emphasis on basic research.[18] The proportion of the total federal R&D expenditure earmarked for basic research rose from 3.5 to 14 percent.

Support of education and nonprofit organizations

To expand this nation's capability to advance knowledge, government has also greatly increased its support for the training of scientists and engineers.[19] This effort began in 1958 with the National Defense Education Act which provided support to high schools for science education and provided financial aid to college and graduate students.

Government's principal support for education in the sciences, however, is provided through contracts and grants to universities and their associated research centers. Federal research and devel-

[18] "Basic research shows continued growth because of general recognition that a portion of the national output should be purposely so assigned as a foundation for technological and cultural advance. . . . Since the mid-1950's basic research has shown the most rapid rise among the three R&D components. Its funds gained added impetus in the post-Sputnik era when new emphasis was placed both on space research and on education, and all major R&D agencies received increased appropriations for their basic research programs." National Science Foundation, *Federal Funds for Research, Development, and Other Scientific Activities*, vol. XV, 1966, p. 9.

[19] "Government aid to education is based upon the understanding that many more scientists and engineers must be educated to meet the requirements of a technologically advanced society. Accordingly, fellowships, loans, and facilities grants are beginning to have a profound effect on the teaching, as well as the research, side of the university equation. Furthermore, new programs of federal aid to primary and secondary schools will only have the net effect of increasing popular demand for university education. On all sides, universities now find themselves firmly constituted as important components of public policy." J. Stephen Dupre and Sanford A. Lakoff, "The New Partnership," in Roger E. Bolton (ed.), *Defense and Disarmament, The Economics of Transition* (Englewood Cliffs, N.J.: Prentice-Hall, Inc., 1966), pp. 169–170.

opment obligations to such institutions quadrupled over the past decade, standing at over $2 billion in 1969. (See Table 6.1, Chapter 6, page 116.) In addition to research contracts, these universities and related institutions receive grants from the National Science Foundation, the National Institutes of Health, and other agencies. To build this nation's scientific capability and to conduct the research and development required to achieve public goals—e.g., the development of a ballistic missile defense, the landing of a man on the moon, the finding of a cure for cancer or of ways to desalinize water—government has turned increasingly to the universities, colleges, and nonprofit agencies where it could find the personnel, facilities, and intellectual climate conducive to doing basic research.[20]

[20] The extent of the involvement of the universities and associated research centers is suggested by the following summary, published in *Business Week*, June 7, 1969, picturing the university and nonprofit "network" that performed military research in 1968:

Value of government research contracts, fiscal year 1968 (in millions)

Ten universities: 41.8%

M.I.T.	$119.1
Johns Hopkins	57.6
University of California	17.3
Stanford	16.4
University of Rochester	13.1
Cornell	12.5
Illinois Institute of Technology	12.1
Pennsylvania State	10.5
Columbia	9.9
University of Michigan	9.4

Eight "think tanks" and nonprofits: 30.7%

Aerospace Corp.	$ 73.3
Mitre Corp.	35.7
Stanford Research Institute	28.7
Rand Corp.	19.1
System Development Corp.	17.3
Institute for Defense Analyses	11.6
Research Analysis Corp.	10.0
Battelle Memorial Institute	8.3

And 113 other agencies: 27.5%

90 universities	$143.5
10 institutes	21.2
6 federal agencies	13.3
7 others	4.5
TOTAL	$664.4

This growing national dependence was threatened in the late 1960s when some college students and faculty members challenged the ethical right of a university to engage in research related to war (e.g., biological and chemical warfare).[21] The challenge was telling, because the extent to which universities had become involved in and dependent upon research for defense and space exploration had never been illuminated, certainly never made an issue for voter choice. The universities had traditionally avoided any semblance of government control; they had argued when the National Defense Education Act was before the Congress that they wanted no federal subsidy if it were to mean even an iota of control. But in important ways they had lost this treasured autonomy by accepting large proportions of their annual budgets in the form of federal research grants and contracts.

The irony of this situation is that when Vannevar Bush first turned the federal establishment toward the universities, he was seeking not only the able talent on their staffs but the perspective, independence, and objectivity of the university scientists. He wanted the arm's-length contracting which university relationships might assure. But the buildup of this federal support for research became so large that the universities lost many of their options when government grants were paying much of the overhead.

The challenge coming in the late 1960s from some college students and faculty members posed a startling question: Must government build its own in-house capability to carry on much of the basic research for which it had come to rely on the universities? And, indeed, could government attract the scientists needed for such research? The issue, still unresolved, is part of the current general reappraisal of this society's values.

Response of the individual firm

As technology has become more and more dependent on progress in fundamental science,[22] business has perforce focused increased attention on basic research. In 1958 industry performed little federally supported basic research ($25 million), compared to that

[21] This issue was studied by a special committee of faculty members, students, administrators, and alumni of the Massachusetts Institute of Technology in May–June, 1969; their report affirmed the desirability of the continuation of M.I.T.'s government-supported research program, but urged a shift in emphasis toward socially oriented projects.

[22] See Hendrik W. Bode, "Reflections on the Relation Between Science and Technology," in *Basic Research and National Goals, op. cit.,* p. 76.

done by educational institutions and by the government itself (see Table 5.1). By 1969 this amount had grown to $391 million, more than one-third of the funds expended for federally supported basic research in universities and colleges. Most was being performed by corporations themselves; of the total of $391 million, only $32 million went to associated nonprofit research centers.[23] Most of this increased expenditure for basic research was made possible by federal support. Industry's own expenditure for basic research remained almost static.

Government's substantial support of education in the sciences builds essential sources of new knowledge and of trained manpower for industry. Business firms have also taken indirect advantage of government's support of science in the universities by establishing new plants, affiliates, and industry-related nonprofit

TABLE 5.1   *Who Performs Federally Supported Basic Research, 1958–1969 (millions of dollars)*

Performer	1958	1962	1966	1968	1969 (est.)
Total.	$334	$1,106	$1,844	$2,104	$2,146
Federal government	125	251	449	515	547
Industrial firms *.	25	236	325	390	391
Universities *.	161	534	940	1,062	1,074
All others	23	85	130	137	135

* Includes Federally Funded Research and Development Centers (FFRDC's) administered by this sector.
SOURCE: National Science Foundation, *Federal Funds for Research, Development, and Other Scientific Activities,* vol. XIII, 1964, p. 112 and vol. XVIII, 1969, p. 256.

research institutes adjacent to universities (e.g., Palo Alto, California, and Cambridge, Massachusetts) to take advantage of the availability of scientific personnel and the "research climate." Some business firms have come into being in these innovative atmospheres; that is, faculty members or researchers, recognizing the commercial value of scientific work in which they were engaged at a university, have established firms to produce a related product or service. The Massachusetts Institute of Technology alone, it has been estimated, has been responsible for 75 to 100 such "spin-off" firms since World War II.[24]

[23] National Science Foundation, *Federal Funds for Research, Development, and Other Scientific Activities,* vol. XVIII, 1969, p. 256.

[24] On this subject generally, see U.S. Congress, House Select Committee on Government Research, *Impact of Federal Research and Development Programs,* 1964, pp. 25–30.

Government has greatly influenced technological progress in individual business firms in several ways. It has fostered the expansion of basic research, stimulated the provision of scientific manpower, encouraged the association of business with the universities, and even induced the establishment of new firms. In short, in stimulating the advance of science, the government has influenced markedly the evolution of industrial technology. If, as seems likely, technological advance proceeds at an even faster rate in the future, government's assumption of responsibility for advancing science promises to be a persistent and major stimulant to business' utilization of science.

SIGNIFICANCE OF THE PARTNERSHIP

The full significance of the expanded responsibility for nurturing the advance of technology that government has assumed in the United States perhaps can best be seen through the eyes of an astute foreign observer, J. J. Servan-Schreiber. He contends that government support for science and technology is one of the keys (perhaps the chief one) to understanding the progress of American industry, at home and abroad.[25] It is clear that the productivity of American industry has outrun that of its European counterpart. And it is clear that American accomplishments in aerospace, in nuclear energy, and in the application of computers have more than industrial significance.

The partnership that has been developed in the United States to nurture technological advance—a partnership between government, industry, and universities and other nonprofit institutions—is a product of the grants economy that contains great promise. It is more than a contractual relationship between a buyer of services and sellers; it is more than a governmental grant-in-aid to support an ongoing governmental program. It is a new means for developing an American resource perhaps more valuable than the fertility of our lands or the ores that lie under them: a means for public-private collaboration in nurturing the innate capabilities of Americans to advance and utilize science and technology. The ends sought through this partnership—ends of large consequence to a society—are pictured in the chapter that follows.

[25] J. J. Servan-Schreiber, *The American Challenge* (New York: Atheneum Publishers, 1968), pp. 65–66.

CHAPTER *6*

Building National Strength with Technology

U_{NTIL} a very few years ago, there was no general concern as to whether knowledge—the raw material from which inventions, discoveries, concepts, cures, materials, processes, and products are made—was being expanded rapidly enough; as to whether enough scientists, engineers, and scholars were being developed; and as to whether new knowledge was being sought to meet *all* the needs of the society or only the needs of agriculture, national security, aeronautics, and public health. Indeed, the prevailing view was that these questions were not a proper concern of national policy.

"That government governs best," that doughty Virginian Thomas Jefferson had held (more than a century earlier, it is true!), "that governs least." Guided by this precept, we left to the "unseen hand" the cultivation of an invaluable resource. A few exceptions were made; for instance, government encouraged re-

113

search to find ways to increase the productivity of our farms. But by and large government did not interfere with the chance of discovery.

Change changed all that. The needs of a growing population, the exigencies of urbanization, expanding social wants, the emergence of an ever-more beneficent (biochemistry) and an ever-more awesome (nuclear energy) technology, and the expanding threat of attack by a nation possessing a superior technology forced government to take a hand. The grants economy fashioned the tools with which government has slowly and fumblingly nurtured this invaluable resource of technology and harnessed it to this nation's needs.

EVOLVING WAYS TO NURTURE

Although not overly concerned with the expansion of basic knowledge, the federal government, almost since its founding, has engaged in and sponsored research to achieve particular objectives. Two alternative ways have been utilized throughout the years. Government has carried on "intramural" research, with its own scientists in its own laboratories; and, more recently, through contracts and grants it has supported "extramural" research in universities, in private business, and in research institutions.

Most federally supported research other than in agriculture was performed intramurally by such agencies as the Naval Observatory, the Coast and Geodetic Survey, the Weather Bureau, the Army Ordnance Laboratories, the Naval Research Laboratory, and the National Advisory Committee for Aeronautics. Medical investigations were conducted by the Army Medical Corps, by the U.S. Public Health Service, and—to some extent—by the Veterans Administration.

Research in agriculture was carried on in the laboratories of the Department of Agriculture. But in 1862 the land-grant college system was established. Within each land-grant college (roughly, one in each state) agricultural experiment stations were established about 1887. These were supported by the federal government to carry on research in agricultural sciences and thus to supplement what was done within government.

When it became necessary, early in World War II, to develop new and improved weapons (e.g., the atomic bomb) on a crash basis, precedent suggested that the federal government conduct this crucial and secret research within its own laboratories. But the necessity of marshaling the ablest talent this nation had to meet these critical needs induced such men as Vannevar Bush, James B. Conant, and Karl T. Compton to persuade those who had authority to utilize the scientists and facilities of private universities and large corporations.[1]

The Office of Scientific Research and Development, headed by Bush, gave two of the nation's top technical schools—the Massachusetts Institute of Technology and the California Institute of Technology—responsibility for developing radar and rockets, respectively. To split the atom, talent was drawn from industry (from such firms as du Pont, General Electric, and Union Carbide) and from the universities, and this team of scientists was established at the University of Chicago as the Manhattan District of the Army Engineers.[2] A similar team of scientists was established at the University of California and charged with fabricating the bomb itself.

In 1941, 46 percent of government's research and development funds was spent extramurally. By 1945, the proportion had reached 60 percent.[3] After the war, the continued need for large-scale scientific work by government and the notable success of wartime projects carried out by the private sector prompted not only the continuation of, but also the increase in emphasis on, contracting out for research and development.

The wartime peak of annual federal expenditures for research and development had reached $1.6 billion in 1945.[4] After dipping to a postwar low of $855 million in 1948, the level of spending rose above the wartime high in 1952, amounting to $1.8 billion. In the period 1953–1957, when the country was reacting to the Soviet Union's acquisition of nuclear capability, the annual expenditures soared to unprecedented levels—$3 to $4 billion.[5] After the Russians sent Sputnik I aloft in 1957, the annual ex-

[1] Irvin Stewart, *Organizing Scientific Research for War: History of the Office of Scientific Research and Development* (Boston: Little, Brown and Company, 1948).

[2] Don K. Price, *The Scientific Estate* (Cambridge, Mass.: Harvard University Press, 1965), p. 73.

[3] Derived from data in *Statistical Abstract of the United States,* 1960, p. 538.

[4] Including expenditures for requisite plant and facilities.

[5] National Science Foundation, *Federal Funds for Research, Development, and Other Scientific Activities,* vol. XVII, 1968, pp. 216–217.

penditures rose to almost $6 billion in 1959 and to over $10 billion in 1962. More is being spent by government on research and development in 1970 (approximately $17 billion) [6] than was spent annually for all governmental functions in prewar years. By the late 1960s, about 80 percent of federal research and development funds was spent extramurally, and the federal government was relying on nongovernmental agencies to perform more than four times the value of all research and development supported by government 10 years earlier.

Universities and other nonprofit organizations have been tapped to perform an increasing proportion of the research and development supported by government during this period. But half the funds expended by government for research and development in 1956 were disbursed through contracts with private business enterprises, and in 1968, 60 percent was spent through

TABLE 6.1 *Where Federally Supported Research Was Done*
(*billions of dollars*)

Performer	1956	1960	1964	1969 (est.)
Total	$3.0	$7.5	$14.2	$17.3
Intramural	1.0	1.7	2.8	3.8
Extramural: *	2.0	5.8	11.4	13.5
Industrial firms	1.6	4.8	9.1	10.2
Universities and				
colleges	0.3	0.8	1.7	2.4
Other **	—	0.2	0.6	0.9

* Includes research centers administered under these categories.
** Less than $50 million.
SOURCE: National Science Foundation, *Federal Funds for Research, Development, and Other Scientific Activities*, vol. XVII, 1968, p. 227.

such contracts. This increasing proportion, combined with the steep climb in annual expenditure, meant that increasingly large sums of money were devoted to the harnessing of private business effort to carry on research and development to serve public ends.

IMPACT ON INDUSTRY

Before World War II, the bulk of all moneys invested by business in research and development (relatively, a small sum) was

[6] Bureau of the Budget, *Special Analyses, Budget of the United States*, Fiscal Year 1970, p. 250.

provided by business from its own funds. In 1967, American business spent $8 billion of its own funds on research and development.[7] But in that same year, government financed more than half of business' $16.4 billion total expenditure for research and development.

Increased government support brought about the concentration of technological effort in those industries most heavily involved with defense and space work. Approximately half the annual governmental expenditure is made by the Department of Defense (over 20 percent by the Air Force alone); most of the remainder is spent by the National Aeronautics and Space Administration.[8] Hence, four-fifths of all governmental support flows into the aerospace industry (i.e., aircraft, missiles, and spacecraft) and into the related electrical equipment and communications industries.

Four-fifths of all research and development in the aerospace industry and about three-fifths of that done in the electrical industry are done under government contract. Although other industries receive far smaller dollar expenditures, the amount of federal support is substantial in several industries in relation to total sums expended by these industries for research and development (see Table 6.2).

Federal expenditures for research and development are concentrated, in considerable part, in relatively few business firms. In 1967, for example, 4 manufacturing firms received 34 percent of the value of all federal R&D contracts awarded to manufacturing firms; 20 firms received 73 percent; and 100 firms received 95 percent. These firms accounted for 4, 19, and 42 percent of net sales by manufacturing companies. Only a fourth of all manufacturing firms with 1,000 or more employees perform federally financed research and development.[9]

This concentration of federal contracts in relatively few firms reflects the fact that government objectives can only be served by those enterprises that possess scientific capabilities. A considerable, but indeterminate, proportion of the funds awarded by gov-

[7] National Science Foundation, *Reviews of Data on Science Resources,* no. 17, February, 1969.

[8] National Science Foundation, *Federal Funds for Research, Development, and Other Scientific Activities,* vol. XVII, 1968, pp. 108 and 216–217.

[9] National Science Foundation, *Research and Development in Industry, 1967,* 1969, pp. 38 and 39.

TABLE 6.2 *Federal Support of Research and Development in Selected Manufacturing Industries, 1967*

Industry	Federal funds (millions)	Percent of R&D funded by federal govern.
Aircraft and missiles $4,510		81%
Electrical equipment and communication. 2,240		59
Professional and scientific instruments. 147		32
Machinery 393		27
Motor vehicles and transportation equipment. .389		28
Fabricated metal products 12		7
Rubber products 30		15
Chemicals and allied products. 212		13

SOURCE: National Science Foundation, *Reviews of Data on Science Resources,* no. 17, February, 1969.

ernment to these few large firms filters down to other, usually smaller, firms in the form of subcontracts; some subcontracts involve research and development on components of the prime project. The Martin Marietta Company, prime contractor for the launch vehicle in Project Gemini, for example, subcontracted parts of the work to 1,500 to 1,800 subcontractors. McDonnell Aircraft Corporation, prime contractor for the space capsule in this same project, subcontracted with more than 3,000 firms.[10]

BALANCED APPLICATION

To what extent has the concentration of this nation's scientific resources on defense and space objectives limited the application of advancing technology to the satisfaction of other human wants? Would Americans enjoy an even broader range of products in 1970 (e.g., in addition to jet aircraft, satellite television, transistor radios, Dacron and Corfam) if the effort of government to promote technological advance had been concentrated less on defense and space objectives? To what extent would Americans' health care system, their schools, their cities and the environment, the homes they live in, and the trains, planes, and buses they ride serve them better if government had attracted

[10] *New York Times,* Mar. 21, 1965.

less of this country's scientific brainpower to the development of weapons, missiles, and spacecraft?

In short, the problem posed by the concentration of so much of this nation's scientific resources on defense and space objectives is this: Can the American political process be relied upon to provide for the balanced development and application of the benefits of an advancing technology? [11]

Technology to satisfy civilian wants

In the past, the Department of Agriculture (the Agricultural Research Service), the Atomic Energy Commission, the Department of Commerce (the National Bureau of Standards), the Department of Health, Education, and Welfare (particularly, the National Institutes of Health), and the Department of the Interior (the Office of Saline Water), to name a few nondefense or space agencies of government, have performed or supported research to serve civilian wants. The Department of Agriculture has for decades carried on research, in its own laboratories and through the land-grant colleges, to increase the productivity of farm crops (and perhaps they have succeeded too well!) and to improve the strains of livestock; the National Institutes of Health are investing nearly $1 billion each year, principally in grants to university–medical school scholars, to discover the causes and cures of disease; the Atomic Energy Commission contracts for research and engages in cooperative programs with business firms to stimulate the commercial utilization of atomic energy. During the 1960s, expenditures by these and other nondefense-nonspace agencies increased even more rapidly than the expenditures for defense-space-related research and development—but still represented, by the close of the decade, less than one-fifth of the total annual expenditure.

Some government officials—chiefly NASA's officials—contend that research and development for defense and space ends provide basic knowledge, processes, and products which can be developed or adapted for the commercial market and will contribute significantly to the satisfaction of broadening human wants.[12]

[11] For discerning discussion of this and related questions see Leonard S. Silk, "Can We Get Balanced Growth?" *The Research Revolution* (New York: McGraw-Hill Book Company, 1960), chap. 6, pp. 127–152.

[12] NASA has established "technology utilization offices" and regional "dissemination centers" to make available information potentially useful to in-

They cite, as examples, the commercial use of Teflon, developed out of attempts to produce a dry lubricant for defense purposes; the plasmajet, an extremely hot torch used to melt exotic metals; advances in transistor technology; the multifold applications of the computer in business, in education, and in health care; and the application of solid-state bonding and vibrational testing to commercial uses.

That there are some commercial spin-offs and some extra benefits for the society from research and development of weapons and space gadgetry is clear.[13] Most aircraft now used for commercial air transport can trace their origin to research undertaken to develop military planes. So it has been with many electronics and communication devices now in civilian use. A growing number of business firms originated in the recognition of prospective commercial applications by individuals engaged in government-supported research. But profitable commercial spin-off from defense and space contracts has been the exception and has come about only when the contractors were capable of imaginative adaptation and willing to make considerable investments. While it takes about 10 professional man-years of commercial research and development effort to produce a commercially utilized patent, it has been calculated that over 1,000 man-years of research and development effort are needed to adapt technology developed for defense or space exploration to produce a patent utilized in the commercial sector.[14] And as the research for defense and space is designed to meet more sophisticated needs in these fields, the

dustry and to encourage private utilization of discoveries made under NASA contracts. Even the Department of Defense, traditionally and understandably the most tight-lipped of all the departments, was moved to review its policies in order to foster "the transfer of Defense-developed technical experience to the civilian sector." In the spring of 1969, the DOD-sponsored Federal Contract Research Centers (FCRCs), such as the Lincoln Laboratory at M.I.T., were permitted, and even encouraged, to devote part of their effort (up to 20 percent) to non-DOD activity.

[13] For example, new sealants developed for caulking spacecraft now plug the gaps between bathroom tiles. Filament-wound plastics enable North American Car Corporation to make railway cars that weigh 9 tons less than cars made of steel. A so-called "sign switch" by which an astronaut can manipulate a switch by movement of his eyes has been installed in a motorized wheelchair for paraplegics.

[14] *Policy Planning for Technology Transfer,* a report of the Subcommittee on Science and Technology to the Select Committee on Small Business, U.S. Senate, 90th Cong., 1st Sess., Document 15, April, 1967, p. 140.

likelihood of spin-off tends to decline. More imagination, time, and funds must be invested than either government or private enterprise has demonstrated a willingness to make available, if space and defense developments are to be adapted profitably to satisfy private wants.

The most effective means of promoting commercial spin-off is the waiver by government, in advance or shortly after the invention. In some cases the possibility of developing a new commercial product in the course of government-sponsored research is a major inducement to obtaining government contracts. Where government holds the patent to new discoveries, however, few businessmen are likely to risk investing, unless adaptations stemming from the discovery will themselves be patentable.

Technology to serve social wants

The prospect of profit to be derived from the discovery of ways to curb air and water pollution, to dispose of waste, to improve intraurban transport, to devise new forms of housing, to desalinize the water, or to improve the technology of education has not been sufficient to attract substantial investments by private enterprise in research and development in these fields. Nor have these and other social wants (e.g., the discovery of the causes of poverty) attracted federal support of a magnitude approximating that of the annual federal investment in research and development in the defense and space fields.

The slice of the federal research and development budget that is devoted to finding new and better ways of satisfying social wants is growing nonetheless.[15] In 1970, it approximated $3 billion, or less than one-fifth of the total. Consider the effort and the blocks to accomplishment in each of the five following fields.

Federal support of medical and health-related research inched up to more than $1.5 billion in 1969. In this field, privately supported research (e.g., by firms in the drug and chemical indus-

---

[15] Almost one-half of all federal expenditures for research and development in 1970 will be made for the development of weapons and military technology. About three-tenths will be made to further the exploration of space; about one-tenth will be made for research and development on ways of utilizing atomic energy. The remainder will be devoted primarily to funding solutions to problems in the fields of public health, education, transportation, and urban life. While these social wants receive far less support than the nation's military and space programs, they constitute the most rapidly expanding area of federal research and development activity.

tries) is relatively large. Yet the federal government currently provides approximately 65 percent of all funds for health research (25 percent is contributed by industry, and the remaining 10 percent is contributed by foundations and voluntary health agencies).[16] The NIH research contracts and grants (estimated at $868 million in 1969, with only some $56 million going to industrial firms) were concentrated on mental illness, on cardiovascular disease, on cancer, on blinding eye diseases (by a newly created National Eye Institute), and on the development of vaccines against diseases such as rubella (German measles).

The largest provider of non–defense-related federal research and development funds is the National Science Foundation. This agency was created in 1950 to stimulate the conduct of basic research, primarily through grants to colleges and universities. With funds grown ninefold within the past decade, the NSF spent $240 million in 1968, awarding nearly 4,000 research project grants to more than 400 academic institutions.[17] The emphasis is on fields of growing national interest—oceanography, atmospheric science, chemistry, social sciences—in the expectation that more basic research will form the basis for applied research and development in areas such as pollution abatement, weather modification, and urban redevelopment.

The increasing concentration of people in cities has made urgent the discovery of improved means of transporting individuals to and from their homes—to jobs, to doctors' offices, to shopping centers, and elsewhere. The presence of 100 million motor vehicles on this country's highways and the rapid growth of air traffic have created urgent needs for the discovery of ways to make automobile driving safer, to regulate air traffic, and to increase the safety of air transport. The obsolescence of the railroads has aggravated this need for the discovery of ways to improve urban transport.

Until the 1960s, the federal government spent relatively little money on any one of these problems. For example, it was not until May, 1968, that the Department of Housing and Urban De-

[16] Bureau of the Budget, *Special Analyses, Budget of the United States,* Fiscal Year 1970, pp. 148–150.

[17] Bureau of the Budget, *Special Analyses, Budget of the United States,* Fiscal Years 1968 (p. 134) and 1970 (pp. 250 and 272). National Science Foundation, *Federal Funds for Research, Development, and Other Scientific Activities,* vol. XVII, 1968, p. 127.

velopment provided "the first truly comprehensive official look at urban transportation in the light of modern technological capabilities." Meanwhile, that is, over the preceding quarter of a century, the existing subway, streetcar, and bus systems have become largely obsolete, and the cities have been confronted with the "paradox of technological obsolescence [of a critically important public service] in the midst of an abundance of relevant new techniques." [18]

Closely allied with transportation headaches is the mounting problem of air pollution. Los Angeles smog is still a subject for jokes; but 20 deaths resulting from a severe air pollution outbreak in the small Pennsylvania town of Donora tragically underlined what had been learned of the hazards to health. It was determined that motor vehicles are the source of more than 60 percent of air pollution, that industrial plants give rise to 17 percent, and power plants are responsible for 14 percent.[19]

Impelled by these and similar developments, government has gradually increased its support of air pollution control and the research into causes and techniques of control that must precede the elimination of pollution. In 1955, the Congress first authorized a federal program of research and technical assistance to state and local governments. The 1963 Clean Air Act paved the way for direct federal grants to state and local control agencies. In 1967, the National Center for Air Pollution Control was established, and that same year the far-reaching Air Quality Act of 1967 was passed unanimously by the Congress. From less than $2 million in 1956, the annual appropriations to fight air pollution have climbed to $35 million in 1966, and have doubled since.[20]

In March, 1966, federal standards for automotive emissions were established to apply to the 1968 model year. And throughout the decade of the 1960s, the federal government encouraged research and development on fuel cells and batteries as an alter-

[18] U.S. Department of Housing and Urban Development, Office of Metropolitan Development, Urban Transportation Administration, *Tomorrow's Transportation—New Systems for the Urban Future,* 1968.

[19] U.S. Department of Commerce, *The Automobile and Air Pollution: A Program for Progress,* Report of the Panel on Electrically Powered Vehicles, parts I and II, October and December, 1967.

[20] National Center for Air Pollution Control, *The Federal Air Pollution Program,* Public Health Service Publication 1560, October, 1967. U.S. Department of Health, Education, and Welfare, *1968 Annual Report,* p. 292.

native, nonpolluting source of power for vehicular propulsion (see Chapter 8).

In the decade of the 1960s, the federal government spectacularly increased its support for education at all levels, and the budget of the Office of Education climbed approximately 700 percent! [21] But the evidence is clear that private business firms in the educational materials industries have done very little that can be dignified by the description of "research"; what product improvement or discovery effort they have made can only be described as "hiring consultants," market research, or accumulating customer preferences.[22]

This noninvolvement must be attributed in substantial part to the hostility of many teachers and school officials who are often apt to resist change and to be suspicious of the profit-making firm that developed improvements in the teaching process. Their reasoning may be illogical, but it manifests again the belief of many Americans that in certain fields the pursuit of profit is not desirable. The spokesman for a major national education association, testifying before the Senate Education Subcommittee in 1967, decried "direct contracts between the U.S. Office of Education and profitmaking agencies" as "inherently wrong."

This noninvolvement must be attributed also to the long and arduous program of research, evaluation, development, and testing before new educational technology—be it books, slides, testing devices, or whatnot—reaches the classrooms. For example, the development of a new physics curriculum project conducted by scholars at the Massachusetts Institute of Technology cost approximately $5 million. Thus, investment by private publishers and others has not been economically attractive and federal "priming" has been required.[23] Among the prime targets for such

[21] Speech by Samuel Halperin, deputy assistant secretary for legislation, HEW, before the Project Aristotle symposium on education-government-industry of the National Security Industrial Association, in *Congressional Record*, Jan. 18, 1968.

[22] *Research and Development in the Educational Materials Industries*, the report of a study conducted under the sponsorship of the Ford Foundation and the Carnegie Corporation of New York by the Institute for Educational Development, 1969. The educational materials industries include textbook publishers and the producers of film projectors, filmstrips, overhead projectors and transparencies, multi-media packages and instructional systems, manipulative devices and supplementary printed materials.

[23] However, in education and in the satisfaction of other social wants—e.g., the disposal of garbage—the satisfaction does not always require a large in-

federal priming effort are improvement of curricula, individualization of instruction, and application of computers to instructional uses. These are lengthy and costly endeavors.

A recent statement emanating from the Committee for Economic Development pinpoints the problem: it deplores the fact that "there has been little recognition of the importance of educational research," and particularly of "development research" which in industry accounts for some 77 percent of the total research and development expenditure (as compared to 10 to 12 percent in education).[24]

In the final analysis, the measure of our management of the bountiful benefits of science is the effectiveness with which we as a people have utilized science to alleviate the condition of man. Since World War II, the allocation of scientific resources among the various ends they may serve has been substantially taken out of the hands of the market system. That course, with all its consequences, may have been made essential by the persistence of the cold war. But by 1970 there were also accumulating doubts —underlined by the urban crisis; the plight of the poor; and the realization of the inadequacies in the schools, health care institutions, transport systems, and environment—as to whether the American political process had indeed so influenced the application of the fruits of advancing technology as to better the condition of all Americans.

EFFECT ON STRUCTURE
OF THE ECONOMY

The postwar years have made apparent that in a democratic-capitalistic society experiencing rapid technological advance, government inevitably will expand its support of science and, to maintain its capitalistic character, will contract out extensively. But what effects do these two obvious trends have upon the structure of the American economy? That is, how have they affected the relative growth of different industries within the

vestment. It often requires the formulation of simple ideas, unglamorous perhaps, but important and potentially profitable, e.g., the devising of ways to make the school bus, where children spend substantial time, an educational instrument by the use of slide projectors.

[24] Committee for Economic Development, *Innovation in Education: New Directions for the American School*, New York, 1968.

American economy? The degree of concentration that obtains within the American economy? The roles of public enterprise and private enterprise?

Relative growth of industries

A look at the rates of growth experienced by such industries as food and related products, tobacco, paper and allied products, and machinery (other than electrical and automotive equipment) makes manifest that factors other than the government's support of research and development have stimulated their growth. These industries have participated minimally in government's research and development patronage and yet they have grown markedly.

If we examine indices of industrial production (the base period 1957–1959 equaling 100), we find that the value of all manufacturing production rose to 167 in 1968. The rates of growth experienced by several industries which have received little federal R&D support were as follows: paper and products—164; fabricated metal products—168; food—136; and, most spectacularly, chemicals—222, and rubber and plastics—220.[25]

The prescription drug industry offers a striking, if not entirely typical, example. Leery of the possibility that patents could not be had for products or processes developed as the result of research financed with federal funds, the industry chose to finance research almost entirely with company funds. It channeled nearly 13 percent of its total research and development funds into basic research (as compared with the combined average of 3 percent for all other industries). Federal funds support only 3.5 percent of all research and development in the drug industry (as compared with more than 50 percent for all industries in which federal support is provided).

Expansion of firm-initiated research

In the late 1950s and early 1960s, following the federal government's assumption of major responsibility for financing research and development, dire predictions were made. Government, it was suggested, might preempt fields of research in which private enterprise had been active, sap the innovative powers of the private firm, and monopolize the nation's scientific and engineering manpower to such a degree that firm-initiated research would de-

[25] *Statistical Abstract of the United States,* 1969, p. 714.

cline.[26] These predictions have been proven to be in error. Government's share of the financing of industrial research and development has tended to decrease since 1959, and company support has grown (see Table 6.3). The ratio of industrial expenditures for research and development to net sales rose by a third from 1957 to 1967 (see Table 6.4).

On balance, it is obvious that innovation has remained a major concern of the private sector. In those industries where the federal contract is a major source of support for research and development, the growth of company-supported R&D may be largely attributed to attempts to improve the industrial firm's capabilities and to develop new products for the government.

TABLE 6.3 *Growth of Company Expenditures for Research and Development in Selected Industries, 1957–1966*

Industry	Percent of R&D funded by federal government, 1966	Company R&D funds as percent of net sales, 1966	Growth of company R&D funds 1957–1966
Manufacturing industries 53%	2.0%	114%
Professional and scientific instruments. 32	3.8	115
Chemicals and allied products 13	3.7	115
Electrical equipment 61	3.4	132
Aircraft and missiles 86	3.5	153
Machinery 27	3.0	141
Motor vehicles and other transportation equip.. 26	2.6	89
Fabricated metals 10	1.2	50
Petroleum refining and extraction 13	1.0	92
Rubber products 14	1.7	102
Primary metals 3	0.7	115
Paper and allied products 0	0.7	105
Food 1	0.4	111

SOURCE: Derived from National Science Foundation, *Research and Development in Industry, 1966*, 1968, pp. 30, 32, and 73. Updated with some revised figures published by the National Science Foundation in *Reviews of Data on Science Resources*, no. 17, February, 1969.

[26] For example, see Yale Brozen, "The Role of Government in Research and Development," *The American Behavioral Scientist*, 1962, pp. 22–26.

But some of the industries which receive the least federal support have also substantially increased their expenditures for research and development. The concurrence of technological advance, a steadily growing demand for both capital and consumer goods, and vigorous competition to take advantage of this demand, supported by government's dissemination of information and by tax incentives that encourage the firm to expand investment in research and development, have impelled innovation. Note, for example, in Table 6.3, the growth of expenditures for research and development in the machinery, paper, metal, and food industries.

TABLE 6.4   *The Proportion of the Sales Dollar Spent from Company Funds for Research and Development in Selected Industries, 1957–1967*

Industry	1957	1962	1964	1966	1967
Manufacturing industries	**1.5%**	**1.9%**	**2.0%**	**2.0%**	**2.1%**
Chemicals and allied products 3.1		3.4	3.8	3.7	3.7
Machinery. 2.0		2.8	3.2	3.0	3.1
Electrical equipment 2.6		3.5	3.6	3.4	3.5
Aircraft and missiles 2.0		2.7	2.5	3.5	4.1
Professional and scientific instruments . . 3.9		4.1	4.3	3.8	3.7

SOURCE: National Science Foundation, *Reviews of Data on Science Resources*, no. 12, January, 1968, and no. 17, February, 1969.

The lack of direct federal support for research and development has not prevented or dissuaded these industries from maintaining a rapid rate of growth.

Effect upon concentration

Industry-initiated research and development is primarily an activity of large firms. "Most significant research and development," David Lilienthal noted almost two decades ago, "require large resources and often a long period of time during which no results are forthcoming . . . only large enterprises are able to sink the formidable sums of money required to develop basic new departures. . . . Bigness and research activity are largely synonymous whether in business or in government." [27]

Government contracts for research and development (as noted on page 117) are concentrated in relatively few firms. And the

[27] *Big Business: A New Era* (New York: Harper & Brothers, 1952), pp. 69–72.

dollar volume of government contracts with these firms indicates only a part of the effect of government support on industrial concentration. The production contracts which follow successful research and development projects constitute the major profit-making and firm-building opportunity.

Where patent rights to commercial products are waived or government research leads indirectly to commercial spin-off, the firm acquires significant economic power. The capabilities, manpower, and plant obtained through federal support place the firm in an advantageous position both in the commercial market and in regard to obtaining future government contracts, particularly in highly specialized fields.[28]

In most instances the government has few alternative contractors with which to deal. The nature of defense and space research is highly specialized. Much of it requires a highly talented and highly trained staff as well as the extensive facilities and large investment that only a few big firms command. The pattern of concentration is intensified as contracts automatically increase the capability of the firm to win additional federal support.

This relationship between company size and ability to perform significant research and development poses serious questions as to the logic of prevailing antitrust policy.[29] Government's support of research and development, particularly the concentration of its support in a relatively few larger enterprises and the development of the technological capabilities and economic power of these enterprises, patently runs counter to prevailing governmental antitrust policies. The reasons that induce the concentration of government's support of research and development sustain those critics who describe prevailing antitrust policy as "anachronistic." [30]

To some extent the federal expenditures benefit all industry by creating subprocesses, equipment, components, and materials that can be adopted in other industries. The cost and perform-

[28] Federal contracts also provide profits permitting industries to branch into entirely new commercial areas. This is illustrated by the growth of non-aerospace sales by the aerospace industry from $134 million in 1948 to $2.7 billion in 1969. *Aerospace Facts and Figures, 1969*, p. 8.

[29] For a simplified statement of the characteristics of modern industry which make large size essential for the support of research and development, see John Kenneth Galbraith, *The New Industrial State* (Boston: Houghton Mifflin Company, 1967).

[30] *Ibid.*, p. 197.

ance of the products of one industry are influenced by research and development performed by other organizations. Techniques and basic concepts behind various products and processes turn out to be the key to the solution of problems in other industries. It is not seldom that unpatentable aspects of a design concept are more important than a specific patented product or process. At least nine of the fifty major inventions of the first half of the twentieth century were the result of modifying, after considerable additional research and development, a basic concept developed originally in a different context.[31] Finally, most results of basic research are, or must be, published as nonproprietary material (by universities, nonprofit and government agencies, etc.) and thus contribute to the store of knowledge in the public domain. As a result, although the benefits are greatest for industries committed to an intensive research and development effort, they redound to other firms in other industries, and productivity increases are experienced even by industries that spend little or nothing on research and development.

Allocation of scientific and technological manpower

A congressional study has pointed out that "research and development funds act as an important magnet drawing highly trained scientific and technical manpower to the area or establishment in which the funds have been placed. The funds can also be a major factor in making actual scientists out of potential ones, for they frequently stimulate interest in education and the sciences in the affected areas." [32]

The concentration of research and development personnel in particular industries is less marked than the allocation of federal financial support, but follows a similar pattern. Over half the engineers and scientists engaged in industrial research and development are employed in the aerospace or electrical equipment and communications industries. Most others are employed in chemicals, machinery, and motor vehicles and transportation equipment industries. The 10 remaining major manufacturing indus-

[31] Richard R. Nelson, Merton J. Peck, and Edward D. Kalachek, *Technology, Economic Growth, and Public Policy* (Washington: The Brookings Institution, 1967), pp. 66–88.

[32] Committee on Labor and Public Welfare, U.S. Senate, *Impact of Federal Research and Development Policies upon Scientific and Technical Manpower,* 1966, p. 3.

tries, which receive 3 percent of all federal funds for industrial research and development, employ 15 percent of industrial R&D personnel.[33]

The manpower needs of industries unsupported by federal funds are intensified by the ability of firms holding contracts to offer substantially higher salaries and to draw highly qualified individuals away from firms which finance all their own research. As the technological needs of all industries may be expected to grow in future decades, the problems of competition for scarce manpower between contractors and firms engaged in privately funded research may be expected to increase.

The efforts of government and of business to expand the nation's supply of scientists and engineers benefit industry generally. Much of industry support to education through training programs and contributions to educational institutions is concentrated in fields in which scientific and technical personnel are already heavily concentrated. These forces tend to influence further the allocation of this valuable resource to a limited segment of the economy.

Effect on private-public roles

What effect have government's efforts to stimulate the advance of science had on the relative roles of private and public enterprise?

Government's efforts have established an increasing dependence on public financing and on private performance. At the beginning of World War II, the federal government provided relatively little of the funds utilized within the American economy to support research and development (see Table 6.5). Since 1941, an expanded proportion of all research and development has been *financed* by government. After declining from 1948 to 1963, the portion of all research and development *performed* by government has again increased. The proportion performed by nonprofit institutions (especially the universities) has increased markedly. In other democratic-capitalistic nations, government provides less financing and performs more research and development in its own laboratories and offices (see Table 6.6). In none of these countries is the business sector as heavily relied upon to carry out research and development as it is in the United States.

Underlying these shifts in relative responsibilities lies the in-

[33] National Science Foundation, *Reviews of Data on Science Resources*, no. 17, February, 1969.

TABLE 6.5   *Sources and Users of Research and Development Expenditures in the United States, Selected Years*

Year	Percent provided by			Percent used by		
	Government	Industry	Non-profit*	Government	Industry	Non-profit*
1941	41%	57%	2%	22%	73%	5%
1945	70	28	2	28	65	7
1948	53	44	3	22	70	8
1958	62	34	4	13	77	10
1963	65	31	4	13	73	14
1966	63	33	4	15	69	16
1970 (est.)	56.8	39.7	3.5	13.8	70.3	15.9

* Nonprofit sector includes universities and colleges, federally funded research and development centers, and other nonprofit institutions.

sources: Data for 1941, 1945, and 1948 from *Statistical Abstract of the United States*, 1960, p. 538. Later data from National Science Foundation, *National Patterns of R&D Resources, 1953–1970*, 1969.

TABLE 6.6   *Sources and Users of Research and Development Expenditures, Selected Countries*

Country	Percent provided by			Percent used by		
	Government	Industry	Non-profit*	Government	Industry	Non-profit*
Netherlands, 1964 †	40	54	3	3	56	41
Canada, 1963 †	55	34	8	43	41	16
Japan, 1963 †	28	65	7	12	65	23
United Kingdom, 1964–1965 †. . .	54	42	1	25	67	8
France, 1963 †	64	33	nil	38	51	11
United States, 1963 †	64	32	4	18	67	15

* Nonprofit sector includes universities and colleges, Federal Contract Research Centers, and other nonprofit institutions.

† Funds from abroad not included; total may not add to 100. The proportions stated here vary from those stated in Table 6.5 as a consequence of the derivation from different sources. The data presented here adequately reflect the intercountry comparison.

source: Organisation for Economic Cooperation and Development, *The Overall Level and Structure of R&D Efforts in OECD Member Countries*, Paris, 1967, p. 57.

creasingly apparent fact that national goals cannot be achieved without the cooperative efforts of government, industry, and the nonprofit institutions. Our national defense; our goals in space; our growing commitment to advances in health care, to the betterment of education, to the elimination of poverty, and to the achievement of continued economic growth require the participation of all sectors of the economy. The resulting mix of public support and private action to achieve these objectives is the clear consequence of recognition by "those who have shaped the relationship . . . that cooperation is essential if free institutions and individual freedom are to continue to function successfully. They have . . . sought to answer a national need but at the same time to promote institutional pluralism and personal responsibility." [34]

SIGNIFICANCE OF NEW GOVERNMENTAL ROLE

Does this effort by government represent an onrush of socialism in a capitalist state? Not necessarily.

The American federal government has established a new relationship between democratic government and capitalistic enterprise. It has forged a new partnership to share the responsibility for building national strength—military, economic, and technological. But within the partnership, government—the agent of the *demos*—has not demonstrated the ability to make allocative decisions consistently in the interest of all the people. This is the meaning of the recurring outcry against the military-industrial complex; the agents of the military and the agents of the industrial suppliers of defense research, development, and material have been able to influence allocative decisions to advance their own selfish interests.

It seems inevitable that government will in the future (1) continue to stimulate private innovation in each of the ways that has been pictured in this chapter; (2) strive to protect our national interests by developing ever-more lethal weapons and ever-more effective devices for exploration in space and under the seas; (3) increase our supply of scientists and engineers; and (4) increase its support of basic research.

[34] J. Stephen Dupre and Sanford A. Lakoff, "The New Partnership," in Roger E. Bolton (ed.), *Defense and Disarmament: The Economics of Transition* (Englewood Cliffs, N.J.: Prentice-Hall, Inc., 1966), p. 167.

The pursuit of these ends suggests that government will continue to influence the relative development of industries—some more, others less—as the public needs seem to dictate. It also portends that government expenditures for research and development will provide a continuing stimulus not only to the initiative of individual firms, but also to the initiative of the faculties of universities and the staffs of nonprofit agencies. It forecasts that despite the opposition of some faculty members and some students to the performance of much governmentally supported research, the universities will continue to accept such support and perform much or most of such research for the simple reason that their capabilities are needed to serve the public interest. It suggests that the relative strength of the business and nonprofit sectors of the economy will be altered, but that the vigor of the total effort and the probable yield of innovation will continue to grow.

CHAPTER 7

The Evolving Role
of the Third Sector

As the American society has begun to clean up a
spate of "unfinished business" during the post-World War II
years, it has been confronted with the reality that traditional
methods—individual and corporate entrepreneurship, either
alone or supported by governmental subsidies, contracts, or research and development grants—are not suited to many of the
jobs to be done.

With or without government backing, business cannot solve
the problems of the cities—the technical problems of traffic
congestion, of air and water pollution, and of fiscal imbalance.
By its own mores and by the prevailing ethos, business is ill-
suited to cope with the nationwide social problems of unemployment, of poverty, of the physically and mentally unfit, and of the
inadequately educated. And business cannot solve the cancerous
problem of race prejudice.

Business can make, and has made, important contributions to the solution of each of these segments of the unfinished business of the American society. But, with notable exceptions, it has demonstrated little taste for such problems and a marked incapacity for building the political consensus that is required for their solution.

Hence, as such problems—and others—have loomed large, in many instances government has had to devise new arrangements for mobilizing the human talent required. It has turned increasingly to a variety of existing nonprofit institutions and has established others to do specific jobs. Through the use of the mechanisms of the grants economy—i.e., through subsidies, grants, and (more often) contracts—it has contrived to have a growing, if still small, proportion of the public business done by the nonprofits, the "third sector." The purpose of this chapter is to indicate the magnitude of what is going on and to suggest why.

KINDS AND USES
OF NONPROFITS

The large number of nonprofit institutions of various sorts to which government has turned can be categorized in terms of the kind of service rendered to either the defense or the civilian sector of government. Some nonprofit institutions have an inconvenient way of defying tidy classification. And though the very categorization of these institutions reads like a dull catalog, such categorization is needed if we are to understand the evolution that has taken place.

Functional categories

A substantial number of nonprofit institutions carry on research or manage research for federal departments and agencies. This category includes:

■ Defense-oriented institutions such as the Lincoln Laboratory of M.I.T. and the Applied Physics Laboratory of Johns Hopkins University

■ Atomic energy–oriented agencies such as the Associated Universities, Inc., which manages the Brookhaven National Laboratory (as well as the National Radio Astronomy Observatory); the University Research Association, Inc., which will manage the high-energy proton accelerator when it is built; Stanford University, which manages a linear accelerator; Princeton University and the University of Pennsylvania, which jointly manage still another accelerator; the University of Chicago, which manages the Argonne National Laboratory

■ Housing- and urban-oriented agencies such as the American Institute of Planners, National League of Cities, National Association of Housing and Development Officials, and the National Homeownership Foundation created to encourage homeownership and increased housing opportunities for low-income families

■ Health-oriented institutions such as most of the medical schools of this country, which carry out federally supported biomedical research

■ Economics-oriented agencies such as the Institute for Research on Poverty (University of Wisconsin) which carries out economic studies for various federal departments and agencies.

Another category (which to some extent overlaps the category just described) includes those which provide systems engineering or technical management services. For the defense sector, the Aerospace Corporation and Mitre provide such services. For the civilian sector, an analogous service is performed under contract with the Agency for International Development by the universities that have accepted responsibility for establishing medical, agricultural, or business schools in the developing countries. As yet, such systems engineering and technical management services are not contracted for by other civilian agencies, but precedents are now being established in the transportation and housing sectors.

Other nonprofit institutions conduct policy studies and evaluations and provide advice. This group includes such institutions as the Rand Corporation, Research Analysis Corporation, Institute for Defense Analyses, Analytic Services, Inc., the Center for Naval Analysis (administered by the Franklin Institute of Philadelphia), Logistics Management Institute, Human Resources Research Office, and Special Operations Research Office. The function performed by these agencies in the defense field has been replicated at times by the Educational Testing Service in the field of educational policy (under contract with both the Office of Education and the Office of Economic Opportunity), by the Brookings Institution and the Center for Behavioral Studies at the University of Michigan (for the Federal Reserve Board) in the fields of economic and social policy, and by some universities in the field of health policy (e.g., the University of Michigan's School of Public Health in the administration of the Medicaid program).

A fourth category of nonprofit institutions provides a wide as-assortment of services, including ad hoc studies. In the defense, atomic energy, and space fields, Battelle Memorial Institute, Southwest Research Institute, Stanford Research Institute, and the System Development Corporation have provided such services. In the field of foreign affairs, the Department of State and the Agency for International Development have been served by Education and World Affairs, Governmental Affairs Institute, the Institute of International Education, the American Field Service, and the International Executive Service Corps. In the field of health affairs, a particularly notable service was rendered to the Food and Drug Administration by the National Academy of Sciences in evaluating the efficacy of a large number of drugs; an equally significant and continuing service is rendered by the nonprofit hospitals in the care of Medicare patients and by the Blue Cross associations in many states in receiving and processing claims under Medicare for the Social Security Administration. The Housing and Urban Development Act has provided funds to nonprofit groups to renovate houses for low-income families. In the field of welfare and training, still other nonprofit institutions have served the Departments of Health, Education, and Welfare; Housing and Urban Development; and Labor and the Office of Economic Opportunity. These include the Child Welfare League of America, the Family Service Association of America, the National Council on the Aging, the National Council on Crime and Delinquency, the Community Service Society of New York, the National Council of Jewish Women, and the National Urban League.

A fifth category includes institutions to which government entrusts decision making that is of special consequence to particular groups (e.g., the historians or the poor). For example, the Department of State contracts with the Conference Board of Associated Research Councils for the management of activities involved in the selection of individuals to receive scholarships or lectureships for service in other countries under the Fulbright program, and the HEW contracts with the American Psychological Association for the evaluation of graduate departments of psychology. While the academics would not want officials of a government department evaluating their scholarly capabilities, they are committed to accepting the evaluation of their peers! Similarly, the prime objective of the support by the Central Intelligence Agency of a limited number of institutions (e.g., the Afro-American Institute, the American Institute for Free Labor Development, and the National Student Association) was to enlist this country's intellectuals—its spokesmen for labor, for students, and others—in the continuing propagandistic dialogue with the advocates of communism throughout the world.

The same principle applies to the Office of Economic Opportunity's contracting with the so-called "community action agencies"; a major objective is to involve individuals, including the poor, in actions to overcome poverty. A related objective of this contracting is "the quest for community."[1] The deeply rooted and pervasive belief is held that if cities are to be "managed," much authority must be fixed at the neighborhood level. This authority must be adequate to cope with the need to create jobs, to help minority group members (particularly Negroes) establish their own businesses, to control schools, to provide social services (e.g., the management of day-care centers), and to provide health services (e.g., comprehensive, family-oriented medical and social care through a neighborhood health center).

The mechanism that has emerged from this quest for community takes various forms but may loosely be described as "the neighborhood corporation." It may trace its genesis to the Poverty Program and to the establishment of the community action agencies. Out of that womb have grown such enterprises as the Bedford-Stuyvesant Corporation in New York City and the United Planning Organization in Washington, D.C.

Out of the same intellectual womb has grown an idea much discussed in 1969 and included in the Community Self-Determination Act, a statute proposed for enactment by Senators Javits, Percy, Hart, and Nelson. This bill proposes to set up, with the aid of established business enterprises, community development corporations that would be owned by shareholders resident in the community, would enjoy significant tax exemptions, and

---

[1] See, for example, D. P. Moynihan, "The Quest for Community," *Maximum Feasible Misunderstanding* (New York: The Free Press, 1969), chap. 1; and "Table Talk—Finding the City," in *The Center Magazine,* a publication of the Center for the Study of Democratic Institutions, Santa Barbara, Calif., vol. 1, no. 4, May, 1968.

would utilize a substantial portion of their profits for the financing of needed community social services. A central objective of the establishment of such neighborhood corporations would be to develop a flow of income that the community might control and utilize for those social needs it deemed urgent.[2]

Structural types

The nonprofit agencies to which government has turned include a number of freestanding nonprofits (e.g., Brookings, Aerospace, and Rand); universities; university medical schools; and consortia of universities (e.g., Associated Universities, Inc., and the University Research Association Inc.); hospitals; and long-established educational, health, and welfare institutions that have undertaken services for government within relatively recent times (e.g., the Family Service Association of America and the National Urban League). But government has come to rely as well on nonprofit institutions newly created at the instigation of the government to provide specific services for them (e.g., Women in Community Service, an association of women's organizations created to assist in recruiting for the women's Job Corps training centers, or the educational laboratories created by the Office of Education).

Those that have been cited as examples constitute only a fraction of all nonprofit institutions, an increasing proportion of which are utilized by government to get its work done. Robert S. Lesher has suggested that there are "three basic types of nonprofit corporations"[3]:

■ Private (i.e., those "organized for a private purpose such as social, fraternal, civic, literary, patriotic, athletic, agricultural and the like"), including:
   Mutual insurance companies
   Savings and loan associations
   Chambers of commerce
   Farmers' cooperatives
   Consumers' cooperatives

---

[2] A similar proposal was advanced by Professor Richard S. Rosenbloom in an article entitled, "Social Entrepreneurship" (*HBS Bulletin*, May–June, 1969, pp. 23–26). Rosenbloom emphasizes the utility of such community development corporations in involving private business firms in resolving social problems.

[3] "The Nonprofit Corporation—A Neglected Stepchild Comes of Age," *The Business Lawyer*, July, 1967.

Trade associations
Trade unions
Professional societies
Churches
Recreational and welfare agencies
Social clubs

- Quasi-public (i.e., those "organized for a purpose which is currently recognized as relating to a public interest"), including:
Blue Cross–Blue Shield
Foundations
Museums and libraries
Colleges and universities [4]
Voluntary hospitals [4]
Research organizations [4]

- Public (i.e., those "created by government to fulfill one or more public purposes outside of the usual government establishment"), including:
Public "authorities"
"Public benefit corporations"
Government corporations
Colleges and universities [4]
Hospitals [4]
Research organizations [4]

The first two types of nonprofit institutions (the private and quasi-public) are organized by private individuals to serve social ends that they deem to be desirable, ranging from the encouragement of homeownership and savings or the stimulation of ethical practices among business and professional men to the education of the young, the care of the ill, and the assistance of the orphaned and the poor. Many of these institutions—the cooperatives, professional societies, colleges, hospitals and clinics, museums, and recreational and welfare agencies—have enabled the citizens who gave their money and time to establish, maintain, and operate them to understand better the processes of democracy; have distributed power widely throughout the society; and

[4] The duplication of "colleges and universities," "hospitals," and "research organizations" is made necessary by the fact that in each of these categories there exist simultaneously two kinds of institutions: (1) those organized by private individuals to serve ends they deemed important and financed in whole or in major part through private endowments or other nonpublic sources of support and (2) those that are essentially a part of government and draw all or most of their support from government.

have provided a mechanism for the continual promotion of social change.[5]

The nonprofit institutions of the third type (the public) are organized by government. The oldest of such institutions are the public authorities utilized alike by federal (the Tennessee Valley Authority), state (the New Jersey Turnpike Authority and the New York Port Authority), and local governments (the local housing or urban renewal authorities). These institutions perform functions identical, or very similar, to those performed by traditional governmental agencies (e.g., the operation of an airport). Each has its independent and continuing existence separate from government. Each is subject to some measure of political control and relies in whole or in part on sources of support other than tax revenues or government contracts. Each was organized "outside the usual government establishment" because, for various reasons, the function to be performed in each case (e.g., developing a river valley, managing and developing ports, operating hospitals) was believed to require a degree of autonomy in operation (e.g., the university) not available to in-house government departments.

THE GROWING NONPROFIT SECTOR

These several types of institutions, when taken together, assumed a substantial role in the American economy.[6]

A realistic model of the American economy must include greater recognition of the nonprofit and governmental enterprise activities than has been customary in the past. Measured in terms of the "growth of expenditures" or the "growth in employment," the not-for-profit sector of the economy has grown more rapidly over the past three decades than the profit-making sector.[7] No

---

[5] See Alan Pifer, "The Quasi Nongovernmental Organization," an essay included in the 1967 *Annual Report* of the Carnegie Corporation of New York.

[6] Eli Ginzberg, Dale L. Hiestand, and Beatrice G. Reubens estimate in *The Pluralistic Economy* (New York: McGraw-Hill Book Company, 1965) that not less than one-third and possibly almost two-fifths of all employment is accounted for, directly or indirectly, by the activities of the not-for-profit (including government) sector and that during the decade 1950–1960, nine out of every ten new jobs were created by this sector.

[7] See *ibid.*, "The Scale and Scope of the Not-for-Profit Sector," chap. 5, and "Employment Trends in the Not-for-Profit Sector," chap. 6, for detailed presentation of these developments.

single measure of expenditures by the nonprofit institutions is available, but data as to the growth of expenditures by universities and by nonprofit (voluntary) hospitals illustrate the rate of growth. As for employment, the proportion of all employees in the United States employed directly by the nonprofit sector increased from 2.8 percent in 1929 to 5 percent in 1960 (or from 9.7 to 20.5 percent, if we include the government sector). Also significant is the fact that while the not-for-profit sector accounted for only 20 percent of all employees, it employed more than half of all "professional, technical, and kindred" workers.[8] By 1968 the nonprofit sector provided 7 percent of all employment (25 percent, including the government sector). The following figures will illustrate some aspects of this growth: the "nonprofit membership organizations" expanded the number of their employees from 831,000 (1.2 percent of total employment) in 1960 to 1.3 million (1.7 percent of the total) in 1968; employment in "educational services" (the bulk of which is in public or nonprofit agencies) increased from 676,000 (1 percent of the total) to 1.2 million (1.5 percent of the total) during the same period. During the years 1960–1968, employment provided by the nonprofit sector showed a 39 percent growth (from 5 to 7 percent of the total), while employment in the governmental sector rose by 20 percent (from 15 to 18 percent of the total). [9]

So astigmatically have Americans focused their attention and concern on the profit-making enterprise that this development of the nonprofits has gone substantially unrecognized. Moreover, what is public, what is private profit making, and what is private nonprofit is increasingly difficult to distinguish.

Much confusion prevails. Citizens, businessmen, government officials, and even executives of the nonprofit institutions manifest this confusion. For many citizens there is little apparent difference between the nonprofit institution (like the Blue Cross associations) and the profit-making business enterprise (like the Metropolitan Life Insurance Company). For many businessmen the nonprofit institution is a competitor which is unfairly ex-

---

[8] Daniel Bell predicts the continuance of this relative emphasis when he writes (*Daedalus*, Summer, 1967, p. 667), "I would assume that in a postindustrial society . . . the major new institutions of the society will be primarily intellectual institutions."

[9] Data derived from *Survey of Current Business*, July issues of 1962, 1964, 1966, and 1969.

empted from taxes that profit-making enterprises must pay. Many government officials view the nonprofit institutions as one more would-be seller with goods or, more often, services for the government market. The executives of nonprofit institutions view their agencies as service organizations that, having forsaken the pursuit of profit, merit especial public favor.

WHY USE NONPROFITS?

Straight thinking about the evolving role of the nonprofit institution in the American economy is needed. To achieve that, let us consider *why* the number of nonprofit institutions and the range of functions they perform have expanded. And let us consider the related question *why* government has utilized through contracts or grants an increasing variety of nonprofit institutions and has fostered the establishment of others (the Logistics Management Institute and the educational laboratories, for example) to carry out what have been, and are, public functions.

A prime reason *why* is that government has found in these institutions a handy vehicle for obtaining talent to work on public tasks that it cannot recruit under archaic civil service rules and at comparatively low salaries.[10] The intensive specialization that has accompanied the advance of technology has created an urgent need for trained and experienced technical and professional personnel. Government has found much of the needed expertise on the staffs of nonprofit institutions, and it has encouraged the creation of other nonprofits to assemble such expertise.

A second reason *why* is that these nonprofit institutions are concentrated, for the most part, in five rapidly growing fields: the persistence of the cold war has enhanced their importance in defense and space; our growing national affluence has lent added importance to their role in the fields of health, education, and welfare.

A third reason for the utilization of nonprofit institutions is that they can operate more flexibly than bureaus and depart-

[10] It is not the federal government alone that has found a valuable resource in these nonprofit institutions. For example, the RAND Corporation, created originally to provide an independent nonprofit research center to serve the U.S. Air Force, has broadened its capabilities over two decades and has been called upon to serve other departments of the federal, state (e.g., Arkansas), and local governments (e.g., New York City) and private agencies (e.g., the New York and American stock exchanges).

ments of the government. This reason prompted state and local governments as well as the federal government to contract with such agencies to perform public tasks.[11] The external nonprofit institution is free of the constraining influence of prescribed public budgetary, personnel, purchasing, and auditing procedures, and of congressional surveillance. It is able, hence, to act more promptly and to tailor its actions to the exigency of immediate problems.

A fourth reason for the increasing utilization of nonprofit institutions may be found in the desire to provide an antidote for the insularity of large-scale governmental organization. Rand, one of the earliest of the nonprofits, was established outside the U.S. Air Force to give the top command independent and objective advice, to provide judgments not winnowed and tempered by successive layers of the Air Force hierarchy. Analogously, Aerospace emerged from the Air Force's need for an agency independent of the large contractors in the missile development and production field and capable of evaluating the technical and production proposals of the developers of missiles.

This reason is rooted in the traditional American belief in pluralism and in the social benefit that is derived when independent and competing units stimulate each other and thus promote advance by government and by private enterprise. Much of the advance in public health in the Southern states, for example, was stimulated by programs (launched by the Commonwealth Foundation and, separately, by the Rockefeller Foundation) to eradicate tuberculosis, venereal disease, and the ravages of hookworm. Much of the technological advance in private enterprise is attributable to the inventiveness and drive of independent and competing small enterprises; both Polaroid and Xerox were small, inventive, and driving enterprises only a few decades ago, and many profitable products of du Pont, General Foods, General Electric, General Motors, and other large enterprises were created by small, independent, and competing enterprises that were subsequently acquired.

This national belief in pluralism has enabled us to adapt to the changes of the postwar decades. It has enabled us to reaffirm

---

[11] This is not a uniquely American practice. Great Britain established a National Ports Authority in 1969 to plan the renovation and operation of all British ports—a task requiring introduction of far-reaching technological developments and new employment and operating practices. *The British Record*, British Information Services, Feb. 14, 1969.

our belief in the worth of the individual by reaching out through profit-making and nonprofit enterprises to obtain talent wherever it is located. And, as a people, by building up a network of independent nonprofit institutions to aid, but also to challenge and to evaluate, the policy directions of an increasingly powerful central government, we have reaffirmed our traditional belief that we do not want an all-encompassing government.

A fifth reason *why* is that business has been adjudged unsuitable to provide or incapable of providing some needed services.

Historically, Americans have not expected business enterprises to provide the basic services needed by the poor, the delinquent, the uneducated, and the ill because these people are unable to pay for the services they need (health care and housing, for example)—and which the body politic wants them to have—a price that would yield a profit to the supplier. And, deep in their conscience, Americans do not believe that some should make a profit out of the distress of others. This fact is affirmed by the increasing frequency with which it is suggested that drug manufacturers should not be privileged to make a profit from the sale of drugs which some individuals must have to live. It is affirmed even more vigorously by obvious and spreading dissatisfaction with the fact that, while great advances have been made in the caliber of medical care, steeply rising doctors' fees and hospital charges effectively deny many families (particularly those with annual incomes from $3,000 to $8,000 per annum) the health care they urgently need.

Business, simultaneously, has generally been regarded as incapable of carrying on basic research as effectively as other institutions. The rigorous regulation of the marketing of new drugs is premised in substantial part on the fear that such drugs would be sold for human consumption before their safety and efficacy had been adequately tested. Similarly, much research underlying the development of weapons, space vehicles, and satellites is entrusted to universities or other nonprofit institutions on the grounds that the enterprise oriented toward production as a principal source of profit cannot provide an objective climate for research.

Basic research, many researchers hold, simply does not flourish in a profit-making environment.[12] There are notable exceptions

[12] See essays by Carl Kaysen and Paul W. Cherington in *Public Policy*, a Yearbook of the Graduate School of Public Administration, Harvard University, 1963, pp. 219–285.

—the Bell Telephone Laboratories, General Electric, du Pont, and the Hoffman-LaRoche and Schering pharmaceutical research laboratories, for example. But experience suggests that, by and large, fundamental inquiry does not flourish in a climate dedicated to applying new knowledge to the making of a profit within a pragmatically limited time period.

Finally, business has not been credited with the capacity to make objective decisions in instances where the well-being of the individual or the buyer and the profit of the supplier are at issue. This belief is manifest in the general distrust of the privately owned (usually, doctor-owned) profit-making hospital; experience with such institutions suggests that the admission and length of stay of patients in the hospital may be influenced more by the prospect of profit for the owner-doctor than by the health care need of the patient.[13] This belief is also manifest in the contracting for research and development by the Department of Defense and the National Aeronautics and Space Administration; much of such contracting is not placed with profit-making enterprise on the theory that its decisions and recommendations as to research and development will be unduly influenced by the desire to profit from prospective production contracts.

A sixth reason why government has used nonprofit institutions is to aggregate a problem and thus to permit identification of pieces which business enterprise can undertake at a profit. Much is heard in 1970 of the "systems approach"; by that term nothing more is really meant than the antithesis of the "piecemeal approach." [14] In other words, we have learned of late that solutions to many problems require that the problem be looked at as a whole.

The Tennessee Valley Authority provides an early example of a governmental attempt to deal with a problem—the economic and social development of a then "depressed area"—as a whole. A more recent example is afforded by the creation of the New York City Health and Hospitals Corporation.

Looked at as a whole, the delivery of health services to all low-income persons in New York City involves more than 5 mil-

---

[13] The nursing homes, where admission and length of stay are less dependent on the judgment of the physician, are generally operated as profit-making enterprises.

[14] The clearest and most effective articulation of this idea that I have found is Simon Ramo's *Cure for Chaos* (New York: David McKay Company, Inc., 1969), p. 116.

lion people: thousands of physicians and more thousands of nurses; scores of hospitals, nursing homes, outpatient clinics, and related facilities; and the governmental agencies that provide public health services, furnish income for the needy, and administer Medicaid and Medicare. To cope with the whole problem, the New York State Legislature established in 1969 a "public benefit corporation." [15] That nonprofit institution will assume responsibility for the operation of all public hospital and health care facilities. It is expected to perfect the "system" made up of all the pieces enumerated above.

If the newly created corporation is successful in perfecting the system, then it is likely that pieces of the total problem (perhaps feeding in the several hospitals, a television network for communication between all related health facilities, or simply the transportation of doctors and patients within the system) can be identified and contracted out to private enterprise. The hope that the zeal of private enterprise will be attracted to finding profitable opportunities to provide much needed new goods and services that will satisfy expanding social wants—notably health, education, and housing—lies in the establishment of nonprofit institutions to perform such an aggregating, planning, and system-building function.

PROSPECT FOR THE FUTURE

What is the prospect for the future? Do these reasons for the development of this third sector of the American economy suggest further growth in the relative use of nonprofit institutions to get done what the society wants done? Do these reasons suggest a steadily lessening (although still major) dependence upon private profit-making enterprise?

The answers to these questions flow from the reasons that have been spelled out as to *why* the number and the function of nonprofit institutions have grown so substantially. A contrasting, but supporting, vision of the prospect for the future was presented by Richard C. Cornuelle in his book, *Reclaiming the American Dream.*[16] "As a frontier people, accustomed to interdependence,

---

[15] The New York Port Authority has essentially performed a similar "aggregating, planning, and system-building function" for the transportation needs of the New York metropolitan region.

[16] New York: Random House, Inc., 1965, pp. 21–24 and 118.

we developed a genius for solving common problems," he wrote. "People joined together in bewildering combinations to found schools, churches, opera houses, co-ops, hospitals, to build bridges and canals, to help the poor." But "a mounting agenda of problems" has caused citizens to feel "that only government seems big enough to work on them." This attitude was "born of the Depression" which "marked the end of automatic confidence in our traditional way of doing things," i.e., through independent, nonprofit agencies supported by private philanthropy, membership fees, and charges for services and managed largely by businessmen and their wives. "To restore the traditional American system in the modern context, businessmen must exercise their trusteeship of the independent sector with imagination and drive comparable to that which they use in business," concluded Cornuelle.

In the light of what has happened during the past three decades and the reasons for these happenings, the prospect envisioned by Cornuelle seems, at the least, unlikely. The role as well as the "imagination and drive" of the nonprofit sector of the American society has been made vital, as Cornuelle might wish. But these nonprofit institutions—private, quasi-public, and public—have been stimulated, supported, and utilized not by "businessmen and their wives," but by government; nor have they found the increased support that permitted their growth in "private philanthropy, membership fees, and charges for services."

In the light of what has happened during the past three decades, one perforce must answer the questions posed at the start of this section, as follows:

■ The prospect is that during the 1970s the nonprofit sector of the American economy will play a role substantially greater than heretofore. It will be increasingly utilized to mobilize the expanding range of human talent required to satisfy the society's need for new knowledge—whether for new death-dealing weapons or for life-preserving drugs—and to satisfy social wants that the society has now identified and can afford to meet.

■ The substantially greater role of the nonprofit sector will be defined in principal part by government and will be financed largely by government and only in small and declining part by private philanthropy, membership fees, or charges.

■ The causes that have given rise to the growth of the role of nonprofit institutions suggest their further growth and a somewhat—not greatly—lessened dependence of the American economy upon private, profit-making enterprise.

FORESEEABLE CONSEQUENCES

A relatively lessened demand for the services of profit-making enterprise does not necessarily mean a displacement of profit-making enterprise from the tasks it has traditionally performed. In substantial part this lessened demand is the result of the *expansion* of the wants of American people for services that have traditionally been supplied by agencies other than business enterprise:

- By the family
- By the churches, schools, colleges, hospitals, and other agencies created and supported voluntarily by those citizens who could afford and would contribute money and time
- By government

The expansion of what we have called social wants promises to claim an increasing share of the annual gross national product, and the provision of the services that satisfy these wants will be assured, in substantial part, by institutions other than business enterprises.

The future growth of the role of nonprofit institutions, while seemingly assured, seems destined to be accompanied by a harrowing sequence of trials and errors. A rash of problems flow out of the new and expanded relationship with government.

The need for the talent found in the nonprofit institution (talent which government is unable to obtain and retain on its own payroll) gives rise to important questions as to what public policy issues can be entrusted to private agencies. In turn, the performance of public or quasi-public functions by a private agency places on the nonprofit institution responsibility for a degree of accountability to the contracting government agency (and, in notable instances, to the Congress) to which it is little accustomed. Indeed, since the nonprofit institution is often performing services for which there is no "market" (e.g., the monitoring of the government's missile development program or the development of new techniques of learning to overcome the school dropout problem) and since there is no measure of profit, no adequate criteria exist for the appraisal of the contribution made by the nonprofit institution.[17] The government contracting officer, in most instances, shows little recognition that these agencies are "different" from profit-making enterprises. Yet, if the vital innovative spirit which has brought these institutions into being is to be maintained, they must be given a degree of independence consonant with the research or professional service activity in which most are engaged.[18] And the dependence of the federal government on the talent found in these agencies has in some instances made the nonprofit institution a subservient creature of government and not an independent organization capable of providing objective, detached advice or service.

These problems need to be recognized and resolved if the nonprofit institutions are to fulfill their very substantial promise.

[17] This accounts for an increasing effort to find new measures of benefits in relation to costs. For example, what is a new learning process that holds in school 10 percent of the kids that now drop out before completing high school worth to the society?

[18] The issue is dramatically spelled out in a report by the Comptroller General of the United States on an examination of the performance of the Hudson Institute under a contract with the Department of Defense, May, 1968.

PART 3

Regulation to Achieve Public Purposes

O NLY a minority—even though a large minority—of
American business enterprises are directly affected
by the grants economy pictured in the preceding five
chapters. A larger number of business enterprises
are affected by governmental regulation. The traditional forms of regulation of enterprises "affected with
the public interest" reach a limited proportion. But
that portion is being steadily expanded by the extension of older forms of regulation and by the introduction of new ones. That extension and its implications are dealt with in the four chapters that follow.

CHAPTER *8*

How Much Competition and How Much Regulation

M*OST* of this country's private enterprises are not supported by government subsidies, contracts, or research or development grants and are not nonprofit enterprises. But the forces that have impelled government to expand greatly its use of these mechanisms have simultaneously given rise to the extensive expansion of government regulation of private enterprises.

Businessmen are ideologically and emotionally committed to the idea of competition [1] and generally allergic to government regulation. Competition, the businessman argues, "serves as a regulator and reducer of prices, as an incentive to improved production efficiency, as a guarantor that we [the consumers] shall

[1] Francis S. Sutton, Seymour E. Harris, Carl Kaysen, and James Tobin, *The American Business Creed* (Cambridge, Mass.: Harvard University Press, 1965), p. 366. For excellent analyses of business' views toward competition see "The Functioning of a Competitive System," chap. 8, pp. 161–183.

get what we want, and as a protector of the freedom of opportunity." [2] Regulation, on the other hand, many businessmen contend, discourages initiative, contributes nothing to the efficiency of operations, and limits the rights of private property owners.

But in the real world of the late twentieth century, as J. K. Galbraith has suggested in a typically challenging fashion, "competition was abridged by custom, monopoly, trade unions, torpor, legislation, and even a degree of compassion." [3] And as a society, it can be added, we have been unwilling to let competition work in many areas, for when it does work, it works in brutal ways its benefits to provide!

Competition today is no longer among many sellers of relatively equal economic strength, as classical economic theory assumed. Consider the three "giants" of the automobile industry, the status of International Business Machines in the computer industry, or the status of International Telephone & Telegraph or Ling-Temco-Vought in the several industries each inhabits. In the words of one businessman:

> Today's competition is the competition of pricing policies, of quality, of consumer surveys, of mass advertising and of mass distribution devices, of research and of production practices and conditions of employment. This kind of competition is the only kind that is workable in a society like ours which requires large productive groups. [4]

And competition is no longer among buyers who are well informed as to the quality, content, and character of the products or services they buy. When the individual who buys advertised drugs, cigarettes, automobiles, or garden pesticides cannot know whether the product he is buying is safe or is worth what he is asked to pay, the venerable rule of caveat emptor is, indeed, a merciless rule. It is equally merciless for the small investor who must evaluate common stocks, mutual funds, and variable annuities or for the borrower who signs an installment loan contract.

Moreover, business has never been free of all restraint other than competition. From the days of our Founding Fathers, the

[2] National Association of Manufacturers, *The American Individual Enterprise System: Its Nature and Future*, 1946, vol. I, p. 59.

[3] *The Affluent Society* (Boston: Houghton Mifflin Company, 1958), p. 42.

[4] Roger M. Blough, *Free Man and the Corporation* (New York: McGraw-Hill Book Company, 1959), p. 15.

Congress and state and local legislative bodies have established laws to restrict competition, to permit it only in accordance with established standards, or to replace it in areas where it was believed continued competition was not in the public interest. Among the earliest of such laws were those establishing fair weights and measures for shopkeepers, standards of cleanliness for public eating places and barber shops, and the chartering of corporations; those providing for the supervision of banks and insurance companies; and those controlling hours and conditions of work for women and children. As time has passed, government regulation has been introduced in a variety of situations ranging from the prescription of quality standards as a protection against fraud to the imposition of detailed control over prices, outputs, and investments.[5]

FIRST USES OF REGULATION

From the earliest days, there was public regulation of canals, turnpikes, toll roads, ferries, inns, and gristmills. This regulation was founded on the reasoning that it was uneconomic to have competition in those industries deemed to be "natural monopolies." The railroads illustrate the point; duplicate investments in rights-of-way and rolling stock were deemed uneconomic and a burden rather than a benefit to consumers. Hence, as the railroads developed they were granted exclusive rights to transport persons and goods by rail over specified routes. In exchange for such exclusive rights, they were required to conform with specified safety provisions, to adopt schedules and fares approved by government, and to earn only what was determined to be a "fair return" on the stockholders' investment.

As other natural monopolies developed—gas, water, telephone, electricity, radio, and television—providing services in varying degrees essential to the public or utilizing a publicly owned resource (e.g., water or the airwaves), each has been subjected to regulation. Usually regulation was imposed first by the state gov-

[5] "Increasingly, under the legal and moral control of Federal agencies and, to a lesser extent, of state and local agencies, free enterprise is limited and no longer recognizable in terms of the social Darwinism of Sumner or of the natural rights of Adam Smith. The economic rationality of laissez faire gives way to the moral and legal power of the national community." W. Lloyd Warner, *The Emergent American Society*, vol. I, *Large-scale Organizations.* (New Haven, Conn.: Yale University Press, 1967), pp. 7–8.

ernments and assumed by the federal government when the economic area served extended beyond state boundaries. When the reach of many banks had been thus extended and it had become clear that their stability was of national concern, the National Banking Act of 1863 was enacted. Two decades later, dissatisfaction with the states' regulation of railroads that had extended their rights-of-way over several states resulted in enactment of the Interstate Commerce Act of 1887.

In subsequent decades, as business grew to serve markets encompassing several states, the federal government acted to meet additional problems. Federal food inspection was launched in 1890, with enactment of the Meat Inspection Act. The outlawing of "combinations in restraint of trade" and attempts to monopolize came with the Sherman Antitrust Act of 1890. The original Pure Food and Drug Act was passed in 1906; the Federal Trade Commission Act and the Clayton Act were both enacted in 1914; and the Packers and Stockyards Act was passed in 1921. Effective federal regulation of the electric power industry came with enactment of the Federal Power Act in 1935, strengthening the existing 1920 legislation and replacing the old Federal Power Commission (consisting of the Secretaries of War, Interior, and Agriculture) with an independent body consisting of five full-time commissioners. By that year an increasing proportion of all electricity was being transmitted across state lines, and many local electric companies were owned and controlled by holding companies with interests in two or more states.

Regulation of air transport and radio-television communications came in response to the chaos created by technological innovation in each field. The Federal Radio Act, enacted in 1927, was superseded by the Communications Act in 1934. The Civil Aeronautics Act of 1938 introduced safety, licensing, traffic control, and route and rate regulation of air transport; earlier, this industry had been controlled through payments for carrying the mail.

The Depression of the 1930s revealed in stark clarity the need for federal regulation to protect depositors, investors, and workers. This need gave rise to enactment of much New Deal legislation and particularly to the establishment of bank deposit insurance (1933), the Securities and Exchange Commission (1934), and the National Labor Relations Board (1935).

These steps highlight the gradual substitution of government regulation for market competition.[6] They suggest also *why*—as new industries have emerged; as technology has created new products, services and problems; and as the inability of the consumer, the depositor, the investor, the listener-viewer, or the worker to protect his own interests has become increasingly clear —new forms of regulation have been introduced. Subsequent sections of this chapter illustrate this trend, picture the forces that have impelled its development, and examine its impact on business' freedom.[7]

EVOLVING INDUSTRIES IMPEL REGULATION

Only two essentially new federal regulatory agencies have been established since World War II—the Atomic Energy Commission in 1946, and the Federal Water Pollution Control Administration in 1965 (absorbed in the Environmental Protection Agency proposed by President Nixon in 1970). Yet, federal regulation has not remained static. It has been extended in rapidly developing industries, intensified in areas where the consumer cannot make effective choices, and established "to protect the consumer against himself" where his health or life is at stake—even while increasingly vigorous efforts have been made to preserve and strengthen competition throughout much of the economy.

Communications industry

After World War II, the substantial and rapid expansion [8] and development of radio and television made necessary the recasting of old regulatory rules, the updating of engineering standards,

[6] For a useful chart of the history of federal regulation, see Emmette S. Redford, *American Government and the Economy* (New York: The Macmillan Company, 1965), pp. 362–364.

[7] Despite the continuing extension of regulation, American businessmen generally assume that they have greater freedom from governmental control than their British contemporaries—and certainly greater freedom than the counterpart nationalized industries. Yet Andrew Shonfield, the British economist and journalist, has written: "Coming from Europe and observing the behavior of people in industry and commerce, one may well be struck by the way in which it seems to be accepted that it is part of the lot of businessmen to be pushed around intermittently by one Federal agency or another." *Modern Capitalism* (New York: Oxford University Press, 1965), p. 299.

[8] A total of 48 FM stations and 6 television stations were operating during the war. By mid-1967, more than 2,000 FM stations and nearly 800 TV stations were on the air.

and refinement of the system by which scarce frequencies and channels were assigned to private owners.

No sooner were these tasks undertaken than a succession of technological refinements (in the FM field—facsimile and stereophonic broadcasting; in TV—color transmission, ultrahigh-frequency transmission, and community antenna transmission systems) created the need for further regulation. For example, enactment of a federal law banning the manufacture and importation (after April 30, 1964) of all television sets not able to receive the UHF channels followed the introduction of ultrahigh-frequency transmission.

In addition, regulation had to be instituted for such new means of communication as radar (for aviation and maritime use), microwave transmission, electronic "snoopers," and communication via satellites. When Congress established the Communications Satellite Corporation (Comsat) [9] in 1962 to develop and operate an international satellite communications network, it authorized the Federal Communications Commission to regulate the altitude of satellites, their radio transmission standards, the rates charged by Comsat for transmission, and the corporation's issuance of stocks and borrowings.

The need for possible further extension of regulation in the communications industry arises periodically. For example, in 1966, Comsat sought recognition as the sole authorized operator of domestic communications satellite systems. No determination of this issue had been reached by early 1970, but reactions to the proposal forecast that new forms of government control rather than competition will govern.[10] The computer service industry

[9] Comsat is a private, profit-seeking corporation owned by private communications companies (for example, American Telephone and Telegraph Company and International Telephone and Telegraph Corporation) and public shareholders. The federal government owns no stock in the corporation, but the President of the United States names three of the fifteen directors.

[10] McGeorge Bundy, in *The Strength of Government* (Cambridge, Mass.: Harvard University Press, 1968), p. 17, asks: "Do communications satellites constitute a new kind of common carrier, or is it better to conceive of such an information service as a form of free press? What is the place or places for competition here? How far can there be provision for kinds of information that are usually regarded as matters for philanthropy or public service? Should such a system or systems be directly assimilated to the processes of public education, and if so, how are the economics of both the system and the schools affected? What about governments as consumers of this information as well as regulators?"

poses a similar problem. The computer has become increasingly valuable, even essential, to the operation of many businesses. Its services have been made available to many smaller firms by virtue of "time sharing" on a central computer accessible via telephone lines. The emerging question is: Will the rates charged for access to and time on the computer be subjected to governmental regulation? [11]

Nuclear power industry

So far as one can see into the future, the nuclear power industry will never be as free from governmental regulation as even the most natural private monopoly can be. This is true because the awesome force of nuclear energy can end modern society overnight, and government must maintain such control as will ensure that it can prevent that catastrophe.[12]

The Atomic Energy Act of 1954 relaxed government's initial monopolistic control in this field. Private firms, it provided, could be licensed to build and operate nuclear power plants and to utilize this form of energy in other ways. In 1964 private ownership of all components of a nuclear power plant (including the heretofore excepted enriched uranium fuel and the plutonium produced in the reactor) was authorized. In 1969 a further step toward private ownership was taken when the AEC authorized the enrichment of privately owned uranium for a charge ("toll enrichment").[13]

These moves placed in the hands of private profit makers a

[11] Manley R. Irwin, "The Regulatory Status of the Computer Utility," *Land Economics*, May, 1967, pp. 223–227. *Business Week* (Nov. 22, 1969) poses these further questions: "Ought communications companies be allowed to supply unregulated data services? Should the FCC involve itself in ensuring the privacy and security of information stored in data-processing systems that use communication links? Where does communication stop and computing begin?"

[12] In discharging that responsibility, government is handicapped by the so far insuperable difficulties of communicating about nuclear energy—between specialists, between military and civilian officials, and between officials and private citizens. For elaboration of this point see McGeorge Bundy, *op. cit.*, pp. 20–22 and 46–55.

[13] As of January, 1971, the AEC distribution of special nuclear materials for use in power reactors will be only by sale. No new lease agreements for power reactor fuel can be entered into by the AEC after that date, and all existing lease arrangements must terminate by July 1, 1973. U.S. Atomic Energy Commission, *The Nuclear Industry, 1968*, p. 23.

new technology, the use of which involves hazards to the lives of employees and others. Hence, the legislation authorizing private ownership in the nuclear power industry simultaneously established extensive government regulation. The Atomic Energy Commission regulates through a licensing system the construction of nuclear power plants and their operations, and controls the ownership of nuclear fuels. In addition, the AEC, ICC, Federal Aviation Agency, Coast Guard, and the Post Office Department regulate in detail how all radioactive materials must be packaged, labeled, loaded, shielded, and stowed when transported.[14]

Drug industry

Biomedical research has produced during the postwar decades a succession of new life-lengthening and lifesaving drugs and vaccines. These discoveries have made Americans, particularly the aged,[15] increasingly dependent, some for the very maintenance of life, upon the continued availability of drugs; they also have enabled the drug industry to enjoy substantial and profitable growth.

Total drug sales rose from nearly $3 billion in 1957 to about $5.6 billion in 1968, and the drug industry "has maintained an annual profit rate based on net worth which is substantially higher above that of the average major American industries." One study showed that among 31 major industries, drug makers have averaged an 18.1 percent return on capital, as compared with 9.7 percent for the several industries.[16]

These developments have been accompanied by an intensification of regulation. The 1951 Humphrey-Durham amendment to the Food, Drug and Cosmetic Act of 1938 clarified prevailing law

[14] See Atomic Energy Commission, *Handbook of Federal Regulations Applying to Transportation of Radioactive Materials*, 1965.

[15] The aged represent less than 10 percent of the United States population, but account for 23 percent of all drug expenditures and spend three times as much for prescription drugs as those under 65. In addition, a large proportion of their drug expenditures goes for "long-term maintenance drugs, used primarily for the control of chronic diseases." *Competitive Problems in the Drug Industry, Hearings before the Subcommittee on Monopoly of the Select Committee on Small Business, on Present Status of Competition in the Pharmaceutical Industry*, U.S. Senate, 90th Cong., 2d Sess. part 9, Sept. 18, 19, and 25, 1968, pp. 3761–3762.

[16] *Ibid.*, pp. 3770 and 3793–3794.

as to what drugs could be sold without prescription and what drugs could not. In 1953, another amendment gave Food and Drug Administration inspectors authority to enter manufacturing establishments, warehouses, and drug stores without the permission of the owner and without a search warrant, provided notice was given.

In considerable part as a consequence of drug-caused thalidomide tragedies, the most substantial extension of drug regulation in this country's history became law in 1962.[17] Among other things, these amendments (1) authorized the FDA to set standards for good manufacturing practice; (2) required that all "new drugs" be proved by the manufacturer as being *effective* for the purposes claimed as well as being safe; [18] (3) authorized review for efficacy and safety of drugs introduced previously, even though already approved; (4) gave FDA new powers in policing the testing, experimental use, and reporting of side effects of drugs; (5) further broadened factory inspection powers; (6) permitted the FDA to establish generic names for drugs and to require inclusion of the names on labels and advertisements; and (7) introduced surveillance of pharmaceutical advertising in medical journals.

Chemical industry

The postwar years ushered in a seemingly endless parade of new products and services placed at man's disposal by technological advance in other fields of chemistry. Their blessings were readily hailed. Their consequences were not immediately perceived [19]

[17] A succession of reports that pregnant mothers who had taken a drug called thalidomide, experimentally available in the United States market and commercially available in Europe, had given birth to children with deformities, and the further revelation that a single analyst on the staff of the FDA, Dr. Frances Kelsey, had prevented approval of this drug and its marketing generally throughout this country created public concern sufficient to overcome long-standing opposition in the Congress to amendments proposed by Senator Estes Kefauver and others. See Richard Harris, *The Real Voice* (New York: The Macmillan Company, 1964).

[18] The definition of new drugs encompasses not only newly developed drugs but also new uses prescribed for existing drugs and new forms of previously approved drugs. Subsequent analysis of almost 4,000 new drugs by the National Academy of Sciences–National Research Council, under contract for the FDA, revealed that "a few drugs, about 7 percent of the total, were rated ineffective for all cited claims," while others were rated effective against only one or some of the diseases that their labels claimed they cured.

[19] Jacob Bronowski illustrated this fact dramatically when he wrote: "Who would have thought that the unfortunate character who invented photo-

until sometime later when they inevitably prompted either the extension of already existing government regulation or its introduction in new forms.

The new miracle products, it turned out, called for new ways to protect the consumer. New detergents, solvents, polishes, and cleaners were perhaps more effective, but they required the passage of the Hazardous Substances Labeling Act (1960).[20] Nylon, rayon, Dacron, or Fortrel were a joy to wash and wear, but the early synthetic fibers made it necessary to pass the Flammable Fabrics Act (1953). Food preservatives, emulsifiers, sweeteners, all those activities that made oranges more orange and cosmetics more glowing necessitated a string of amendments to the Food, Drug and Cosmetic Act and a further measure of protection through the provisions of the Fair Packaging and Labeling Act (1967).

But the greatest battle was sparked by the gentle middle-aged lady from Silver Spring, Maryland, Rachel Carson, whose famous book, *Silent Spring,* sounded the alarm against the new pesticides and was largely instrumental in strengthening their regulation during the early 1960s.

Pesticides have contributed greatly to agricultural productivity and to human comfort. But many of them proved hazardous to those who applied them, remained in the environment for a long time, and left in agricultural crops and in animals a residue that endangered humans. The most famous of those new pesticides, the once hailed DDT (dichloro-diphenyl-trichloro-ethane), has been accused of causing cancer in mice, poisoning the Lake Michigan Coho salmon, contributing to the virtual disappearance of the peregrine falcon on the East Coast of the United States, and upsetting whole ecosystems. Already banned in some

graphic film would have been responsible for the California film industry? And thus, indirectly, for contracts that would prevent film stars from having affairs that might give rise to gossip and scandal? That consequently stars would lead their love life in public, by repeated divorce and marriage? That therefore the beautiful pinups of films, in time, become the models of the divorce business? And the climax, that one-third of all marriages contracted this year in California are going to end in divorce—all because somebody invented the process of printing pictures on a celluloid strip?" *Saturday Review,* July 5, 1969, p. 44.

[20] The Caustic Poison Act of 1927 covered only 12 chemicals and corrosives (such as lye) and in short shrift became totally inadequate to protect consumers against new hazards.

European countries, DDT will also be banned in the United States by 1971. Late in 1969, announcing a drastic phaseout of DDT, HEW Secretary Finch admitted sadly that even if the use of DDT stopped immediately, "it would take 10 years or longer for the environment to purge itself."

To deal with problems of such magnitude obviously requires a vast regulatory apparatus. Some evidence of what extended regulation of the drug and chemical industries means is afforded by the growth of one regulatory agency. In the first years following the war, the FDA had a staff of about 800 employees and an annual budget of $3 to $5 million. By 1969, it employed more than 5,000 people and its annual budget was over $60 million.

Natural gas industry

Between 1947 and 1958, oil and gas producers fought vigorously to keep the Federal Power Commission from regulating the prices at which natural gas is sold at the wellhead by independent producers to interstate pipeline companies. The producers contended that competition between producers to sell gas to the pipeline buyers afforded adequate assurance of a reasonable price. Spokesmen for the companies distributing gas in the larger urban centers contended that competition did not in fact obtain. The producers of gas eventually lost, partly because of the unsavory tactics they used in striving to influence the Congress in 1956 and again in 1958.

The FPC interpreted the Natural Gas Act of 1938 to mean that the Commission had no jurisdiction over the field price at which natural gas was sold by producers to pipelines; the Commission thus confined its regulation to prices charged by pipelines to local distributors. A Supreme Court decision of 1954 made clear that the Commission's authority did include power to regulate field or wellhead rates.[21] Thus saddled with unwanted regulatory powers, the Commission was faced with the difficult task of determining field prices for thousands of individual producers. The backlog of pending cases grew until, in September, 1960, the foreseeable work load was enough to consume the staff's time until the year 2043! [22]

The FPC then developed the concept of area regulation. In

[21] *Phillips Petroleum Co. v. Wisconsin,* 347 U.S. 672 (1954).

[22] Arthur M. Johnson, *Government-Business Relations* (Columbus, Ohio: Charles E. Merrill Books, Inc., 1965), p. 270.

Opinion No. 468 (August, 1965) the Commission, differentiating between "new" and "flowing" gas, established a two-price system for sales of gas by all producers in the Permian Basin in the Southwest. The Permian Basin action not only determined the price at which the product could be sold, but also was designed to encourage the search for new natural gas sources. This method of regulation was affirmed by the Supreme Court in May, 1968.[23]

Four other area proceedings were initiated following the Permian Basin action. When completed, they will establish prices for approximately 93 percent of the sales volume of natural gas subject to FPC jurisdiction. It is estimated that the FPC action in the important southern Louisiana area alone "will result in annual rate reduction of about $49 million by the area producers which supply gas to pipeline companies serving a 28-state area of the eastern and central United States." [24]

Securities industry

The growth of corporate organization and the purchase of corporate securities as a method of savings by a steadily increasing number of Americans have made the securities distribution industry a prime candidate for government regulation. Within the decade ending in 1969, the number of stockholders more than doubled. Approximately one out of every four adult Americans now owns corporate shares. Additionally, the growth of investment by pension funds, mutual funds, and insurance companies has created an estimated 100 million "indirect investors." This combination of broad individual participation and growing institutional activity has resulted in the trading on all markets of an average daily volume of over $825 million and over 22 million shares.[25]

As a result of these developments as well as disclosures of some law violations,[26] Congress authorized in 1961 the first exhaustive

---

[23] *Permian Basin Area Rate Case*, 390 U.S. 747 (1968).

[24] Federal Power Commission, *Annual Report*, 1968, p. 54.

[25] Securities and Exchange Commission, *34th Annual Report*, 1968.

[26] The most spectacular of these disclosures was perhaps the Re affair which broke out in 1961 and marked the first time that the SEC took action against a stock specialist. Gerald A. Re and his son Gerald F. were charged by the SEC with "deliberate and gross" violations of law. The Res were selling unregistered securities and engaged in flagrant manipulation of prices. They were expelled from the American Stock Exchange and the broker-dealer license of their firm (Re, Re and Sagarese) was revoked.

study of the operations of the securities industry since the 1930s. The earlier inquiry, prompted by the disastrous stock market crash of 1929, resulted in enactment of the Securities Act of 1933 and the Securities Exchange Act of 1934 (creating the regulatory Securities and Exchange Commission). The report of the 1961 inquiry, *Special Study of the Securities Markets,* prompted the Securities Acts amendments of 1964; the adoption of new rules and regulations by the SEC; and the intensification of federal regulation of the activities of brokers, dealers, investment advisors, and specialists.[27] This extension of regulation was also attributable in part to what *Fortune* described as "probably the greatest business scandal of our era," i.e., the failure in 1963 of a respectable 36-year-old stock and commodity brokerage house, Ira Haupt & Company, through which the Allied Crude Vegetable Oil and Refining Company had gambled on vegetable oil futures.

Subsequent extension of securities regulation was clearly the consequence of the same factor which has prompted the extension of regulation in other industries—technological advance. It has manifested itself in the evolution of institutions which have made possible and encouraged investment in equities by many more individuals, and particularly by the small savers. These are generally known as "investment companies," and the best known of this genre are the "mutual funds."

The number of investment companies registered with the SEC increased during the 1960s, and by 1970 approximately 1,000 were registered with assets approximating $75 billion. Most of

[27] Specifically, the amendments and new rules and regulations provided for (1) direct SEC supervision of those securities firms that are not members and hence not subject to the rules of the stock exchanges or to the surveillance of the National Association of Securities Dealers; (2) submission of information to the SEC on all sales above a minimum size by all firms that trade or deal in securities listed on the exchanges, but do not do so on the exchanges (the so-called "third market"); (3) maintenance by all securities-trading firms of larger minimum capital to support their transactions; (4) prohibition of "floor trading" (i.e., trading stocks for themselves when handling public orders) by firms belonging to stock exchanges; (5) regulation of the specialists whose function is to moderate market fluctuations; (6) quarterly reporting by broker-dealers to the SEC on the investment of their own capital, amounts and sources of their revenue, and costs of operation, thus revealing profits and losses from each separate source—underwriting, stock brokerage or investment counseling. One additional change is that "full disclosure" rules were applied to the over-the-counter market, i.e., stocks traded outside the exchanges.

this growth was accounted for by the mutual funds. In 1940, less than 300,000 people held mutual fund shares; by 1970, more than 4 million people held them. In the mid-1960s, there were already 19 mutual funds, each of which held assets greater than those held by the entire mutual fund industry in 1940.[28] In 1968, of the 967 investment companies registered, 558 were mutual funds with total assets of $53.5 billion.

Small wonder that other financial institutions hastened to adopt the concept of the investment companies. First among these were the insurance companies. Noting a "broadening of interest in equity products," they began "looking more closely into the merits of mutual fund programs and individual variable annuities for their policyholders." [29]

In 1966, the SEC reported that these developments had created "a need for additional protections for mutual shareholders in areas which were either unanticipated or of secondary importance in 1940," when the Investment Company Act was enacted. Accordingly, the Commission proposed amendments relating primarily to the costs passed on to shareholders by investment companies for management and the acquisition of additional shareholders. Although passed by the Senate in July, 1968, these amendments were not considered by the House and died in the Ninetieth Congress.

The foregoing examples illustrate but a small part of the technological advance that has bettered the living standards of the American people during the postwar era—and, simultaneously, has impelled the extension of regulation. They illustrate not only the demands that technological advance has created (or helped to create) for government regulation, but also the government's growing concern with the interests of the consumer—his health, his welfare . . . and his pocket book.

COMPETITION AND COMPASSION

The classical concept of competition was a harsh one. It allowed for no compassion for the weakest members of society—the less capable producer, the less aggressive shopkeeper, the less efficient

---

[28] *Public Policy Implications of Investment Company Growth,* **Report of** the Securities and Exchange Commission, Committee on Interstate and Foreign Commerce, House Report 2337, December, 1966.

[29] *Life Insurance Fact Book 1968,* Institute of Life Insurance, New York, p. 6.

worker, or the less knowing consumer. Let the producer, the shopkeeper, the worker, and the consumer all mind their own interests.[30]

Practice has varied from theory. Some producers, some shopkeepers, and some farmers manifested a compassion in dealing with their competitors, their workers, their customers, and their communities that was inconsistent with the working of competition as the textbooks picture it. But society's increasing concern with the quality of life has posed a succession of problems that could not be met by competitors within the bounds of compassionate profit making. Consequently, the government has resorted to new forms of regulation.

Product regulation

Scores of drug and food products, refrigerators that become deathtraps for children climbing inside, toys that present electrical, mechanical, or heat hazards—all these present an illustration of the fact that competition alone was not sufficient to ensure the quality, the purity, or the safety of products offered to consumers. Indeed, these examples demonstrate that not only the consumers but also the ethical and compassionate competitors suffer if competition alone controls.

One product that has attracted regulation in lieu of the working of competition is the cigarette. A 1964 report of the Surgeon General of the U.S. Public Health Service, entitled *Smoking and Health*, revealed a high correlation between smoking and cancer and concluded that "cigarette smoking contributes substantially to mortality." This report gave rise to a federal statute (1965) requiring that "Caution: Cigarette Smoking May Be Hazardous To Your Health" be printed on cigarette packages. The

---

[30] "The economic system pictured in the central tradition was a thing of peril for those who participated in it and so, *pro tanto*, was economic life at large. The peril was a virtue, and the purer the peril the better the performance of the system. Yet the intrinsic insecurity was disturbing in two respects. The vulnerability of the weakest members of the society could not entirely be ignored. An economic system which of constitutional necessity was so unfeeling, so intolerant of weakness, was troubling. Even in the best of causes compassion is difficult to control. And equally disturbing was the unwillingness of ordinary men—businessmen, farmers, workers, reformers—to live with that peril. At every turn they showed their inclination to press collectively or with the aid of the government for measures designed to make their life more secure." J. K. Galbraith, *op. cit.*, p. 42.

use of such a warning to the consumer (rather than a required modification of the cigarette, e.g., a strengthened filter) followed the well-established pattern of regulating the sale of drugs and household cleaners. Subsequently, further forms of regulation— printing an even stronger warning on each package, providing free TV time to the American Cancer Society and other organizations to rebut cigarette commercials, or even outright banning of all cigarette advertising from TV and radio—have been proposed with increasing frequency. This apparent public demand for strengthened government regulation has grown despite the well-publicized effort of cigarette manufacturers to develop self-regulation among competing producers.

In the case of cigarettes, the public interest (i.e., the well-being of consumers) demanded regulation rather than competition. A similar case could be made for automobile safety.

The expanded use of the automobile in the United States was responsible for the most attention-attracting instance in which government regulation of the character of a product has been substituted for competition. In 1945 there were 31 million motor vehicles registered in this country; in 1970, their number exceeded 100 million. In 1945, more than 28,000 Americans died in automobile accidents; this figure was doubled by 1968. And, as this threat to the quality of life became increasingly apparent, the companion threat to health, caused by the spewing of exhaust fumes into the air by an ever-growing number of cars, came to be recognized.

Competition among automobile manufacturers during the years following World War II resulted in vast improvements in the appearance, the speed, and generally the caliber of the automobile. Competition did not—it is clear in retrospect—stimulate manufacturers to carry on research that would enable them to build into the cars they offered for sale all the mechanisms that would minimize threats to user safety and public health.

Though long concerned with highway safety,[31] the federal government did not direct its attention to these threats until relatively late. But by 1960, Congress was sufficiently concerned to direct the Surgeon General of the United States to make a study of the health effects of exhaust fumes. The report *Motor Vehi-*

---

[31] In 1924 Secretary of Commerce Herbert Hoover convened a National Conference on Street and Highway Safety.

cles, Air Pollution, and Health, presented to the Eighty-seventh Congress in 1962, provided the basis for subsequent regulatory legislation.

Congressional concern resulted in the enactment in 1964 of a law requiring that the General Services Administration, the government's purchasing agent, prescribe safety standards for the automobiles it buys for federal departments and agencies. GSA issued in 1965 a list of 17 features it would require in all the 1967 vehicles that it purchased. These features included exhaust fume controls, collapsible steering wheel columns, and dual brake systems. (Additional standards were published subsequently.)

Although the government purchases only a tiny proportion of commercial motor vehicle production each year (80,000 units at a total cost of $175 million in 1967), the automobile manufacturers responded quickly to this form of government regulation. The Chrysler Corporation announced promptly that 12 of the 17 features would be incorporated in all 1966 Dodge cars, and the Rubber Manufacturers Association revealed that automobile tire standards were being raised.

This "regulation by purchasing" (used earlier by the Department of Defense) was reinforced by a growing trend toward compulsory regulation to force manufacturers to incorporate both antipollution and safety features into automobile design. The state of California pioneered requiring that all 1966 cars sold within its borders have an exhaust control device that would meet the strictest emission standards in the nation. The federal government followed when the 1965 amendments to the Clean Air Act authorized the establishment of federal standards for the control of exhaust emissions from motor vehicles, beginning with the 1968 model year.

A giant next step came in the form of the Highway Safety Act and the National Traffic and Motor Vehicle Safety Act passed by Congress in 1966. Implementation of the latter act resulted in the announcement on February 1, 1967, of 20 "motor vehicle standards." They seemed to please no one. Critics—even those less single-minded than Ralph Nader, author of *Unsafe at Any Speed* and self-appointed defender of the consumer—thought they reflected excessive concessions to industry pressures. The industry, on the other hand, asked for further changes in 18 out of the 20 new standards. By February, 1969, there were 28 standards issued, and stiff violation penalties ($1,000 for *each* nonconformity, up to $400,000) had been announced.[32]

In 1966, John S. Bugas, speaking for the Automobile Manufacturers Association, argued against the legislation establishing federal regulation and pleaded in favor of industry self-regulation,[33] admitting, however, "what we [the Ford Motor Company] and others have done in the past is no longer sufficient to meet today's and tomorrow's needs." Though his plea was rejected, two years later, Lloyd Cutler, the perceptive counsel for this same association, spoke of the ensuing standards as a boon which freed the manufacturers to better their products in needed ways; car buyers, he contended, had never been willing to spend the relatively few added dollars for seat belts or other safety devices and hence, so long as competition was unbridled, a manufacturer could build added safety or antipollution devices into his product only at the risk of a lesser profit or the loss of sales to his competitors.

Casualty insurance—another automobile-related product—poses a similar problem as to the functioning of competition and the need for regulation. The automobile has become essential for many people in their jobs; consequently, automobile insurance is an essential form of protection today. Yet critics claim that the present system of automobile insurance is costly,[34] incomplete, and stacked against the poor and certain other groups; that it

[32] Contemporaneously, the federal government sought to improve highway safety through the maintenance of a nationwide register of drivers whose licenses had been withdrawn or revoked for more than six months and by influencing the state governments, through the prospect of the loss of federal grants, to tighten up motor vehicle inspection, driver regulation, highway design and maintenance, and the conduct of traffic courts.

[33] The banner of self-regulation was hoisted again late in 1969, when an advisory group of the U.S. Chamber of Commerce proposed a broad program of voluntary business reforms to meet the challenge of "new consumerism." Drawing a parallel with the civil rights movement, the report stated that "current consumer activism . . . has gone beyond protest to the formulation of legislative reform programs" and that new self-regulatory initiatives by business were needed "to minimize ill-conceived legislation and to offset the impact of new Federal regulatory programs."

[34] During the 1968 congressional hearings, Insurance Commissioner of Pennsylvania David O. Maxwell stated that "most authorities agree that no more than 55 percent of the premium dollar is being used to pay claims." In his article on automobile insurance in *New York Times Magazine* (Aug. 27, 1967), Daniel P. Moynihan quotes the results of a Michigan study: ". . . for every $1 actually paid into the hands of the injury victim, $2.20

maximizes "delay, fraud, and contentiousness" and clogs United States courts with an avalanche of cases which in metropolitan areas take, on an average, 30 months to come to trial.

In response to these criticisms, the Department of Transportation began in 1968 a two-year study of automobile insurance, and the Senate Antitrust and Monopoly Subcommittee opened hearings on what has become a $10 billion industry.

There were solid reasons for congressional concern. In part they stemmed from the excesses of competition among insurance companies striving for this growing volume of business. The regulation of insurance companies had been left up to the states by the 1945 McCarran-Ferguson Act; the inadequacy of this system was highlighted by the House Antitrust Subcommittee in an earlier report, which emphasized the many variations in insurance company regulation presently operative among the 50 states and the overresponsiveness of state "regulators" to the interest of the "regulated" industry.[35] The implication was that stronger and more uniform regulation by the federal government is needed.

Environmental protection

One of the most rapidly expanding ideas of the post-World War II era is that government should do whatever is needed to protect the environment in which more and more people live. Government—predominantly, local governments—had early assumed responsibility for purifying the water we drink and disposing of trash and garbage. But, until fairly recently, neither the meaning of "environmental pollution," "smog," and "thermal pollution," nor their effects on human, animal, and marine life were recognized as the threats they are.

The House Subcommittee on Science, Research, and Development warned in 1968 that "a well intentioned but poorly informed society is haphazardly deploying a powerful, accelerating technology in a complex and somewhat fragile environment." [36] Each year this problem has become more painfully clear to peo-

must be contributed by insurance policyholders and taxpayers." This, he claims, compares with $1.07 for the Blue Cross and Blue Shield operations.

[35] *Automobile Insurance Study*, a Report by the Staff of the Antitrust Subcommittee of the Committee on the Judiciary, House of Representatives, 90th Cong., 1st Sess., Oct. 24, 1967.

[36] *Managing the Environment*, Report of the Subcommittee on Science, Research, and Development to the House Committee on Science and Astronautics, Committee Print, Serial S, 1968.

ple choked by smog; irritated by the smoke from industrial chimneys or from the exhausts of an increasing number of automobiles; denied recreational or simple bathing and washing facilities by the dumping of refuse into our streams; threatened by nuclear fallout or, more frequently and more subtly, by the emission of radioactive rays from industrial and service facilities; and distressed by the generally little known consequences of pesticide use.

Inevitably, the business firm that ejects filth from its plants into the air or into streams, the municipal government that similarly pollutes the air or the water, and the automobile manufacturer whose product belches gas into the air have become the objects of new regulatory activity. Industry, being the leading producer of wastes because of the very nature of its activity, has been subjected to a new and rapidly growing form of regulation.

Water pollution

As early as 1899 federal law prohibited the discharge of wastes into a stream in such a way as to impede navigation, but federal action to limit pollution of water dates from passage of the Federal Water Pollution Control Act in 1948. This act provided for research on the causes and ways to curb pollution and for cash assistance to state and local governments. It also established a procedure (clarified and strengthened in subsequent years) by which the federal government could compel a municipality or an industrial firm to adopt pollution abatement programs. Although few enforcement actions were being taken under this procedure, the handwriting on the wall was made clearer to those businessmen who read in a succession of reports about the mounting threat of water pollution.

It became known that the water Americans drink in a substantial number of communities did not meet Public Health Service standards; that New York City dumped 200 million gallons of raw sewage into the Hudson River every day; that the oil-slicked Cuyahoga River, flowing through the middle of Cleveland, could and did burn so fiercely in 1969 that two railroad bridges were nearly destroyed; that the annual fish-kill census indicated that in 1967 nearly 12 million fish were killed by pollution in the streams of 40 states; that the discharge of hot water into the streams by a growing number of nuclear power plants threatened aquatic life.[37]

An editorial in a business magazine drew the obvious conclusion, "It's inevitable that your company, if it is responsible for pollution, will be forced to act." [38]

Many business firms did act. A survey of 2,800 member companies of the National Association of Manufacturers indicated that whereas in 1949 only 18 percent of the sample had water treatment facilities, by 1964 more than two-thirds of the sample had installed them. The total annual investment by manufacturers in such facilities amounted to about $100 million. The chemical industry alone was reported to be spending $40 million a year.

This apparent effort to curb water pollution has not stemmed the tide of new pollution regulation. In a decade of burgeoning industrial growth (the source of two-thirds of the nation's water pollution), expanding regulation was inevitable. The Water Quality Act of 1965 created the Federal Water Pollution Control Administration and required the states to adopt and enforce standards designed to "enhance the quality of water." If a state failed to do so, the federal government could, for the first time, superimpose its own standards and enforcement procedure. The Clean Water Restoration Act was passed in 1966 (unanimously, as was its predecessor act of 1965). It provided federal funds to speed up introduction and enforcement of water standards; it included, for the first time, a provision for federal assistance for research on industrial pollution; it required registration of existing or potential sources of pollution (with the proviso that no trade secrets need be revealed); it made available grants for coordinated river basin planning and increased research. A legislative effort to stimulate the construction of waste treatment plants with federal money—the Water Quality Improvement Act—was vigorously advanced in 1967 and in 1968 but did not become law. Meanwhile, implementation of the Water Quality Act of

[37] Alarmed biologists estimated that by the year 2000 "the use of natural waters to cool the condensers (when perhaps 125 nuclear power plants exist as contrasted with 14 in the fall of 1968) would entail the heating of an amount of water equivalent to a third of the yearly fresh water runoff in the U.S." John R. Clark, "Thermal Pollution and Aquatic Life," *Scientific American*, March, 1969.

[38] "It All Comes Out of Mr. Jekyll's Hyde," *Mill & Factory*, November, 1966.

1965 proceeded, and by 1969 the Secretary of the Interior moved to institute the first federal proceedings to "prosecute those who pollute": four large steelmakers, a Kansas mining company, and the city of Toledo. The mood of the country was further reflected by the action of Congress in November, 1969, when the National Environmental Policy Act was passed and $800 million was appropriated to help the states fight water pollution; this was a larger sum than had ever previously been appropriated and more than half a billion dollars more than had been requested by President Nixon. This mood was further reflected in January, 1970, when President Nixon devoted a major section of his State of the Union address to stressing the role of government in combating pollution.

Air pollution

Government efforts to control the principal source of air pollution—motor vehicle exhausts—have been pictured. In view of the rising number of motor vehicles, the pollution caused by this source can only be kept from getting worse; existing and foreseeable devices can markedly reduce exhaust gases, but not eliminate them. Thus the neutralizing of air pollution from other sources—customarily called "stationary"—acquires added urgency.

Yet control of air pollution from these sources (industrial plants, for example) on a national scale is singularly complex. Unlike motor vehicles, these sources vary tremendously as to type and region. Proposals for a national standard, or set of standards, have met with strong opposition from various industries on the grounds that the uniformly applicable emission standards would "serve administrative convenience only," would be "scientifically untenable," and possibly even "economically wasteful." [39]

Despite growing concern with the quality of air, it was not

[39] During the hearings on the Air Quality Act of 1967, a representative of the Manufacturing Chemists Association (an organization whose members reportedly have invested half a billion dollars in control programs since World War II) expressed the industry's fear that "the tendency . . . would be to set standards restrictive enough for the worst situations, resulting in arbitrary regulation that would incur unnecessary hardship and expense elsewhere" and could "discourage the future development of industry in areas away from pollution-plagued industrial centers." U.S. Senate Public Works Committee, *Hearings on the Air Quality Act of 1967*, 1967, vol. 3, p. 1783.

until enactment of the 1955 Air Pollution Control Act that the Department of Health, Education, and Welfare was authorized to initiate regulations to curb air pollution. Eight years later, the Clean Air Act of 1963 authorized two major new federal actions: (1) direct grants to state and local agencies to foster air pollution control programs and (2) a limited federal role in control of specific interstate pollution problems. Subsequently, amendments to the Clean Air Act of 1963 authorized control of automobile emissions and permitted the use of federal grants for maintaining state, local, and regional pollution control programs. But only with enactment of the Air Quality Act of 1967 was a significant expansion of the federal, state, and local air pollution control responsibility established.[40]

Solid waste

Commencing later but gaining rapidly in intensity is government's effort to limit the pollution of the environment by the accumulation and disposal of solid wastes. Waste accumulates in garbage pails, trash cans, dumps, and incinerators at a rate of about 5 pounds per day for each person in the United States.[41] It is estimated that up to 7 million automobiles are junked each year, and most of these accumulate in dumps and along highways. Even while spending $3 billion a year, we have not been able to keep up with the collection and disposal of such waste.

New technology is both an ally and a foe in this struggle. While it produces new ways of coping with solid waste, it also creates new problems. For example, 48 billion cans are produced in the United States each year. The old-time tin cans used to rust away, but today we have to cope with the improved "unrustable" aluminum cans and with plastic containers that may gladden the heart of an archaeologist 5,000 years hence.

[40] In February, 1969, in the first federal action of this kind, the Justice Department asked the U.S. District Court in Baltimore to order the Bishop Processing Company closed down for alleged violation of the federal clean air statutes.

[41] *Environmental Pollution, A Challenge to Science and Technology*, Report of the Subcommittee on Science, Research, and Development to the Committee on Science and Astronautics, U.S. House of Representatives, 89th Cong., 2d Sess., 1966, p. 30. See also *Environmental Quality*, Hearings before the Subcommittee on Science, Research, and Development, 90th Cong., 2d Sess., 1968.

Under the terms of the Solid Waste Disposal Act of 1965, federal funds are available to support the development, evaluation, and demonstration of various methods of disposal (incineration, sanitary landfills) and new devices, equipment, and techniques (crushing, baling, grinding) used to reduce the staggering volume of solid waste. Federal grants (e.g., in Maryland) support programs showing how solid waste can be used to reclaim the blight of strip mines.

As in the case of water and air pollution, this "study" phase of regulation will inevitably develop into mandatory regulation.

PROMOTING INNOVATION
THROUGH REGULATION

Large institutions find it difficult to adapt to changing circumstance. Governmental regulators are impelled to "emphasize law and regularity against the day they are challenged in court or denounced in public." [42] The industries, in turn, emphasize the rituals of regulation to limit its scope and to maximize predictability. The complexity and obscurity of the regulatory process prevents the public from prodding for change. The consequence is a relatively closed system in which the regulator and the regulated measure success in terms of the maintenance of the status quo. [43]

Yet the increased dependence of consumers dictates the need for progressive change and particularly the need for forcing technological advance in those industries where the stimulus of competition is lacking or limited. These needs for change, in turn, dictate the need for modifications in the regulatory process. In subsequent paragraphs these needs for change and the currently inadequate responses to them are pictured.

Electric power

Much of a relatively high annual rate of productivity improvement in the electric power industry through the years must be at-

---

[42] For excellent statement of this theme see Richard E. Stewart, "Ritual and Reality in Insurance Regulation," an address before the Joint Convention of the National Association of Casualty and Surety Executives, White Sulphur Springs, W. Va., Oct. 7, 1968.

[43] Federal regulatory agencies have tended, in the words of one observer, "to learn to live in amiable comfort with the regulated industry." Sidney

tributed to the development of new equipment by the manufacturers of electrical generation and transmission equipment. The electric utility companies have themselves invested little in research and development. In several technological areas the industry has fallen behind levels of efficiency achieved in Europe and in the Soviet Union during the postwar period. The industry also has lagged in the coordination and integration of power systems across the country; in 1964 only a third of installed thermal capacity was planned and built on a coordinated basis.[44]

Not until the mid-1960s did the Federal Power Commission begin aggressively to promote national integration and technological advance. The primary tool for this has been an exhaustive inquiry into the present state and future potentialities of the industry, known as the *National Power Survey*. Completed in 1964, the survey, made in cooperation with leaders of the electric utility industry, urged a full coordination and interconnection of the nation's 3,600 power systems. This would permit, the survey argued, greatly increased efficiency and as much as a 27 percent decrease in the average retail price of electricity. Larger and more efficient generating units could be used, thermal plants could be located more advantageously, the benefits of nuclear power could be exploited, surpluses of power could be shunted about more widely, and the reliability of the power supply improved.[45]

Industry leaders who participated in the survey did not envisage compulsory implementation of its recommendations by the FPC. On the contrary, the study was presented as a "guideline pattern for development" rather than a compulsory plan, an illustration rather than a "blueprint." Moreover, the survey em-

Robbins, *The Securities Markets: Operations and Issues* (New York: The Free Press, 1966), p. 77.

[44] "The Electric Power Industry in the Decades Ahead," an address by Joseph C. Swidler, chairman of the Federal Power Commission, before the American Power Conference, Apr. 16, 1964.

[45] *National Power Survey: A Report by the Federal Power Commission,* 1964, 2 vols. The extremely rapid growth of the electric utility industry brought in its wake new challenges, foremost among them, perhaps, the industry's increasingly heavy reliance on nuclear power generation and the mounting public concern with the impact of power systems on the quality of the environment in which we live. These developments have prompted the FPC to undertake the updating of the 1964 survey. The new National Power Survey report will extend the period of analysis to 1990 and is scheduled for publication in 1970.

phasized that achievement of a national power grid through government ownership was not under consideration. In July, 1967, in a report to President Johnson precipitated by power failures that blacked out large areas in the Northeastern and Middle Atlantic states, the FPC recommended the expenditure of $8 billion for the construction of extra-high-voltage transmission lines and proposed the setting up of public planning machinery to spur the utilities on in the development of improved coordination among electric power systems. In response, utilities have taken steps in a number of regions to form coordinating councils, and in June, 1968, an agreement forming a National Electric Reliability Council was signed by 12 coordinating organizations and utilities.

Banking

In 1961 the Commission on Money and Credit urged that government regulation of private financial institutions be made generally more flexible in order to achieve a more efficient flow and utilization of private capital. With respect to commercial banks, the Commission recommended, among other proposals, that restrictions on lending over wider geographical areas and restrictions on bank investments be liberalized. Present regulations, according to the Commission, "often discourage initiative and competition." [46]

During the early 1960s, one federal regulatory office, the Office of the Comptroller of the Currency, responded to this urging.[47] Comptroller James J. Saxon (1961–1966) chartered an unprecedented number of new national banks (627 in 4 years). He encouraged the branching of banks, which allows more geographical mobility of loan funds and more competition for savings by banks. He generally supported the merger of banks on the grounds that larger institutions could take advantage of economies of scale such as the use of data processing systems. He relaxed interpretation of the principle that a bank cannot invest in the

[46] *Money and Credit: Their Influence on Jobs, Prices, and Growth* (Englewood Cliffs, N.J.: Prentice-Hall, Inc., 1961), p. 161.

[47] There are three federal agencies with authority to regulate various aspects of banking: the Federal Reserve Board, the Federal Deposit Insurance Corporation, and the Office of the Comptroller of the Currency. Their efforts do not always add up to consistency in regulation, a fact which lends some weight to the proposal advanced in recent years that they be merged into a single agency.

common stock of a company whose business is other than banking and thus allowed new flexibility in banking enterprise, permitting, for example, a bank to enter the credit-card business.[48] In 1964 Mr. Saxon also proposed that all federal regulation of state banks, which is carried out by the FDIC and the Federal Reserve Board, be removed and transferred to the states.

But federal reins were tightened in 1966, when the amendments to the Bank Holding Company Act of 1956 repealed that act's two major exemptions. That same year, amendments to the Bank Merger Act of 1960 endeavored, not wholly successfully, to clarify the applicability of the antitrust laws to bank mergers and to establish standards for consideration of mergers by federal regulatory agencies and by the courts. Finally, the Financial Institutions Supervisory Act of 1966 empowered federal bank regulatory agencies to issue cease-and-desist orders against banks and suspension-and-removal orders against bank officials engaged in unsafe or unsound banking practices.

Over the past three years a new controversy over banking regulation had been gathering momentum and resulted, in 1969, in congressional hearings. The debate centered on bank holding companies, more specifically, on *one-bank* holding companies. Their exemption from regulation under both the 1956 act and the 1966 amendments allowed many a large bank to get around the prohibition to diversify by acquiring nonrelated, nonbanking business interests. Urging the passing of new regulatory legislation, President Nixon noted "a disturbing trend . . . toward erosion of the traditional separation of power between the suppliers of money —the banks—and the users of money—commerce and industry."

Transportation

The transportation industry of this country has benefited from numerous innovations during the postwar decades; for example, the introduction of jet aircraft and the V / STOL planes, containerized shipping, and high-pressure, large-diameter pipelines. While the railroads have manifested less change in equipment and in processes, rail transportation has been improved by the increased use of diesel locomotives, the development of "piggyback" trailer-flatcar service, the development of the high-speed-train concept, the introduction of the "Big John" hopper cars

---

[48] This proved so attractive that by mid-1968 there were 416 banks operating credit-card programs, double the number of the year before.

capable of carrying 100 tons of grain, the "Rent-A-Train" concept, and other innovations.

By and large federal regulatory agencies in transportation—the Interstate Commerce Commission (ICC), the Civil Aeronautics Board (CAB), and the Maritime Commission—resisted the technological advance manifest in these innovations, at least in notable instances. In the early postwar period, the CAB discouraged air coach travel when the nonscheduled lines pushed for it against the wishes of the major carriers. In the early and mid-1960s, the ICC, prompted by opposition from barge lines and truckers who feared new competition from the railroads, refused to accept reduced railroad rates made possible by new freight cars. In the ocean shipping field, the Maritime Commission has opposed change in the operating and construction subsidies granted to the private United States merchant marine, even though the importance of a merchant marine has declined and the subsidization tends to inhibit the creation of a more efficient and competitive fleet.

But the winds of change blew. In 1962 President Kennedy recommended a number of reforms. To make regulation less restrictive, he proposed reduction of minimum rate regulation, decreased use of subsidies in aviation, additional employment of the "user charges" principle and joint rates, and federal assistance to urban mass transit. The coal industry, barge shippers, and other opponents were successful in defeating all the proposed reforms except the last, which was enacted in the form of the Urban Mass Transportation Act of 1964.[49]

This law seeks to promote innovation in the transportation industries by providing financial assistance. It authorizes general improvements grants and loans, as well as grants for research and demonstration projects. Simultaneously, the federal government sponsored two significant development efforts. One was the development, in large part through federal financing, of a supersonic air transport (SST) for commercial use, which would fly 1,800 miles per hour. The second was the so-called "Northeast Corri-

---

[49] The Kennedy message was by no means the first such effort to achieve de-regulation of transportation. In 1949 the Commerce Department, at President Truman's direction, issued a report along these lines (the Sawyer Report), and in 1955 a Cabinet committee established by President Eisenhower made recommendations urging less government regulation. Both came to nought.

dor" project, a research effort designed (1) to improve existing rail technology generally, as the Japanese have done in the development of the Tokaido line and (2) to explore radically new means of travel, such as enclosed tubes with rocket propulsion and air or liquid suspension. President Johnson called for a third effort in March, 1966, when he proposed in a message to the Congress that the federal government undertake research in traffic safety and oceangoing vessels. Also he proposed that the new Department of Transportation "plan and fashion research and development for a total transportation system." [50]

In the field of maritime regulation, the relentless pressure of technological advance, overseas competition, and this country's balance-of-payments vicissitudes gave rise to proposals for change. In his 1965 State of the Union message, President Johnson promised "a new maritime policy for this nation." But the political strength of an industry in which change is urgently needed has been sufficient to prevent technological advance and the reduction of government control.

COMPETITION AND ANTITRUST POLICY

Clearly, the years since 1946 have been marked by the extension of regulation (and a lessened dependence on competition) to control more and more areas of this country's economic activity. Yet simultaneously there has been an intensified effort by government (under both Republicans and Democrats) to maintain and to strengthen competition throughout the economy. This effort is apparent in legislation (e.g., the Celler-Kefauver Act of 1950), in the enforcement efforts of the federal government, and in recent court decisions which extend the reach of the existing antitrust laws and make them more effective.[51]

The central objective of these laws is to outlaw any action ("in the form of trust or otherwise, or conspiracy") designed to restrain trade or commerce, create a monopoly, or lessen competition. The original Sherman Act was a "trust-busting act," and since its enactment in 1890, much of the antitrust effort has been

---

[50] *President Johnson's Message on Transportation,* Mar. 2, 1966.
[51] Particularly the Sherman Act of 1890; the Federal Trade Commission Act of 1914; and the Clayton Act of 1914, amended by the Robinson-Patman Act of 1936.

concentrated on breaking up—or, more recently, on preventing the formation by merger or acquisition—of large corporations that could exercise some monopolistic power. To achieve the objective of maintaining competition, the enforcement agencies and the courts have found it necessary to prohibit businesses from collaborating with other firms in joint ventures, through trade associations, or directly for the exchange of information, agreement on prices, output, division of markets, or other matters. And to achieve this objective, antitrust activity has included a continuing effort to outlaw trade practices that are restrictive or monopolistic, such as price discrimination, exclusive dealing and tying contracts, acquisitions or mergers of competing companies, or interlocking directorates.

Eight decades of antitrust legislation have done much to maintain competition, to prevent unfair competition (for example, false advertising and misbranding), and to eliminate trade practices that would limit competition. At the end of these eight decades, however, there still remains a substantial controversy as to whether the major effort—aimed at limiting mergers—is in the public interest.[52]

To the corporation or bank president seeking larger volume, security through diversification, and lower overhead costs, the opportunity to acquire another enterprise offers the prospect of profitable growth which his stockholders and directors expect him to attain.[53] To the members of the Federal Trade Commis-

[52] The issue, said Henry H. Fowler, Jr. (later Secretary of the Treasury, but at the time a private attorney) in an address before the Business Council in 1964, "is whether the growth and development of sizable business units shall be limited to processes of internal expansion. Or, putting it in question form—is the mating instinct of business organizations of substantial size and scope to be outlawed as incompatible with the maintenance of the competitive system?" Mr. Fowler added that "there is ground for some apprehension that bigness is about to be put under attack if it has resulted in some measure from the processes of external acquisition, however normal and proper the acquisitive acts at the time."

[53] J. Fred Weston, in *The Role of Mergers in the Growth of Large Firms* (Berkeley: University of California Press, 1953), analyzed the asset growth of 74 firms from approximately 1900 to 1948 and estimated that 22.6 percent of the growth was accomplished by external acquisition and 77.4 percent was accomplished by internal expansion. By arbitrarily treating the assets owned at the beginning of the period surveyed as having been acquired externally, the percentages work out as 36.3 and 63.7 respectively. Industries were found to vary widely in the degree to which they had grown by acquisition; whereas the largest motor vehicle firms had averaged 16.4 to 20.8 percent external growth (depending upon the method of calculation), the largest steel

sion (FTC), the staff of the Antitrust Division of the Department of Justice, and members of the federal judiciary, the acquisition by one corporation of others poses a threat of lessened competition and the prospect that the new, combined enterprise will wield its greater economic power to the disadvantage of consumers and competitors.

Both the businessmen and the government officials entrusted with enforcement of antitrust laws consciously or unconsciously make judgments as to the desirability of acquisitions and mergers in a changing context. Population growth and concentration in urban centers provide markets for much larger enterprises than were visualized when this country's antitrust laws were conceived. Technological advance makes possible vastly greater production, and some enterprises may be too small to take advantage of the advanced equipment and new processes, which are the consequences of substantial investment in research. Upon occasion, the threat of "political" competition by the nationalized industries of the U.S.S.R. or the cartels of Western Europe raises the question of the ability of American enterprise to compete in rapidly enlarging international markets. These and other evolving factors require the evaluation of acquisitions and mergers on other bases than the wielding of economic power in a domestic economy peopled by many small enterprises.

J. K. Galbraith has led the attack on the antitrust laws. He charges that these laws are "an anachronism," "a charade," and that they constitute a "legal condemnation of monopoly and its *de facto* acceptance in slightly imperfect form as oligopoly."[54]

To appraise the merits of this indictment requires consideration of these issues:

■ *Economies of scale.* Galbraith contends that the antitrust laws discourage the development of large firms that can realize all potential economies of scale. Those holding opposing views counter that available evidence suggests that many firms in concentrated industries are larger than necessary to produce goods at the lowest possible cost.[55]

companies had accomplished from 40.2 to 53.0 percent of their growth by this route.

[54] J. K. Galbraith, *The New Industrial State* (Boston: Houghton Mifflin Company, 1967), p. 186.

[55] Contrary views presented here are summarized from a paper by Donald F. Turner, Professor of Law, Harvard University (and formerly Assistant Attorney General of the United States) delivered before the Institute of Advanced Legal Studies, London, England, June 5, 1967.

■ *Technological progress.* Galbraith contends that the anti-trust laws limit the amount of research and the efficiency of research done by private business firms, because only the larger firms can afford to mobilize the substantial annual expenditures that are required. Those who hold contrary views contend that while it is true that many more large firms (with 5,000 or more employees) than small firms (with less than 500 employees) conduct research, once a firm gets large enough (say, $50 million annual sales), there is no evidence that further growth is needed to support research. Moreover, they contend that many smaller firms tend to spend on research proportionately as much as do large firms and that a study of patents indicates that the smaller firms turn out proportionately as many inventions.

■ *Efficiency in managerial planning.* Galbraith contends that to achieve the full economy of management planning that present techniques permit, firms must be allowed to grow large. His opponents argue that while the computer has greatly expanded corporate management's ability to handle great masses of operation information, there is no evidence that these computer-aided planning processes can be used only by "giant-sized firms." They hold that after a certain minimum size is reached, firms become less, rather than more, efficient in terms of management.

Galbraith's indictment has received no support that gives promise of any reversal of the 80-year effort to maintain competition by limiting the growth through acquisition of individual enterprises. Yet there is accumulating evidence that oligopolies are often characterized by efficient production, expansive output, and prices that are generally thought rather favorable to the public. In the face of the underlying forces that are changing the American society, the advice of John M. Clark seems particularly relevant: The task, he has advised in effect, is how to ensure workable competition among oligopolists.

SIGNIFICANCE FOR THE FUTURE

Businessmen, economists, public officials, and journalists all profess their belief that competition is the most efficient and the most productive way of organizing the American economy. Each would hold, too, that competitive capitalism provides more personal freedom than does any other social system. Yet this canvass of some happenings during the postwar years makes clear that regulation has been substituted for competition in an increasing number of instances and that governmental efforts to maintain and strengthen competition through enforcement of the antitrust laws have been subjected to significant challenge.

There is some evidence that businessmen, despite their traditional antipathy toward governmental control, have not been particularly concerned by the manifest extension of regulation. An analysis of references to federal regulation in a business journal during the years 1934–1940 and 1946–1948 suggested that "there has been a long-term and steady decline in business hostility toward government regulation from 1935 (omitting the war period) until 1948." This does not mean, the author cautioned, that there has been an increase in favorable opinion toward regulation; it suggests only that businessmen "worried" less about regulation at the end of this decade than at the start.[56]

This general conclusion is essentially confirmed by polls conducted at intervals during the postwar era by the Opinion Research Corporation. Businessmen and the general public were asked: "What is your feeling about government regulation of business—would you say it is better to regulate business pretty closely, or would you say the less regulation of business the better?" The results are as follows (omitting the "no opinion" percentages): [57]

	1946	1955	1962	1967
Regulate pretty closely				
Businessmen:				
Proprietors and managers 23%	27%	38%	
Business executives 8	15		
Small businessmen 20	25		
General public 35	34	39	35%
Less regulation of business				
Businessmen:				
Proprietors and managers 69	66	48	
Business executives 87	80		
Small businessmen 72	68		
General public 52	55	39	47

[56] Robert E. Lane, *The Regulation of Businessmen: Social Conditions of Government Economic Control* (New Haven, Conn.: Yale University Press, 1954), pp. 38, 54, and 55.

[57] Opinion Research Corporation, Public Opinion Index for Industry, *Collectivist Ideology in America*, 1946, p. A-4; *Socialist Thinking in America*, 1953, p. A-1; *Free Enterprise in America*, 1962, p. A-1; *Free Market vs. Socialistic Thinking*, 1955, p. A-1; and letter to the author dated Dec. 31, 1968.

If competition is eminently desirable and yet regulation is being persistently extended and accepted, what is ahead?

Even as the laws of physics explain why, when a pebble is dropped in a still pond, the impact spreads in a series of concentric circles, so the forces that are changing the society we live in —the changing composition of the population, urbanization, technological advance, the growth of organizations, chronic war, the collapse of space, growing affluence, and increasing concern with the quality of life—explain the steady extension of regulation.

The prospect is for further limitation of competition to protect the public interest. This prospect creates three urgent needs. The first is for the reappraisal of the role that competition can play effectively in the American society of the 1970s. There will be opportunities to abandon regulation in fields where competition reappears (e.g., railroad passenger and, to some extent, freight transportation). There will be an even greater opportunity to utilize competition as the governor of the economy if economists, businessmen, legislators, and public officials can find ways of ensuring effective competition among large enterprises.

A second need is for a commitment to research on the part of regulators. There is an urgent need for basing regulation (or the abandonment of regulation) on facts rather than on arbitrary, legalistic determinations of a situation that has existed whether or not the situation still exists. It would be better if a decision as to airline fares were founded on some knowledge of the elasticity of demand for air transport. It would be better if decisions as to what rate of return American Telephone and Telegraph should be permitted to earn were based on research-based findings as to the needed cost of continuing technological innovation. It would be better if the FTC's determinations as to mergers were based on some real study of the nature of competition in concentrated industries. Decisions, dozens of them each month, are made now without the aid of research. Established concepts of competition and legal rituals are rough and obsolete instruments for regulation in a time of rapid change.

The third need is for a new theory of regulation. The limited regulation of pre-World War II days relied heavily on the yardstick of "a fair return on a fair valuation." The much more extensive regulation of the 1960s has no such yardstick. The assignment of air routes, the issuance of TV franchises, the fixing of quotas for oil imports, the labeling of cigarettes, and the approval of new drug applications all rest on judgments as to what is in the public interest, and these judgments are deeply rooted in scientific considerations. For such judgments there are no generally accepted yardsticks; there is only the increasing reliance that Americans place on the effectiveness of the democratic process and on the disinterested competence of public officials. Stated thus baldly, this thought makes many businessmen tremble.

CHAPTER 9

Prices and Wages: The Growth of Informal Constraints

A CORNERSTONE notion of the free enterprise system has been that businessmen must be free to set prices and to bargain with their employees as to wages without government interference. In recent years, however, most Americans have gradually accepted the idea that the public interest requires governmental influence over at least some, if not all, private wage and price decisions.

The traditional notion is founded on the concept of a highly competitive market in which sellers are numerous and entry is easy and in which the individual firm or union has little power to limit supply. As it has become clear that the American economy is replete with instances in which such a competitive market does not exist, governmental intervention to provide or supplement market forces to protect the consumer or the worker has become increasingly accepted—and expected.[1]

Historically, government control over private price and wage decisions rests on formal authority granted by a legislative body and is exercised by well-established agencies (e.g., regulatory agencies) or the courts. Such legislation and the Federal Administrative Procedure Act assure the individual or the enterprise the due process of law. In short, when government has intervened in decisions traditionally within the province of the business firm, it has done so through legislatively established institutions and processes designed to protect private interests.

Exceptions, prior to the 1960s, were few, brief, and impelled by emergencies—war or a national strike. During World War II, in the weeks prior to passage of the Price Control Act, and during the Korean War before the Chinese intervention, exhortative or "jawbone" price control was employed. Periodic congressional investigations of prices—of steel in 1957 and 1962, of automobiles in 1958, and of drugs in 1957 and 1962—may also be viewed as attempts to influence private pricing decisions by means that provide the businessman with inadequate opportunity to protect his interests. But with such exceptions, the purposes of government intervention have been to supplement the functioning of the market (e.g., through the regulation of utilities and antitrust enforcement) and to meet emergency needs (e.g., wartime controls.) [2]

Since 1960, however, a pattern of informal constraints over wages and prices has developed which differs from these traditional forms of intervention both in objectives and in administration. It is exercised at the discretion of the President, with greater flexibility than formal controls; with all the power of the federal government's role as a subsidizer, purchaser, lender, and manipulator of public opinion; and with considerable danger of bias and inequity. It is aimed at more than protecting the public from improper pricing practices or oppressive strikes. This new pattern of constraints provides a continuing measure

[1] Governmental programs to support farm prices and to control agricultural output provide an early illustration of governmental intervention. For a summary analysis of these efforts, see Paul A. Samuelson, *Economics, an Introductory Analysis,* 7th ed. (New York: McGraw-Hill Book Company, 1964), pp. 399–423.

[2] In the enforcement of anti-price discrimination legislation the FTC markedly influences the setting of some prices—e.g., gasoline, beer, cigarettes.

of control over prices and wages as a key part of government's overall economic objectives. The primary purpose is to prevent an inflationary wage-price spiral from offsetting the gains of full employment and economic growth.

WAGE AND PRICE CONTROLS
AND THE PUBLIC INTEREST

The continual striving of this country's government to avert (or, at least, to limit) inflation provokes consideration of three basic questions: What causes inflation? Why must government assume this responsibility that used to be borne by the market? Why must the federal government increasingly intervene in the determination of prices and wages within private enterprises?

First, the American people have determined that they want full employment, and they want it continually, not only at the peak of recurring booms. And they have determined that they want economic growth, for they have learned that only a growing economy can provide an increasing number of jobs for an increasing population—and also rising incomes for most families.

Second, after years of experimenting as to *how,* Americans have chosen to underwrite the economic lot of the farmers and at least the lowest-paid wage earners. They have built into the economy farm price supports, minimum wages, and governmental support of collective bargaining.

This twofold expansion of the concept of the public interest makes a continual price climb inevitable. The effect of this price climb is further reinforced by two characteristics of the evolving economy:

■ *The fixity of wages.*   In most of the American economy—particularly the organized labor and the public segment—wages rise but do not go down, and it is difficult to envision a period when wages would be lowered comprehensively and kept down for a year or more. The last yearly decline in hourly wages in production occurred in 1933.

■ *The fixity of prices.*   In a substantial segment of the American economy that is marked by a concentration of industry (e.g., cigarette manufacturing, gasoline distribution, electrical equipment manufacture, and steel production), prices do not fall. In those industries where only a few producers compete, they can hold prices up even when demand falls off. Again, this characteristic of an increasing, even if relatively small, part of all American industry keeps the price curve slanted upwards. In only 2 out of the past 30 years was there a reduction (1949 and 1955), and it was so small as to be negligible.

Together, these factors make persistent rising prices inevitable in the kind of economy developed during the postwar era. But must government assume the responsibility for controlling such inflation, a responsibility that was left to the market in the past? This question has been substantially answered: Government must intervene because the market economy—when there are strong labor unions and large and strong oligopolies—is unable to control prices effectively. And the consequences of an unlimited, continuing rise in prices are inconsistent with the humane economy.

Rapid inflation can wipe out many or all economic and social gains achieved through full employment and economic growth. It can reduce the demand for goods and services and create unemployment. It can dissuade businessmen from making capital expenditures by limiting the foreseeable demand for the goods that might be produced and thus slow down or stunt economic growth. It can discourage exports and thus weaken this nation's balance of international payments. It can play havoc with the living standards of persons whose incomes do not expand as prices rise (pensioners, for example). It can impair the efficiency with which this nation's resources are allocated among the various demands for goods and services.[3] And, once begun, the inflationary spiral is easily accelerated, difficult to slow down, and can only be unwound at the expense of substantial unemployment.

But cannot government control inflation through monetary and fiscal measures? Must the federal government increasingly intervene in the determination of prices and wages within the individual enterprise?

Historically, government has tried to moderate the declines as well as the rises in demand for goods and services by the use of monetary and fiscal measures, by shoring up competition as best it can, and by stimulating increased productivity. The insufficiency and political unacceptability of these measures became patently clear in the late 1960s. Despite general agreement that the imposition of mandatory controls over pricing and wage setting by the individual business firm is the least desirable and

---

[3] For effective description of the consequences of inflation, see *Annual Report of the Council of Economic Advisers*, 1968, pp. 82–84.

least palatable way of curbing inflation,[4] this country's government has moved steadily toward the establishment of such controls.

STEEL PRICES: EVOLVING CONTROLS

The steel industry has long been looked upon—despite growing competition from aluminum, plastics, reinforced concrete, titanium, and other new products—as a bellwether industry. Changes in the price of steel, it has been assumed, foreshadow the ups and downs of prices throughout the economy.[5] Moreover, as President Kennedy noted, steel prices affect "the cost of homes, autos, appliances, and most other items for every American family" as well as the equipment that produces many or most of the facilities they use.[6]

In addition, the steel industry is highly concentrated. The four largest producers represent 50 percent of the output, and the twenty largest manufacture virtually all domestically produced steel. These firms generally follow one another in making price changes. Declines in demand are met by cutting back production rather than by lowering prices, so that steel prices, like prices in other oligopolistic industries, generally move in only one direction. In 1958, for example, the steel industry increased its prices while operating at little more than half its rated capacity.

These characteristics—the central significance of steel as a product and the oligopolistic character of the industry—made the steel industry a prime candidate for governmental controls over prices. Consider the development of such controls during the period 1958–1969.

[4] The unpalatability of wage and price controls was illustrated during the early summer of 1969 when, in the course of the Nixon administration's effort to obtain congressional approval of the income tax surcharge, White House spokesmen twice "corrected" Secretary of the Treasury Kennedy when he stated publicly that if the surcharge were not extended it might be necessary to consider establishment of wage and price controls. The White House spokesmen indicated that wage and price controls would *not* be considered.

On the other hand, the public favored such controls in mid-1969 by a 47 to 41 percent margin according to a Gallup poll (*Time,* July 18, 1969), while a Harris poll showed wage and price controls favored by 50 to 26 percent (*Time,* July 4, 1969).

[5] The relationship between steel prices and the wholesale price index from 1953 to 1969 is pictured more fully in *Studies by the Staff of the Cabinet Committee on Price Stability,* January, 1969, pp. 40–41.

[6] News Conference, Apr. 11, 1962, in *Public Papers of the Presidents, John F. Kennedy, 1962,* p. 316.

The Eisenhower approach

The economy had hit the bottom of the third postwar recession in the spring of 1958. Production was well below capacity. Nevertheless, the consumer price index had been rising by about 3 points a year in 1956 and 1957, an inflation traceable to the wage-price spiral rather than to excess demand. Steel prices had risen $3 to $10 a ton each year, and hourly steel wages had risen 15 to 19 cents annually.

Early in 1958 a poll among steel producers revealed their intention to raise prices that summer. The United Steel Workers of America demanded a substantial wage boost. Senator Estes Kefauver, chairman of the Senate Subcommittee on Antitrust and Monopoly which had investigated steel prices in 1957, urged the President to use the full powers of his office to prevent a new round of wage-price increases. Mr. Eisenhower refused to take public action.

Late in July all major producers announced increases. The Federal Reserve Board increased the margin requirements on stock market credit, but no other anti-inflationary moves were made by the federal government. The President expressed anger over the steel industry actions at his next press conference but took no steps to ward off inflation other than an unsuccessful attempt to reduce government spending.

The Kennedy approach

Four years later, President Kennedy faced a similar rise in steel prices. Early in 1962, in response to administration urgings, the steelworkers had accepted a more moderate wage increase than they had demanded in the course of their negotiations, substantially lower than previous settlements. Government economists opined that this wage increase created no need for a rise in steel prices. But on April 10, Chairman Roger M. Blough of the U.S. Steel Corporation paid his famous call at the White House to inform the President that his firm was increasing prices by $6 a ton. Most other major steel companies promptly followed suit.

Mr. Kennedy denounced the action as "a wholly unjustifiable and irresponsible defiance of the public interest." The Justice Department initiated an antitrust investigation, for which FBI agents made early morning calls on reporters to check on remarks attributed to a steel official. The Federal Trade Commission began an informal inquiry to see if the steel companies had violated a consent decree handed down a decade earlier. The Senate and House Antitrust Subcommittee agreed to launch congressional investigations of the price increase. Several bills that would impose price-wage mechanisms on the industry were studied. The Defense Department announced that a $5 million armor plate order had been placed with one of the smaller producers that had not raised prices. The President and high government officials personally called executives to persuade them not to raise prices or to rescind increases already announced. Five of the twelve largest producers held back from the increase.[7]

On April 13 Bethlehem Steel, a major producer which had raised prices, suddenly announced a cutback. Later that day, just 72 hours after Mr. Blough had called at the White House, U.S. Steel rescinded the increase in prices it had announced. Other firms quickly followed suit.

The incident shocked businessmen. Governmental power, in various forms, had been utilized to deny business firms freedom to determine prices that they deemed in their own best interest. Mr. Kennedy had used the power of the Presidency in unprecedented ways to protect what he regarded to be the public interest. In the perspective of time, his objectives, if not his methods, have gained substantial sanction.

The Johnson approach

In contrast to the 1962 incident, President Johnson's denunciation of the steel industry's recurring price hikes was generally restrained. Other officials in the Johnson administration (such as Gardner Ackley, chairman of the Council of Economic Advisers) did most of the scolding and pushing, but the government finally preferred to accept a compromise settlement rather than force a rollback of the price increases.[8] When, on the last day of 1965, Bethlehem Steel unexpectedly announced a substantial increase, President Johnson voiced wearily the customary complaint about "unwarranted price increases" and the failure of Bethlehem to inform the administration in advance and exerted considerable pressure (partly successful) to prevent the rest of the industry

---

[7] Inland, Kaiser, Armco, McLouth, and Colorado Fuel and Iron companies.

[8] President Kennedy had had additional provocation in that government intervention was responsible for the "noninflationary" wage increase for steelworkers that preceded the attempted price increase.

from following Bethlehem's lead. As a result, when U.S. Steel made additional price adjustments in February, 1966, it notified the government of its intentions three days before the price changes were publicly announced and met no objections from the administration. Thus was the precedent of prior consultation on specific price increases by major corporations effectively established.

Two years later, in the wake of the triennial settlement with the United Steel Workers of America, the companies revised prices upward by about 5 percent (July, 1968). The Johnson administration protested publicly, with the result that about half of this increase was rolled back.

Following the inauguration of President Nixon in January, 1969, the steelmakers posted a number of increases on specific steel products without provoking any reaction from the new President or his Council of Economic Advisers. The pacemaking U.S. Steel Corporation observed the anniversary of the steelmakers' defeat at the hands of the Johnson administration by announcing price increases averaging 4.8 percent on a broad range of products; its lead was followed by other major producers. Adverse reaction came not from Washington, but from General Motors. Taking the unprecedented step of notifying the press about what otherwise may have been a routine action, G.M. requested that U.S. Steel stop shipments pending a "reevaluation of the competitive situation with respect to prices," thus in effect inviting bids from those steelmakers who had not raised their prices. According to seasoned steel-watchers, this was the first instance of a major steel customer acting publicly to thwart a price increase. But the revolt was short-lived and its epilogue made front-page headlines just one month later: "G.M. Lifts Prices of 1970 Cars 3.9%; Cites a Cost Rise." [9]

Despite variations in government's interventionist policy aimed at controlling steel prices and despite the progressively bolder pricing tactics of "selective increases" employed by the steel in-

[9] *New York Times*, Sept. 12, 1969. This was the sharpest increase in more than a decade by a maker controlling about half of the market, yet the Nixon administration neither asked for nor received prior notification of the price increase; it also refrained from any comment, as it had done in the case of other equally "visible" industries such as steel, copper, aluminum, and oil. Secretary of Commerce Maurice Stans commented merely that the price increases were "a consequence of inflation we are fighting, and not a cause." Ford followed G.M.'s lead within less than a week.

dustry, the sequence of events related here suggests that Americans have come to conclude that:

1. Steel prices—and, presumably, the prices of other products as basic and essential to the economy—affect the public interest.

2. Government must develop effective means for utilizing its various powers to control prices that affect the public interest, while assuring equitable treatment for private business enterprise.

THE WAGE-PRICE GUIDEPOSTS

Prior to 1961, federal officials frequently spoke out against the dangers of inflation and urged restraint in specific cases, but no general principle was offered to guide business or union behavior, and no controls were established. The need for at least guidance became clear after 1961, when the federal government became fully committed to expansionist policies to "close the gap" between the actual and the potential output of the nation's economy. Fiscal and monetary policies were adopted to raise aggregate demand to the point at which the nation's manpower and industrial plant capacity would be fully utilized. Such policies greatly intensified inflationary pressures and created new needs for restraint. The wage-price guideposts, first enunciated in the 1962 *Economic Report of the President,* were meant as a response to these needs.

Kermit Gordon, one of the prime architects of the guideposts, described them as "an effort to give some operational content to the notion of responsible wage and price behavior" for, the argument ran, "so long as responsible behavior was left undefined, it was of little utility as a guide to conduct." [10] The guideposts offered a definition of the public interest in the area of prices and wages. They established standards to be followed by unions and industries with sufficient economic power to administer prices and bargain for wages without many of the limits imposed by open competition. They were designed to dissuade the unions and industries from taking "full advantage of every opportunity to charge what the traffic will bear—in their own longer run interest and in the general interest of the economy." [11]

---

[10] U.S. Congress, Joint Economic Committee Hearing, *Twentieth Anniversary of the Employment Act of 1946,* 89th Cong., 2d Sess., p. 63.

[11] *Annual Report of the Council of Economic Advisers,* February, 1968, p. 120.

The primary target of the guidepost concept was the wage-price spiral, the tendency of wages and prices to chase each other upward. This tendency is particularly strong in industries dominated by a few large firms. These firms are relatively free from competitive pressures to keep prices low. In addition, they tend to set prices below the level of maximum profit, at the level which contributes most to security and long-term growth, and consequently they can raise prices to meet higher labor costs without reducing demand.

The guidepost concept was an attempt to end this cycle by limiting wage and price increases to the rate at which productivity increases throughout the nation. If wages increased at the same rate as productivity, it was reasoned, unit labor costs would not increase because a given man-hour of labor would yield added output proportionate to the rise in wages.

To balance these wage increases among industries with varying rates of productivity increase, industries were asked to base their price behavior on a comparison between their own productivity growth rate and that of the economy as a whole. In industries where productivity was equal to the national rate, prices were to remain stable. Prices were to rise in industries where the increase in productivity was below the national rate and to fall where productivity increased more quickly than in the nation as a whole. In this way, prices on the average would remain stable and profits would experience the same proportionate rise as wages.

In an economy operating at less than full capacity, it was hoped, these limitations on wages and prices would retard inflation without acting as a brake on economic growth, because they would place no restraints on aggregate demand. It was recognized, however, that once unemployment fell to 4 percent, excess demand would create pressures greater than the guideposts alone could meet. Kermit Gordon has described this limited workability in terms of "a band of unemployment rates, above which the guideposts were superfluous and below which they would be largely ineffective." [12]

It was also recognized that the existing distribution of income between capital and labor was not immutable and that wages and prices must be responsive not only to changes in productivity, but also to changes in supply and demand. Consequently, a

---

[12] *Twentieth Anniversary of the Employment Act of 1946, op. cit.,* p. 64.

number of exceptions were permitted. For example, industries suffering from chronic shortages of labor could raise wages above the standard to attract workers, and industries showing profits insufficient to attract capital could raise prices above the norm. Where wage rates were exceptionally low or nonlabor costs had risen exceptionally quickly, the guideposts were not applied. By permitting these and other exceptions, the guideposts were intended to remain consistent with basic concepts of efficiency in resource allocation. They would permit changes in precisely those situations where purely competitive markets would yield increased prices or wages and allow the guideposts to alter in response to changes in supply and demand.

Changes in emphasis

Between 1962 and 1969, successive volumes of the *Economic Report of the President* and of the *Annual Report of the Council of Economic Advisers* reflected, with increasing precision, what government expected of the guideposts.

In the 1962 report, the guideposts were introduced simply as a means to "suggest to the interested public a useful way of approaching the appraisal" of a particular wage or price decision.[13] In 1964 it was said that "the most constructive private policy in the great majority of situations would be to arrive at price decisions and wage bargains consistent with the general guideposts."[14] In 1966, the report claimed that "the overwhelming majority of private wage and price decisions in recent years has been consistent with the guideposts, whatever the extent to which the guideposts may have consciously entered into the decisions reached."[15]

The tone of these reports was increasingly positive and aggressive. This trend was paralleled by a tendency for the guideposts to become increasingly specific. In 1962 the Council stressed that "the most that can be done at present" in determining the national rate of productivity increase "is to give some indication of orders of magnitude, and of the range within which most plausible measures are likely to fall."[16] In addition, the need for flexibility was stressed, and cases in which the guideposts should not apply were detailed.

[13] *Annual Report of the Council of Economic Advisers,* 1962, p. 188.
[14] *Ibid.,* 1964, p. 119.
[15] *Ibid.,* 1966, p. 89.
[16] *Ibid.,* 1962, p. 187.

In 1964, although the Council did not overtly assert a specific standard, a series of productivity tables were presented, and the "trend productivity" figure of 3.2 used in these tables, described as the "annual average percentage change in output per man-hour during the latest five years," came to be considered the specific standard to be followed. It was also asserted that "the general guideposts can cover the vast majority of wage and price decisions." [17] The 3.2 figure appeared in tables again in the 1965 report.

In 1966, the nature of the guideposts was fundamentally changed. A guidepost of 3.2 percent was reaffirmed, but no claim was made that this figure measured the year's increase in productivity. Instead, this figure was set forth as a judgmentally established measure to guide wage and price decisions that would make for stability in the economy.[18]

By 1967, the rise in consumer prices (3.3 percent) and the increase in corporate profits (considerably higher than the aggregate labor income) pointed up the futility of setting the trend of productivity as a numerical target for wage increases. This was recognized in the *Annual Report of the Council of Economic Advisers,* 1968, which admitted that "it would be patently unrealistic to expect labor to accept increases in money wages which would represent essentially no improvement in real hourly income." The Council, however, repeated that "the only valid and noninflationary standard for wage advances is the productivity principle. If price stability is eventually to be restored and maintained in a high-employment U.S. economy, wage settlements must once again conform to that standard." [19]

Within four years since their formulation, the guideposts had evolved from a basis for discussion concerning responsible wage-price behavior to a means of control, informal at least. Simultaneously, the guideposts had evolved from a guide based on the

---

[17] *Ibid.,* 1964, p. 119.

[18] In a lengthy passage the Council stated that (1) revisions of past productivity data revealed that the percentage should have been 3.4 instead of 3.2 in 1964 and 1965; (2) if a moving five-year-average method of calculation were employed in 1967, the figure would be 3.6 percent; (3) this method of calculation would no longer give "a reasonable approximation of the true productivity trend" because five unusually good years would be averaged; and (4) the true long-term trend, independent of cyclical swings, would be slightly over 3 percent.

[19] *Annual Report of the Council of Economic Advisers,* 1968, p. 126.

analysis of economic behavior—a guide that was to be adopted in application to situations in particular firms and in different industries—to a broad and unilaterally determined assertion of what was expected of all business enterprises.[20]

The evolution of the wage-price guideposts was not the consequence of communication between government and representatives of private business.[21] Recognizing the shortcomings of this one-sided approach, the President instructed the Cabinet Committee on Price Stability (established in February, 1968) to "work with representatives of business, labor and the public to enlist cooperation toward responsible wage and price behavior." In its report (issued in December, 1968) the committee noted that a disturbing inflationary pattern developed in 1968 with consumer prices up 4 percent, wage settlements averaging about 6.5 percent, and widened average profit margins. A plea was made for a new attempt to curb inflation through voluntary compliance with guideposts. It was recommended that wage settlements be held to "a little below 5 percent" and that employers make no price increases boosting their profit margins, before taxes, above the 1967–1968 level; also, it was recommended that they absorb out of profits "increases of 1 percent in unit costs" of production in 1969. This marked the first time that a formula for limiting profits was suggested.

Inflationary pressures began to build up seriously by late 1965, as the unemployment level neared 4 percent. Although the administration continued to use the guideposts in 1966, these efforts were increasingly unsuccessful, because the principles on which the guideposts were based were not applicable to periods of genuine shortages and excess demand, and the system of voluntary restraint and informal control was insufficient to with-

[20] "What the guideposts did was to provide a coherent background, without which the steps chosen might have been more hesitant and differently directed. In return, the actions gradually defined the applicable content of the principles, and got it taken seriously. General policy and specific action grew together." John Sheahan, *The Wage-Price Guideposts* (Washington: The Brookings Institution, 1967), p. 33.

[21] The *Annual Report of the Council of Economic Advisers*, 1969, p. 121, stated that "in the past neither labor nor business played a major role in the development of the guidepost approach. In the future, effective cooperation is much more likely, if those to whom the standards will apply participate in their development. Persuasion can be helped by representation."

stand such pressures. The government then tried to achieve economic stability through fiscal and monetary policy rather than by direct intervention in price and wage decisions. When these tools proved insufficient to limit inflation,[22] government sought still other means of control. A summary of the means by which government sought to control prices and wages suggests the nature of what may be in the offing.

A WIDENING RANGE
OF ACTION

From 1965 on, government experimented with a variety of tools —weapons in its economic arsenal—in its effort to control prices. Each instance illustrated particular circumstances that provoked the use by government (and demonstrated the availability) of additional means of enforcing the evolving policy of price control. Actions were taken in the steel, aluminum, copper, and automobile industries. Price increases were fought on far-flung battlefields: industries producing fuel oil, shoes, corn, quinine, cigarettes, sugar. In an effort to keep prices from rising, government dipped into national stockpiles (aluminum, copper, corn, quinine), suspended import restrictions (sugar), added extra import quotas (fuel oil), used its purchasing leverage (shoes, textiles, or substitution of margarine for butter), and applied persuasion and pressure (automobiles, prime interest rates).

Government's concern with the rising prices of medical services, hospital services, and drugs—impelled by welfare as well as inflationary considerations—was first manifested by exhortative protest. The prices of medical care and of hospital care rose sharply during 1966 and 1967.[23] The price of drugs had not risen but its increasing significance to a growing body of aged and ill persons was reflected in increasing concern. This concern over rising health care prices was manifested in congressional investi-

[22] The consumer price index rose by no more than 1.3 percent per year from 1961 to 1965. In 1965 it rose by 1.7 percent, and in 1966 and 1967 it rose by 2.9 and 2.8 percent respectively. But 1969 became the worst inflationary year since 1951 (6.1 percent). Department of Labor, Bureau of Labor Statistics, *Monthly Labor Review;* Council of Economic Advisers, *Economic Indicators.*

[23] Since 1961, consumer prices have risen about 25 percent, while medical costs went up 50 percent and hospital costs skyrocketed 250 percent. *New York Times,* June 26, 1969.

gations, in the holding of a National Conference on Medical Costs in June, 1967, and in widespread attention by the communications media. In 1969 the Nixon administration took aggressive action to halt the rise of doctors' fees by use of its strength as the principal purchaser of medical services through Medicare, Medicaid, and other health programs (annual expenditures in excess of $5 billion offer the opportunity to extend government control over drug prices and charges for medical and hospital services) and through the neighborhood health centers of the Office of Economic Opportunity.[24]

MORE LIMITED CONTROLS
OVER WAGES

Attempts to avert inflationary wage increases were generally less successful, largely because excess capacity of the economy was substantially exhausted, fewer means of constraint existed, and voluntary compliance of unions was less often forthcoming. Considerable voluntary restraint was apparent during the first few years of the guideposts, but opposition to them grew as the unemployment rate declined and consumer prices rose. The refusal of industries with rising rates of productivity to lower prices in accordance with the guideposts was cited by unions to explain their own growing unwillingness "to go along." Restraint in wage demands in 1962–1965 meant, the unions contended, that profits rose substantially in relation to wages.

In one significant case, the government was able to enforce compliance with the guideposts in spite of strong union opposition. In June, 1965, the Seaman's Union demanded a wage increase well in excess of the guideposts. Wage demands in the past had not been seriously contested by the shipping industry because government subsidies covered the difference between European and the American operating costs. In this case, however, the Maritime Commission announced that government subsidies would not be expanded to cover wage rises in excess of the guideposts. Consequently, industry opposition strengthened, and after a lengthy strike a 3.2 percent settlement was reached.

Similar tools were available to government to strengthen employer resistance to inflationary wage increases in other industries. Where government licenses or restricts entry to an industry,

[24] *White House Report on Health Care Needs*, released July 10, 1969.

as in transportation or communications, or when import quotas, credit, depreciation allowances, or other government policies are of substantial importance to an industry, government may find similar (perhaps extralegal) ways of bringing influence to bear on the employers to combat union wage demands deemed to be against the public interest. But peaceful settlements of wage disputes were generally preferred, even when they resulted in subsequent price increases and in wage increases in excess of the guideposts. For example, the government sat by while a substantial wage increase was won by the union as a consequence of the airlines strike of mid-1966; no apparent effort was made through the Civil Aeronautics Board to influence the airlines to withstand union demands. The New York transit workers, New Jersey construction workers, and others succeeded in 1965 and 1966, in spite of administration opposition, in getting wage increases higher than the guideposts. Only the wages of civil servants were forcibly held down, when the Presidential veto threatened any civil service pay boost that violated the guideposts.

By the end of 1966, the guideposts as government policy gradually faded from view, and both prices and wages began to move upward at a more rapid pace. Settlement wage-and-benefit packages won by the unions in 1967 averaged a 5.6 percent increase, and this figure rose to 6.6 percent in 1968 contracts (affecting some 4.5 million workers). Wary unions were also unwilling to sign any contract that would bind them for more than three years. (For example, ironworkers in St. Louis refused the employer offer which would raise their wage-plus-benefits package from $6.03 to $9.03 an hour over the next five years.)

THE FUTURE OF GOVERNMENTAL CONSTRAINTS

No new attempts were made during the years 1967–1969 to refurbish principles of governmental intervention in wages and prices, after the guideposts were made obsolete by the substantial increase in demand for goods and services and the marked decline in unemployment in 1966–1968. Yet the dangers of inflation became increasingly apparent. The urgent need for effective means of combating inflation even while a high level of employment is maintained became generally recognized as essential to the public interest in a highly industrialized society. It also became generally recognized that we have advanced beyond the "Post-Industrial Society"—to borrow a phrase from Daniel Bell—and its concentration on the extension of services rather than the production of goods. In the Humane Society we are trying to build and expand services that contribute to the quality of life for all; the kind of inflation buffeting our economy in 1968–1970 imperils this goal, threatening particularly those individuals whose needs are greatest and whose claims on the society are therefore most justified. This explains why public opinion in this country seems ahead of legal authority in its readiness to accept government control of prices. The question is: What means of control are likely to evolve?

The tremendous buying power of government, especially obvious in the fields of defense and space, is increasingly apparent in other fields (including health care), and the accumulation of massive stockpiles of strategic materials endows government with substantial market power. The extension of regulation and increasingly vigorous enforcement of the antitrust laws have created still additional powers, particularly over large firms and concentrated industries. Trade restrictions, though powers of long standing, have been used more flexibly in response to changes in supply and demand, as illustrated by government responses to price increases in copper, shoes, and fuel oil. The vast expansion of subsidies—in the form of credit, tax concessions, services, and direct grants—has further increased government influence.

The withholding of contracts, depression of prices by sales from stockpiles or by the release of import quotas, restriction of exports, antitrust investigations, tax inquiries, rigid enforcement of regulations, and similar actions by government can be used to induce economic behavior believed to be in the public interest. Conversely, government can also exert powerful pressure for conformity to its wishes by the placing of orders, the making of loans, the adjusting of tariffs, and the providing of still other benefits.

Is such a system of penalties and rewards doled out by the government acceptable in a society that depends upon the initiative, enterprise, and freedom of the individual firm and the labor union? [25] This question gains added significance when five factors are recognized:

[25] Some critics, notably Milton Friedman, have seen informal controls as an invitation to the use of extralegal powers to produce compliance with government wishes. See "What Price Guideposts?" in George P. Schultz and

■ The first is that government power in the marketplace must be expected to grow, despite even the seemingly contrary indications given by the Nixon administration.

■ The second is that the evolving system of penalties and rewards provides for no effective review or appeal of the rights of the individual firm or union, no "due process of law." The firm which is denied a substantial contract or the industry threatened with competition from stockpile sales because it has not acted in accord with a stipulated price or wage policy has no effective, built-in means of appeal.

■ The third factor is the difficulty government encounters in enforcing wage-price restraint evenly throughout the economy. Industries heavily dependent on government contracts and forms of governmental aid must conform, while others, less dependent on government actions, can disregard federal guidelines. Firms with influence in Washington may find it easier to have their views heard sympathetically. The more conspicuous industries and unions, those regarded as bellwethers of general price and wage trends or involved directly and indirectly in production of essential goods, are more frequent targets of government intervention. Fewer sanctions can be raised against labor than against business. Less can apparently be done to achieve reductions in prices than to prevent prices from rising. The consequent unevenness in application of government constraints alters prices and wages in ways unrelated to supply and demand. This unevenness in application, hence, may seriously undermine the market incentives normally relied upon to allocate resources. For example, if government has more power to prevent a price rise of copper than of other minerals, the demand for copper will be greater than the demand for other metals which might be substituted, although it may be in shorter supply. Critics of the guideposts have noted the need to "watch carefully for areas of slippage by which an impact achieved in one area is canceled out by indirect effects in another and related area." [26] The indirect and long-term repercussions of government intervention in wage and price decisions are difficult to foresee or control. The monetary and fiscal policies needed to prevent aggregate demand from rising above supply are not sufficiently flexible to maintain the

Robert Z. Aliber (eds.), *Guidelines, Informal Controls and the Market Place* (Chicago: University of Chicago Press, 1966).
    [26] *Ibid.*, p. 8.

economy continuously within the range of demand and employment at which wage and price controls can be most effectively applied.

■ The dependence of this evolving system of price-wage control on voluntary compliance is a fourth factor requiring consideration. The lack of evenness in application tends to lessen the willingness of firms and unions to abide by guidelines voluntarily, as they feel the impact of wage and price increases achieved elsewhere.[27]

■ Finally, in appraising this evolving system it must be recognized that most tools used to induce desired price and wage behavior are increasingly employed for purposes other than wage and price control. So long as threats alone are sufficient to bring about compliance, so long as only a few firms and unions resist government guidelines, this presents no great difficulties. But when inconsistencies in application of government controls and shortages of labor and goods lead to widespread resistance, the cost of using these tools for price restraint becomes apparent. Shifts in contracts to penalize uncooperative firms may mean delays or the purchase of inferior materials and can be made only when there are some producers within the industry who behave in the manner prescribed by the government. Relaxation of import restrictions to bring prices down may be harmful to the balance of payments. Surplus stockpiled materials can be sold only once, and perhaps at the expense of national security.

The 1968 *Economic Report of the President* notes that "neither the United States nor any other free industrial nation has yet learned how to couple steady growth at high employment with reasonable stability of prices." The guideposts, and the means used to compel compliance, must be regarded as an experiment. Even economists who designed the guideposts have agreed that the treatment of wages and prices was not balanced, that productivity rates were hard to measure, and that many complexities of the economy were overlooked by the relatively simple standards. Similarly, early efforts in West Germany and the Netherlands to tie desirable wage increases to forecasts of productivity rates were limited by inaccuracy in the forecasts and later

---

[27] "We, of organized labor, are prepared to sacrifice—as much as anyone else, for as long as anyone else—so long as there is equality of sacrifice," asserted George Meany, president of the AFL-CIO, in 1966, speaking at the New York University School of Commerce.

abandoned. Informal constraints in France and Italy, exercised through exhortative pressures by political leaders, proved insufficient. In Great Britain, controls moved from "pay pauses" requested under the Conservative government to a formal "incomes policy" under the Labour party, and as even this was insufficient to correct a drastic decline of export trade, devaluation of the pound became necessary.

No one can yet foresee how the informal constraints that have been utilized to date will evolve or by what alternatives they will be replaced. The experience of the European democracies prophesies the prospect of more stringent and formalized controls. The pressures created by the Vietnam War, the inherent weakness of the system of constraints itself, and a continuing and relatively substantial increase in consumer prices foreshadow the development of a greater degree of control.

THE TRENDS AND THE PROSPECT

This chapter posed the question: When is the public interest so affected as to warrant intervention by government in the price and wage decisions of private firms and unions? It pointed out that price and, to a lesser degree, wage controls have not been unknown to the American economy. Indeed, they have been more widely applied than businessmen generally recognize or approve. But during recent years, particularly during the 1960s, governmental efforts to control the price and wage decisions of the private sector have been substantially increased.

Probably the most notable excursions of government into this field were President Kennedy's efforts to prevent an increase in steel prices and subsequent efforts by President Johnson to control the prices of this industry. While steel was the prime target of governmental action during the years 1962 to 1969, a number of other industries, including those involved in the provision of medical care and the manufacture of drugs, attracted governmental concern.

Political action and the utilization by a President or the Council of Economic Advisers of purchasing proscriptions, sales from the stockpiles, changed import quotas, or exportation increases are measures not likely to be the consequence of a single, simple cause. The actions enumerated in the chapter, which have accumulated into a system (loose and informal as it yet is), were impelled by the need for maintaining some measure of economic stability during a period when government was taking steps to increase the aggregate demand for goods and services in order to achieve two evolving objectives of government: the maintenance of a high level of employment and the stimulation of economic growth. And this effort to achieve economic stability was coupled with a growing desire to protect the welfare of less fortunate citizens—those who must meet rising medical charges, who require costly drugs to sustain life, who suffer from the lack of low-cost housing, or who become the especial prey of rising prices because of their low incomes.

The first step toward achieving these objectives was the announcement of the wage-price guideposts by the Council of Economic Advisers in 1962. This tentatively stated proposal was the first concrete effort to induce a wage and price behavior, by private firms and by unions, that would be responsive to the public interest without obstructing freedom of enterprise. But the years 1962–1968 showed that the promulgation of guidelines was not enough. Hence, a variety of tools created for other purposes (e.g., contracting for defense equipment and maintaining stockpiles of essential materials) have been utilized to add compulsion where needed in a voluntary system. The resultant system—if it can be said to be that—has manifest shortcomings.

Despite the fact that the price and wage controls were specifically disclaimed by the Nixon administration and not fashionable among economists at the onset of the last third of the twentieth century, Galbraith's was not the only voice suggesting that they may be inevitable.[28] Wage and price curbs were urged in November, 1969, by key officials of five large apparel companies; [29] several labor officials at the AFL-CIO biennial convention in October, 1969, asserted that legal controls over wages, prices, *and profits* may be "the only way out" to stem the rising inflationary tide; [30] public opinion polls showed that substantial majorities endorsed the notion of controls. (It was suggested by

[28] "Yet, while there may be difficulties, and interim failures or retreats are possible and indeed probable, a system of wage and price restraint is inevitable in the industrial system . . . neither inflation nor unemployment are acceptable alternatives." *The New Industrial State* (Boston: Houghton Mifflin Company, 1967), p. 259.

[29] *Wall Street Journal*, Nov. 21, 1969.

[30] *U.S. News and World Report*, Oct. 13, 1969, p. 75.

Robert Lekachman that the public "may have a better grasp of the necessities of national economic policy than do the professional economists, who are perhaps too bedazzled by the beauties of free markets to notice how little of the economy matches their ideal." [31]) Alvin Hansen, a respected economist who has seen in his lifetime many an economic wonder solution come and go, suggested that although rigid price and wage controls may not be acceptable, perhaps "a less ambitious control policy" might be feasible. This might include "a compulsory cooling off period" of perhaps six months during which the corporations would present their case for price increases (with the supporting cost-price analysis), the government would publicize its own analysis of the relevant cost-price data, and "informed public opinion could possibly exert sufficient pressure to moderate price increases." [32]

For the future, it seems inevitable that a system of some kind of governmental controls over prices and wages will evolve. But neither the present makeshift system nor existing means of communication and collaboration between business and government offer any positive, constructive prospect that we shall succeed in devising means of control that will not thwart the motivations of free enterprise.

[31] Robert Lekachman, "Controls—Chapter Two," *Dun's Review*, June, 1969.

[32] Alvin H. Hansen, "Inflation: Korea vs. Vietnam," *The Washington Post*, November 30, 1969.

CHAPTER *10*

Intervention
in the Employment Process

O_{UR} social order has long held to the proposition that an individual's right to enjoy the fruits of production is based on the part he plays in the productive process. John Smith put it simply: Those who don't work, won't eat. Since Smith's colonial days this proposition has developed into the concept that an individual's social and economic worth, in his eyes and in those of his peers, is determined by the job he holds.

But three forces prevailing during the post-World War II years —automation, affluence, and civil rights—have necessitated a complex and arduous readjustment of values. Automation has undermined the validity of the guiding proposition by lessening the need for human labor. Because of the growing wealth of the society, coupled with expanding productivity, the upcoming generation has seen that human wants can be satisfied with less labor and more leisure. And the civil rights revolution of the

213

1954–1970 period has enabled many workers long accustomed to menial, unpleasant, and servile jobs to become competitors for better jobs, while others swelled relief rolls.

Before World War II, nearly every government action that affected the number of jobs, those who worked, and the working conditions was the indirect consequence of efforts to control immigration; to promote the development of the West; to advance education; or to regulate working conditions for, first, children, then women and, during the Depression of the 1930s, workers of all ages and sexes.

Government left the determination of how many and which workers should be employed to private employers, and left the determination of which jobs should be accepted or rejected to the individual worker. Even during the latter part of World War II, when labor was quite scarce in relation to the needs of a war-expanded economy, neither decisions by the firm nor decisions by the individual worker were controlled to the same degree as decisions pertaining to prices of goods or the right to use important materials (e.g., oil, copper).

This chapter pictures the federal government's assumption since 1946—and particularly since 1961—of ever-larger responsibility for the aggregate number employed, what workers are employed, and, less directly, what jobs workers should take. It explains why government has intervened increasingly in the employment process. It offers judgments as to the consequence of such intervention and as to its impact on the character of the American free enterprise system.

THE EMPLOYMENT ACT OF 1946

A new kind of government intervention in the employment process was launched with the enactment of the Employment Act of 1946. This law established, for the first time in this country's history, that it is "the continuing policy and responsibility of the Federal Government to use all practicable means . . . to promote maximum employment, production, and purchasing power." [1]

[1] The full text of the declaration of policy is: "The Congress hereby declares that it is the continuing policy and responsibility of the Federal Government to use all practicable means consistent with its needs and obligations and other essential considerations of national policy with the assistance

The law as passed was a considerably watered-down version of the original Full Employment Bill introduced by Senator James E. Murray and others. The concept of a "right" to employment was omitted and a planning device called the National Production and Employment Budget was left out, but three important features were added: A Council of Economic Advisers in the Office of the President was established; the President was directed to submit an annual economic report; and a Congressional Joint Committee on the Economic Report [2] was created.

The stimulus underlying enactment

Enactment of the Employment Act of 1946 was opposed by many, including many businessmen. But its adoption was propelled by fear that, with the military forces demobilized and the war matériel production no longer necessary, the immediate postwar period would bring with it large-scale unemployment such as that experienced during the 1930s (as much as 24.9 percent of the labor force was unemployed in 1933 and 9.9 percent still unemployed as late as 1941).

This fear prompted both government and business leaders to consider what could be done.[3] A succession of opinion polls conducted by *Fortune* disclosed that "what should be done about preventing unemployment after the war" was the foremost economic question in the public's mind by more than a 2 to 1 margin.[4] A Gallup poll revealed that half of those whose opinions were solicited believed that government would have to provide "WPA-type work" after the war.[5]

and cooperation of industry, agriculture, labor, and State and local governments, to coordinate and utilize all its plans, functions, and resources for the purpose of creating and maintaining, in a manner calculated to foster and promote free competitive enterprise and the general welfare, conditions under which there will be afforded useful employment, for those able, willing, and seeking to work, and to promote maximum employment, production, and purchasing power."

[2] Now referred to as the "Joint Economic Committee." Passage of the law is portrayed in Stephen Kemp Bailey, *Congress Makes a Law: The Story Behind the Employment Act of 1946* (New York: Columbia University Press, 1950).

[3] The Committee for Economic Development, perhaps the most successful of business organizations in influencing national economic policies during the postwar period, was originally established to provide leadership for businessmen in "postwar planning."

[4] *Fortune*, January, 1945, p. 260.

[5] Polls published Sept. 15, 1945, and Aug. 30, 1947.

The feared postwar unemployment did not materialize. Reconversion from wartime to peacetime production was faster than expected. A pent-up demand for goods and services unavailable during the war created a high demand for labor; most returning servicemen seeking jobs found them. Others, with the aid of federally provided "GI grants," continued their schooling. Unemployment stayed, acceptably, between 3 and 4 percent from 1945 through 1948. During the recession of 1949–1950, it temporarily rose above 5 percent, but dropped back to near the 3 percent level in 1951. A recession in 1954, after the Korean War had ended, raised the rate of unemployment above 5 percent, and it remained above 4 percent until 1966 (see Table 10.1).

TABLE 10.1   *Unemployment Rates, 1947–1969* (annual averages)

Year	Total civilian labor force (16 and over)	Groups within labor force		
		Nonwhite (16 and over)	Youth (16–19)	Nonwhite (16–19)
1948	3.8%	5.9%	9.2%	11.2%
1949	5.9	8.9	13.4	16.9
1950	5.3	9.0	12.2	15.3
1951	3.3	5.3	8.2	11.0
1952	3.0	5.4	8.5	10.5
1953	2.9	4.5	7.6	8.0
1954	5.5	9.9	12.6	16.5
1955	4.4	8.7	11.0	15.8
1956	4.1	8.3	11.1	18.2
1957	4.3	7.9	11.6	19.1
1958	6.8	12.6	15.9	27.4
1959	5.5	10.7	14.6	26.1
1960	5.5	10.2	14.7	24.4
1961	6.7	12.4	16.8	27.6
1962	5.5	10.9	14.6	25.1
1963	5.7	10.8	17.2	30.4
1964	5.2	9.6	16.2	27.2
1965	4.5	8.1	14.8	26.2
1966	3.8	7.3	12.7	25.4
1967	3.8	7.4	12.9	26.5
1968	3.6	6.7	12.7	25.0
1969	3.5	6.4	12.2	23.9

SOURCES: U.S. Department of Labor, *Statistics on Manpower, A Supplement to the Manpower Report of the President,* March, 1969; *Employment and Earnings and Monthly Report on the Labor Force,* 1969; *Economic Report of the President,* February, 1970, p. 205.

REASONS FOR INTERVENTION

In retrospect it is clear that the Employment Act of 1946 had:
- Established the principle that the federal government should do what it can to assure a maximum number of job opportunities, if not jobs, for all those able to work and seeking work
- Charged the President with responsibility for seeing to it that the economy was analyzed regularly and that the Congress was informed of the levels of employment, production, and purchasing power obtaining in the United States, as well as the levels needed to achieve the objective of the act
- Committed the President and the Congress to undertake such measures as would increase employment
- Created a mechanism in Congress—the Joint Economic Committee—to facilitate legislative analysis of the state of the economy and the course to take in order to maximize employment

These provisions of the Employment Act were founded in considerable part on philosophical underpinnings supplied by John Maynard Keynes. Essentially, Keynes gave currency during the 1930s to three economic ideas that have changed the nature of the world in which we live.

Idea 1—If people stop consuming and stop investing, national income will fall.

Idea 2—To increase national income it is necessary to increase either consumption expenditures, or investment expenditures, or both.

Idea 3—Government can increase consumption expenditures and investment expenditures if private enterprise alone cannot or will not do it.

Government's responsibility

Despite the commitments established by the act, and in contravention of the growing acceptance of Keynes' ideas, the Eisenhower administration held that government could and should do little to increase the volume of employment. The 1955 *Economic Report of the President,* for example, in listing "Obligations of Federal Government Under Employment Act," mentioned last, in a series of six basic economic issues, the problem of unemployment.[6] The Kennedy administration, in contrast, called for the assumption by government of a larger positive responsibility and undertook a succession of measures "to get this country moving again," as Mr. Kennedy had promised in his campaign speeches. The central concept in the Kennedy interpretation of government's responsibility was that the national economy had been operating at less than capacity from 1955 to 1961. This concept signaled a significant step forward in our reasoning as to what government should do about manpower problems. The postwar planning efforts of 1945–1948 were designed to keep employment up in order to avoid a business depression. Many subsequent efforts were designed to avert the human suffering of the unemployed and their families. But the key idea advanced by the Kennedy administration was that it was in the public interest— in the interest of business, of workers, and of the public as a whole—that manpower should not be wasted in idleness because there were insufficient jobs for many who wanted to work. Thus, government took steps that would stimulate consumer spending and investment spending as a means of increasing employment.

This it did [7] and—without discounting the impact United States involvement in Vietnam had on the American economy— the results are written large in the expansion of the gross national product (1961—$520.1 billion; 1968—$865.7 billion) and in the reduction of the rate of unemployment (1961—6.7 percent; 1968—3.6 percent).

Expanding labor supply

Recognition of the waste involved in unused manpower was the principal but not the only stimulus to governmental intervention in the employment process after 1961. A second contributing stimulus was the growth in the number of individuals "able to work and seeking work."

Beginning in the late 1950s the "war babies," born in the years 1940–1944, entered the labor market. Between 1947 and 1953, the annual rate at which the labor force grew was around 1 percent; between 1953 and 1960, it was around 1.5 percent. For the

---

[6] *Economic Report of the President,* January, 1955, pp. 2–3.

[7] The *Economic Report of the President,* January, 1962, pp. 97–100, listed 17 executive and administrative actions launched shortly after the Kennedy administration assumed office.

1960s, the average annual rate of increase is estimated at around 1.8 percent.[8]

The labor force also grew because more women went to work; the proportion of adult females at work or seeking work increased from 31.8 to 41.6 percent between 1947 and 1968. This percentage meant an increase of nearly 7 million workers in 1968. For married women between 45 and 65, the increase has been particularly great; whereas in 1947 only 18.4 percent of them were in the labor force, by 1967 the proportion had risen to 40.4 percent.[9]

A third factor contributing to the increase in the labor force has been the changing age composition. During the 1950s the proportion of workers aged 16 to 24 increased only 2.2 percent—a consequence of the low birthrates of the 1930s. In the 1960s, however, this body of workers increased by almost half—by 1970 there will be 19 million workers in this age group as compared with 12.7 million in 1960. Simultaneously, the number of older workers—those between 45 and 64—has been growing roughly twice as fast as the labor force as a whole.

In the aggregate all this means that the labor force will include 85 million individuals by 1970 and about 100 million individuals by 1980 (see Table 10.2). The significance of such growth becomes clearer when we realize that its rate is over four times that of the Common Market countries as a group.[10]

TABLE 10.2   *The Labor Force Has Grown—and Continues to Grow, 1950–1980* (*16 years and over*)

Labor force	*Numbers (millions)*					*Percentage change*		
						1950– 1960	*1960– 1970*	*1970– 1980*
	1950	*1960*	*1968*	*1970*	*1980*			
Total labor force	63.8	72.1	82.3	84.6	99.9	12.9%	17.4%	18.1%
Age 16–24.	12.4	12.7	18.2	18.9	22.6	2.2	48.8	19.2
Age 45–64.	19.1	24.1	27.5	29.1	30.5	26.2	20.4	5.1

SOURCE: *Statistics on Manpower, A Supplement to the Manpower Report of the President*, U.S. Department of Labor, January, 1969, Table E-3, p. 78.

[8] National Commission on Technology, Automation, and Economic Progress, *Technology and the American Economy*, vol. I, 1966, pp. 10 and 16.

[9] U.S. Department of Labor, *Statistics on Manpower, A Supplement to the Manpower Report of the President*, March, 1969, pp. 3 and 29.

[10] Richard Allen Lester, *Manpower Planning in a Free Society* (Princeton, N.J.: Princeton University Press, 1966), p. 11. In West Germany, an absolute decline in yearly additions to the labor force is expected.

Structural imbalance

The emphasis of Mr. Kennedy's advisers during the early 1960s was upon fiscal steps to expand the economy and thus to utilize wasted capacity—plant and facilities, as well as manpower. This goal was pursued myopically. Indeed, it was pursued beyond the time when it became painfully apparent that there were many in the labor force who were not readily employable, not even in a substantially expanding economy.

Despite rising prosperity during the years 1964 to 1967, several groups experienced persistent unemployment. The unemployment rates for young people were three times as high as for the rest of the labor force. In addition, Negroes (particularly Negro youth) suffered from a very high level of unemployment; 24 to 30 percent of all Negro teenagers were unemployed during much of the period from 1960 to 1969. The emergence of a militant civil rights movement in the late 1950s and early 1960s was, at least in part, a consequence of the devastating experience of thousands of relatively employable Negroes vainly searching for jobs. Soaring crime and delinquency rates made the public generally aware that such frustrating unemployment among youth, in a time of prosperity, was nothing less than social dynamite.

Unemployment in Appalachia and in other depressed areas (particularly in the urban ghettos) was another manifestation of this structural unemployment problem. Improved coal mining technology, dieselization of the railroads, and the basic lack of resources in Appalachia and other have-not areas made it increasingly difficult to reduce the rate of unemployment there. Those unable to find work because of the character of the area in which they lived and those whose skills had been made obsolete by automation were bound together by the common handicap of an inability to measure up to the prevailing hiring standards of many employers.

Changing demand

Changes in the character of jobs to be filled, i.e., in the demand for workers, constituted another, and related, stimulus to governmental intervention in the employment process.

A continuing and gradual decline in the time spent on the job by the average worker means that more workers are needed. From 1940 to 1968 the average number of hours worked per week dropped from 43.8 to 37.8. By 1976 this figure, it has been estimated, will be 36.6 and by the year 2000—30.5.[11]

But this trend, operating to increase the demand for workers, is offset by the increased productivity of labor. Output per man-hour has risen persistently as technological change has increased worker efficiency. The annual average rate of increase in output per man-hour for the years 1919 to 1965 is 2.5 percent; for the years 1947 to 1965—3.4 percent; and for the years 1965 to 1968 —2.8 percent.[12] This increase has lessened the number of workers required, since the same number of man-hours that produced $69 worth of goods and services in 1947 was producing almost twice as much ($134.3) two decades later.[13]

The character—as distinguished from the sheer volume—of demand for workers has been altered by the increasing importance of the service-producing industries (wholesale and retail trade, finance, insurance and real estate, service, miscellaneous, and government). By 1975, it is estimated, jobs in the service industries will outnumber those in the goods-producing industries by 2 to 1. The service industries use a greater proportion of white-collar workers. They have grown as a consequence of our increasing wealth, technological advance, and commitment to education, health, and welfare. Simultaneously, the goods-producing industries, which tend to use a greater proportion of blue-collar workers, have not grown as rapidly in terms of the number of jobs offered, in part because of the introduction of new labor-saving equipment. The magnitude and pace of this shift in the demand for workers is shown in Table 10-3.

These shifts in the character of the demand for labor have affected youth and Negroes most severely. As the number of young people entering the labor force has grown, the number of blue-collar jobs, through which the young and the inexperienced have traditionally entered the labor market, has declined relatively. The growing number of young Negroes entering the labor market, many of them with less-than-average educational attainment, faced the twin obstacles of a relative decline in the number of

[11] Outdoor Recreation Resources Review Commission, *Projections to the Years 1976 and 2000: Economic Growth, Population, Labor Force and Leisure, and Transportation,* 1962, p. 181.

[12] *Economic Report of the President,* 1966, p. 80; U.S. Department of Labor, *Statistics on Manpower, A Supplement to the Manpower Report of the President,* 1969, p. 103.

[13] *Economic Report of the President,* 1970, p. 216.

TABLE 10.3   *The Character of the Demand for Workers Has Shifted, 1947–1975*

Type of worker	Number of workers (in millions)			Percent distribution		
	1947	*1965*	*1975*	*1947*	*1965*	*1975*
Total civilian employment	57.8	71.0	87.2	100.0	100.0	100.0
White-collar.	20.2	31.8	42.3	34.9	44.8	48.5
Blue-collar.	23.6	26.2	29.7	40.8	37.0	34.0
Service	6.0	8.9	12.0	10.3	12.6	13.8
Farm	8.1	4.0	3.2	14.0	5.7	3.6
Total payroll, nonagricultural establishments *.	43.5	60.8	76.0	100.0	100.0	100.0
Goods-producing industries	18.2	21.9	24.5	41.9	36.0	32.3
Service-producing industries	25.3	38.9	51.5	58.1	64.0	67.7

* Excludes agriculture, self-employment, domestic service, unpaid family work, Armed Forces personnel. "Goods-producing industries" are mining, contract construction, and manufacturing. "Service-producing industries" are transportation, public utilities, trade, finance, insurance, real estate, other private services, and government.

SOURCES: *Historical Statistics of the United States, Colonial Times to 1957,* 1960, p. 73; *Manpower Report of the President,* April, 1968, pp. 270, 304.

blue-collar jobs and racial discrimination. The problem of youth's entry into the labor market has been compounded by periodic raising of the federal minimum wage. Born out of genuine concern for the welfare of low-income persons, these increases have made it impractical in some instances for firms to hire unskilled youngsters. They have had the effect of discouraging the employment of teen-agers, and especially of Negro teen-agers.[14]

Shifts in demand may also result in shortages in the supply of workers with critically needed skills. For example, the demand for professional, technical, and kindred workers possessing relatively high levels of education and experience has increased. During the decade 1965–1975, the need for individuals with such skills will rise by more than 45 percent; the need for managers, officials, and proprietors will increase by 23 percent.[15] The out-

[14] Professor Yale Brozen of the University of Chicago pointed out that the rapid succession of minimum wage increases in the early 1960s resulted in "an unprecedented level of teenage unemployment," amounting to 3.4 times the general level.

[15] *Manpower Report of the President,* 1969, p. 235.

look, however, is that the proportion of workers with such skills and experience will not increase as rapidly.

Implications of supply and demand

The changes in the patterns of labor supply and demand underlie the stubbornly high rates of unemployment that persisted until 1966. Necessarily, they have provoked new and more extensive efforts by government to create employment opportunities.

On the one hand, the aggregate *supply* of labor increased between 1947 and 1965 at about 1 percent a year. On the other hand, the *demand* for labor decreased at approximately 2.8 percent a year, if one accepts the productivity trend rate as 3.3 percent and the drop in hours worked as .5 percent. This means that to *avoid any increase* in unemployment it would have been necessary for the economy to grow at an average rate of 3.8 percent over this period. But the GNP grew at a lesser rate—on the average, 3.5 percent per annum. In only six of the twelve years preceding 1966 did the economy expand enough to absorb the growth in number of individuals able and seeking to work.

For the 1970s the problem and the prospect are these. The labor force will expand during these years at a rate of about 1.8 percent. Assuming that productivity will increase about 3 percent per annum, the GNP will have to increase at a rate in excess of 4 percent if the American economy is to absorb the new workers coming into the labor market. Yet, as the National Commission on Technology, Automation, and Economic Progress warned, "our economy has seldom, if ever, grown at a rate faster than 3.5 percent for any extended length of time. We have no cause for complacency." [16]

MANPOWER GOALS AND PROGRAMS

The prospect is that government will be pressed continually to do what it can to maximize economic growth and to minimize the waste of manpower. Six federal statutes have established an array of manpower programs which constitute government's recent efforts toward these goals. These six statutes—the Area Redevelopment Act of 1961, the Manpower Development and

[16] *Technology and the American Economy, op. cit.,* p. 16.

Training Act of 1962, the Vocational Education Act of 1963, the Economic Opportunity Act of 1964, the Appalachian Regional Development Act of 1965, and the Public Works and Economic Development Act of 1965—reflect a quest for the goals of a humane economy.

The stimuli that gave birth to these statutes also prompted Congress to require in 1962 that the President transmit each year "a report pertaining to manpower requirements, resources, utilization, and training." This annual *Manpower Report of the President* is an effective symbol of the assumption by the federal government of responsibility for the conscious management of what in the humane economy is the most valuable resource of all—manpower.

The Manpower Report serves as a guide to administrative agencies striving to accomplish the objectives set by the statutes enumerated above: first, to maximize the demand for manpower, particularly to create additional jobs in an economy in which unemployment has been a nagging problem; second, to improve the quality and acceptability of the supply, i.e., to train individuals that each might utilize his or her talents to the fullest; third, to match the supply of manpower with the demand that had been expanded.

Maximizing demand

Perhaps the most significant expansion of government's role in the national economy during the postwar decades has been the gradual adoption of fiscal policies designed to maximize demand. This involved abandonment of an annually balanced federal budget in favor of a cyclically balanced budget; that is, in favor of a policy calling for a balanced budget only when there is effective full employment (some would add—"if ever"). The general acceptance by business leaders of the logic and desirability of the positive management by the federal government of the overall economic demand through the active use of monetary, budgetary, and tax changes indicated a striking shift in business philosophy. That shift was gradual in coming, but the support of business leaders for the reduction of federal taxes in 1964 (when the federal budget was suffering a substantial deficit) and their acceptance of the increase in federal income tax in 1968 were notable landmarks in the evolution of business thinking as to the role government should play in maximizing the demand for manpower—while maintaining price stability.[17]

During the four years following John Kennedy's inauguration, the federal sector contributed a surplus of about $2 billion each year to the national economy. Total employment increased from 65.7 to 69.3 million; the rate of unemployment declined from 6.7 percent in 1961 to 5.2 percent in 1964. By the close of the year 1964, it had become increasingly apparent that a continued effort to stimulate expansion of the economy through fiscal measures would yield further reduction of unemployment only at the price of increased inflation. Between 1961 and 1964 the consumer price index (all items) went up from 104.2 to 108.1; in the next five years it rose still faster, climbing to 131.3 in December, 1969.

Recognition that fiscal measures alone would not cure the problem of unemployment gave rise to four other efforts to maximize the demand for manpower. With the launching of the short-lived Area Redevelopment Administration (ARA), the federal government commenced the subsidization of employment in "depressed areas." Other governments (Sweden, France, and Britain) had shown the way, using various means to entice business firms to establish plants in depressed areas.[18] In this country, the Commerce Department's Economic Development Administration (which succeeded the ARA in 1965) offered technical and financial assistance and training grants to those businesses locating in designated "redevelopment areas." At federal expense, a community may contract with a private consulting firm to study industrial possibilities in the area; the results of such study are then made available to interested firms. Grants and loans are made to the community or other public body to make infrastructure investments (e.g., improved roads and water supply) that

[17] The evolution of the public policies providing for the use of fiscal measures to increase the demand for labor over the period 1962–1966 is effectively pictured in James L. Sundquist, *Politics and Policy—The Eisenhower, Kennedy and Johnson Years* (Washington: The Brookings Institution, 1968), chap. 1. Sundquist points out (especially on pp. 47–48) that the U.S. Chamber of Commerce, the National Association of Manufacturers, the American Bankers Association, the New York Stock Exchange, "an array of trade associations," and a businessmen's committee for tax reduction (including such men as Henry Ford II, Roger M. Blough, and Stuart Saunders) worked diligently in support of a tax reduction.

[18] The British government, for example, had offered business firms cash grants of 25 percent of building costs and 10 percent of plant and equipment costs, and discretion in capital depreciation.

would attract industry. The firms themselves are eligible for government loans or loan guarantees at low interest rates, providing they cannot get the financing elsewhere. Finally, the incoming firm is provided with the skilled manpower it needs; this is done by means of precisely tailored vocational (institutional or on-the-job) training carried on at "skill centers" in the locality.[19]

A second effort made by some agencies of business (e.g., the National Industrial Conference Board) and the federal government involved the determination of how many job vacancies exist and where they exist. Efforts to measure job vacancies were designed to facilitate placing unemployed workers. The results were mixed; they indicated that placements could be facilitated, but that employers generally could not state their requirements (i.e., the jobs they would fill at a specified point in time) with the precision that had been assumed.

A third effort, made by two successive Presidents of the United States, was to ask business enterprises to hire unemployed persons from the ghettos, to assume responsibility for making them productive workers, and thus to reduce unemployment further. Business responded through the National Alliance of Businessmen by finding within the years 1968–1970 jobs for some 380,000 individuals, most of them unqualified by prevailing hiring standards. This effort, and the climate of the times, made it clear by the close of the decade of the 1960s that employers would be increasingly expected to "restructure" the jobs in their enterprises, i.e., to redefine what is expected of workers in many jobs. This restructuring of demand—the fourth effort—is impelled by two emerging requirements. It has become clear that in order to employ increasing numbers of hard-core workers, jobs have to be broken down to provide beginning jobs for workers with little or no skill. To provide satisfying jobs (i.e., jobs that hold interest and provide some motivation) for these little-skilled and often discriminated-against workers, these beginning jobs must be related to other jobs in the employer's plant to permit and facilitate the workers' advancement. Alleged unwillingness to work and high turnover rates among the poorly qualified recruits, experience has taught, are attributable in many instances to the dirty or unpleasant character of their work or to the "dead-end" character of their starting jobs. In other words, the demand for

[19] Interviews with Economic Development Administration officials, May 25, 1966.

manpower increasingly must be adapted to utilize the workers available.

To supplement these several efforts to maximize the demand for manpower, the idea that government should become the employer of last resort, i.e., that public employment should be provided for all able-bodied workers who could not be employed elsewhere, was gaining increasing attention by 1970.[20] The idea had been advanced in bills before the Congress and vigorously espoused by some officials of the executive branch and by the mayors of the large cities. It was opposed by such business organizations as the U.S. Chamber of Commerce and the National Association of Manufacturers.

In summary, it became increasingly apparent during the 1960s that:

■ Government could impel the creation of jobs by fiscal measures, and that

■ Such action by government was increasingly approved by spokesmen for the business community, but that

■ The country was confronted with a tough and seemingly insoluble problem, viz.: How can we achieve high-level employment *and* reasonable price stability?[21]

This problem came into sharp focus during the 1968 presidential campaign. Oversimplified as issues manage to become in the course of a political campaign, the belief was emphasized that we cannot have a high level of employment without inflation. Richard Nixon was cast throughout the campaign as the apostle of price stability, and Hubert Humphrey was cast as the apostle of full employment, no matter what the cost. The problem was posed in starkly black or white terms.[22]

[20] The origin and early development of this idea is described by James L. Sundquist in "Jobs, Training, and Welfare for the Underclass," an essay in Kermit Gordon (ed.), *Agenda for the Nation* (Washington: The Brookings Institution, 1968), pp. 49–76.

[21] Garth L. Mangum, codirector of the Center for Manpower Policy Studies has aptly stated a central implication of this question: "We must find some way to quit requiring the poor to be our only stabilizer of the price level. We must find some way of spreading the unemployment around if unemployment must be the balance wheel."

[22] The tenor of the debate is suggested by the remark of Senator Charles H. Percy (Republican, Illinois), formerly an eminently successful businessman, in a speech before the Economic Club of Detroit in November, 1968: "An important segment of business leadership has recently implied that doubling the present unemployment rate to 6½ percent may be necessary to

The truth is not that simple. As drawn originally, the much cited Phillips curve (developed by A. W. Phillips of the London School of Economics) showed that there is a tendency for wages— and, consequently, prices—to rise sharply as unemployment declines beyond a certain point; this has been refined further into a succinct credo: if prices are stabilized, unemployment must go up. No one denies that there is a certain "trade-off" of this kind involved. But experience has shown that government policy can substantially alter the terms of the trade-off, and this the Nixon administration promised to achieve. Paul W. McCracken, Nixon's chairman of the Council of Economic Advisers, voiced this promise at his first press conference, "I hope that, by very careful management of economic policy, we can cool down the price level without having adverse effects on employment."

By the start of their second year in office the efforts of Mr. McCracken and his colleagues in the Nixon administration had met with little or no success: unemployment had increased slightly and prices had risen sharply throughout 1969.

Maximizing supply

Much of what has been undertaken under the six manpower statutes has been designed to maximize and adapt the supply of manpower available. This effort has taken several forms.

Training has constituted an increasingly important part of the cost and effort of many employers; indeed, it has been estimated that employers invest in on-the-job training a sum greater than half of all the moneys spent on public education.[23] Faced with the need of absorbing a million and a half new workers annually, of reestablishing other workers displaced by automation, and of promoting national economic growth, the nation has turned to employers to train still other workers in order to maximize utilization of manpower. Through training, the unemployed can become more readily employable, the employed can develop additional or higher-order skills and become more productive, and

hold down inflation. If this solution is the best that business leadership can come up with, then the business community has abdicated responsible leadership. . . . And ultimately the great losers under such conditions would be the very members of the business community who today can propose no better alternatives to our present problems."

[23] Jacob Mincer has estimated that the total real expenditure for on-the-job training by employers and employees for male employees may be as great as the cost of formal schooling. "On the Job Training: Costs, Returns and Some Implications," *Journal of Political Economy*, October, 1962, pp. 50–73.

the employers can obtain the workers they need and maximize productivity.

Under the Manpower Development and Training Act (MDTA) of 1962 and subsequent amendments, federal involvement in worker training reached unprecedented levels in terms of both financial support and leadership provided.

The MDTA encourages institutional training by providing federal grants-in-aid to the state governments for the support of vocational education in high schools, in technical institutes, and in other institutions. Nearly 850,000 students were enrolled in such vocational programs between August, 1962, and June, 1969. The MDTA encourages expansion of on-the-job training [24] by authorizing the Department of Labor to contract with private organizations to conduct such training. The Department, hence, has contracted with trade associations (e.g., the National Tool Die and Precision Machining Association), community organizations (e.g., the Urban League), labor unions, and private employers (e.g., the Chrysler Corporation or the Tidewater Oil Company). Under these contracts the state public employment service offices recruit the trainees, the employing firm or organization pays their wages, and the Department of Labor reimburses the employer for all training costs incurred. Through June, 1969, some 382,000 men and women had enrolled in on-the-job training, and increasing emphasis was being placed on this program as the central governmental effort.[25]

During the first two years (1963–1965), the training of unemployed persons to fill essential, vacant jobs was stressed. In retrospect this training has been criticized for focusing too narrowly in many instances on the meeting of local shortages of workers rather than on developing the supply needed to meet national manpower demands and for training workers for occupations in which employment prospects are not good.[26]

---

[24] On-the-job training comprehends various forms of learning in the employer's plant, factory, or office, including planned training programs and the informal guidance of employees by supervisors and fellow employees.

[25] *Report of the Secretary of Labor on Manpower Research and Training Under the Manpower Development and Training Act of 1962,* 1966, pp. 5–6, 23–29; *Manpower Report of the President,* January, 1969, p. 238; data provided by U.S. Department of Labor, Manpower Administration (December, 1969).

[26] Lester, *op. cit.,* pp. 159–160. A Department of Labor survey of 366 employers revealed a sharp contrast between the occupations in which these employers sought workers and the occupations for which MDTA training was

During the years 1966–1968, the prime objective of the MDTA program was aiding disadvantaged workers; as much as 40 percent of all training was focused on the hard-core unemployed, 25 percent on disadvantaged youth, and the remaining 35 percent on filling skill shortages. Two groups with high unemployment rates—youth and nonwhites—were more highly represented among the trainees than among unemployed in general.[27]

Special programs for facilitating the employment of disadvantaged workers represent a well-rooted activity of government (particularly, efforts made to aid physically handicapped workers). The racial tensions and the "war on poverty" of the 1960s gave new focus and emphasis to this activity. The Job Corps and Neighborhood Youth Corps, WIN (Work Incentive Program), and other training programs were especially designed to develop the employability of disadvantaged youth and of welfare recipients, most of them black. A special program for mentally retarded persons was launched in cooperation with the laundry industry. Other programs were designed to aid older persons, Indians, and released prisoners. Still other governmental programs were undertaken during the mid-1960s in several large cities to seek out and provide special training for the hard-core unemployed.[28]

The task of aiding such disadvantaged persons involves more than "training" in the conventional sense. It is, in short, the finding of ways of "bringing the individual together." It often in-

provided. Of the employers surveyed, 30 percent reported that they were "very satisfied" with their overall experience with the training programs, 51 percent responded "satisfied," 14 percent responded "unsatisfied," and 5 percent responded "very unsatisfied." *Report of the Secretary of Labor on Manpower Research and Training under the Manpower Development and Training Act of 1962,* 1966, pp. 177 and 178, and data obtained from Office of Manpower Policy, Evaluation and Research, Department of Labor.

[27] *Manpower Report of the President,* January, 1969, pp. 239 and 241.

[28] The National Commission on Technology, Automation, and Economic Progress has proposed a type of "public service employment" for the hard-core unemployed; this would consist of jobs in such areas as health, education, and beautification. The jobs would be sponsored by local government and nonprofit organizations with most of the financing coming from the federal government. This would present to some extent a return to the New Deal idea of created employment, an approach that has been largely avoided in the postwar period. *Technology and the American Economy, op. cit.,* pp. 35–37.

volves the tasks of motivating an individual to want a job, developing his work habits, instructing him on getting along with fellow workers, and developing other personal qualities that are prerequisites to the acquisition of skills.

Actions that eliminate prejudice against some workers also serve to maximize the effective supply of manpower available for jobs. During the Eisenhower administration, government contractors above a certain size were forbidden to discriminate in hiring and in promoting Negroes. Later, a Plan for Progress program was established which urged all large corporations to eliminate discriminatory personnel practices.

The Civil Rights Act of 1964 extended this federal effort to blot out discrimination from government contractors and large firms to all employers of significant size, whether they be business firms, hospitals, educational institutions, labor unions, or other organizations. At first, employers of 100 or more workers were covered by the law, but in succeeding years the provisions of the act have been applied to firms with 75, 50, and—in 1969—25 employees.

An independent federal agency, the Equal Employment Opportunity Commission, was created to receive and hear complaints of discriminatory employment actions and continually to encourage employers by means of personal persuasion to abandon discriminatory practices. This Commission attempts to work out the satisfactory settlement of each complaint or, failing that, encourages appropriate court litigation. The Commission also obtains comprehensive information on the employment status of certain groups.[29]

[29] All employers with 50 or more workers are required to report the number of (1) Negro, (2) Oriental, (3) American Indian, and (4) Spanish-American employees by type of employee (e.g., "officials and managers," "professionals," "technicians," "sales workers"), sex, and plant or other sizable organizational unit. Employers are also required to indicate whether facilities such as rest rooms and drinking fountains are segregated. If an employer refuses to submit such data, the Commission can obtain compliance through reference to a U.S. District Court.

The Civil Rights Act of 1964 also forbids discrimination on the basis of religion, sex, and age. Employment discrimination against older workers has given rise to the Age Discrimination in Employment Act of 1967 and the setting up of some work-experience programs (e.g., Green Thumb, sponsored by the National Farmers' Union, or Foster Grandparents, conducted by the National Council of Senior Citizens and the National Council on the Aging).

Matching jobs and workers

To maximize or manage the effective national supply of workers it may sometimes be necessary to move the unemployed in some depressed areas if they are to find jobs.[30] Hence, in 1963, the MDTA was amended to permit experimentation with the movement of workers in this country. Pilot projects of various types were carried out; some concentrated on a particular type of worker (such as rural farm laborers), others dealt with those laid off from a specific plant. Still other projects were directed to unemployed selected at random from local employment service files. In most cases the move was of a fairly short distance, often within the same state. To be eligible the workers had to be involuntarily unemployed and had to have a bona fide offer of a new job in the area of relocation. They were paid travel costs, moving and storage allowances, and a lump sum for interim living expenses. The 16 pilot projects conducted by the Labor Department in 1965 produced generally encouraging results. By the end of 1969 some 35 pilot projects had been conducted in 28 states, and some 14,000 workers and their families had been successfully moved (at an average cost of $750). Initially concerned mainly with the inroads made by automation, the program has been redirected in the last two years toward the rural poor (nonfarm).

Finally, government has persistently striven to reduce unemployment by improving the means by which employers find workers and workers find jobs. Most jobs are filled without government's help—through personal channels, newspaper advertisements, private employment agencies, and other means. Since 1933, when the United States Employment Service (USES) was created, the federal and state governments have supplemented this process.

The Service is financed and generally directed by the federal government, but there are more than 2,100 local employment offices, operated by the state governments. The system assists em-

[30] In Sweden, where such efforts are most advanced, the National Labor Market Board couples the reporting of prospective layoffs by employers with an efficient job vacancy information network to facilitate the planning of the moving of workers. The Board then provides allowances to meet the cost of travel, subsistence, moving the family and goods, and reestablishing the family in a new location. U.S. Congress, Joint Economic Committee, *Economic Policies and Practices: Paper No. 8, Programs for Relocating Workers Used by Governments of Selected Countries,* 89th Cong., 2nd Sess., 1966.

ployers by referring workers to them, and it assists workers by counseling, testing, and referring them to prospective employers. During the 1960s it made some 6 million job placements in industry and trade per year; job placements in agriculture decreased from 9 to 4.5 million.[31] In addition, the organization makes broad labor market studies and facilitates the various training programs discussed above by advising them of which skills are in demand and by trying to place those who complete the training programs.

Traditionally, the public employment service offices have found low-level jobs for the local unemployed. Steps toward separating the unemployment compensation system from the Service (with which it had been joined since 1939) have been accompanied by efforts to upgrade the Service, i.e., to seek out jobs for professional, technical, and white-collar workers as well as for the blue-collar workers and to bring together men and jobs over wide regions of the country with the aid of electronic data equipment and telecommunications networks. An "early warning system" has been devised whereby cooperating employers notify the Service in advance of pending layoffs. In the late 1960s legislation was sought that would carry these trends further, and steps were taken to transform the USES into "a comprehensive manpower service agency." [32] That objective has not been fully achieved; despite valiant efforts, government's role in the matching of men and jobs continues to be a limited and largely ineffectual one.

IMPLICATIONS FOR BUSINESS FIRMS

What of the future? What will be expected of the business firm? And what part will government play in the labor market?

Influencing factors

The record of recent decades illuminates factors that will determine what will be expected of business and of government in the years ahead.

[31] U.S. Department of Labor, *Fifty-sixth Annual Report,* 1968, p. 74.
[32] See Lester, *op. cit.,* pp. 45–48, and William Haber and Daniel H. Kruger, *The Role of the United States Employment Service in a Changing Economy* (Kalamazoo, Mich.: The Upjohn Institute for Employment Research, 1964).

1. Demographic, social, and technological trends—shifts in the proportion of young and older, white and black, male and female workers in the labor force; racial tensions; shifts in the demand for skilled and unskilled workers resulting from the introduction of new technology (e.g., the computer in the 1960s) and the switch from production to service industries—will keep the problem of unemployment high on the agenda of this country's politico-economy.

2. Changing social attitudes toward unemployment—increasing popular recognition that unemployment not only causes human distress and suffering and creates civil unrest, but also constitutes a waste that can be reduced or eliminated—will give rise to increasing insistence that unemployment be reduced even below levels that are now considered to be acceptable minimums (3.5 or 4 percent).

3. Increasing awareness that unemployment can be reduced—a growing knowledge that employers can utilize even workers traditionally regarded as unemployable and that government can, through fiscal and other means, maximize and stabilize the demand for workers—will result in a persistent and growing popular demand that employers and government do what is needed to reduce this cause of human suffering, of civil unrest, and of waste.

Expanding obligations of employers

The American society has successively attached to the privilege of employing workers a number of obligations that the employer must accept—the maintenance of decent and safe conditions of work, the limitation of hours of work, and the provision of income to workers who are injured on the job or who become unemployed.

The factors enumerated above will attach additional obligations. These will include the hiring of workers who by conventional standards were deemed unsuitable (e.g., those with prison records); the restructuring of jobs so as to permit inexperienced workers to enter employment and to rise through the ranks as their capabilities grow; the further restructuring of jobs not only to eliminate, insofar as possible, drudgery, "dirty work," and routineness but to provide stimulus and the opportunity for the individual to utilize his full capabilities; [33] the conscious and

---

[33] The growing obligation of the employer to provide "satisfying" jobs prompts recollection of Huey Long's promise that "there shall be a real job,

positive upgrading of workers, particularly those who have been traditionally and permanently relegated to lowly jobs; the providing of training, including not only aiding the worker to develop the skills needed on the immediate job, but also educating the worker to enable him to expand as a person and as a citizen and to be more adaptable; and the providing of a variety of supportive services to facilitate the individual's acceptance and holding of a job (e.g., transportation from home to plant, health care for those who might otherwise be unable to hold the job, and day-care services for children).

The cost that the employer will be expected to pay for the privilege of employing other human beings—the wages paid plus the benefits (for conditions of unemployment, illness, death, old age) that are now accepted parts of the cost of employment—will increase substantially. The precedents for each of these additional obligations are already apparent. The cost of these additional obligations is suggested by a prediction that "fringe benefits" will cost as much as 50 percent of wages by 1980.[34] This is a clearly foreseeable cost to be borne by the employer in the humane economy.

Expanding role of government

The general acceptance of government's use of fiscal actions to increase the demand for labor—acceptance by businessmen and citizens generally, Republicans as well as Democrats—portends the increased (and, perhaps, more timely) use of such fiscal actions in the future. Contrariwise, it is not yet clear to what extent reliance will be placed on government subsidization of the creation of jobs by business enterprises. The results of the experiment launched in 1968 by the U.S. Departments of Labor and Commerce and the National Alliance of Businessmen are not yet discernible; this effort has been expanded, and it is likely that more emphasis will be placed on governmental subsidies and less on the voluntarism of business employers.

not a little old sow belly, black eyed pea job, but a real spending money, beefsteak and gravy, Chevrolet, Ford in the garage, new suit, Thomas Jefferson, Jesus Christ, red, white and blue job for everyman." Quoted by T. Harry Williams in *Huey Long* (New York: Alfred A. Knopf, Inc., 1969), p. 700.

[34] The prototype of what is likely can be seen in Japan where, with low wages and a relatively high personal income tax, employees are provided numerous fringe benefits—low-cost restaurants, houses or apartments, and in some instances recreational allowances.

The prospect is quite clear that government will substantially expand its training and placement activities.[35] This expansion will comprehend, in addition to vocational education in the public schools and publicly subsidized on-the-job training, expanded efforts to train men in industry-related skills during their military service and much expanded training for youth and adults in the burgeoning community colleges, whose curricula will be adapted to meet the particular needs of each community.[36]

Effects on business firms

If the prospects that have been delineated prove valid, what effects will such intensified governmental action in the labor market have on the individual business firm? Will business' traditional autonomy in decision making as to the hiring, development, utilization, promotion, compensation, and firing of employees be increasingly constrained?

The answer to these questions seems clear. Business firms will be subjected to increasing pressure to hire individuals they might not otherwise hire—Negroes, the disabled, the unskilled. To enforce equal employment opportunity for minorities, government has used propaganda, the provision for compulsory reporting by employers, and the threat of prosecution. Continuing racial tensions suggest that these efforts will be intensified until employment practices are substantially changed.

Publicly supported training programs will impose on participating business firms increasing obligations to accept the workers —many of them young, old, or black—who are trained in these programs. Similarly, the continued presence of the disabled, the mentally retarded, and the public assistance recipients, and increasing concern as to their well-being, forecast the prospect that the quest for full employment will impel employers to hire disadvantaged individuals.

Government's subsidization of business investment in depressed areas subjects business firms to pressure to employ work-

[35] President Nixon sent to the Congress on Aug. 12, 1969, a message proposing enactment of a "comprehensive manpower training act" to consolidate several existing programs and in some respects to modify, liberalize, and extend their provisions.

[36] For a supporting view see John T. Dunlop, "An Overall Evaluation and Suggestions for the Future," in Robert A. Gordon (ed.), *Toward a Manpower Policy* (New York: John Wiley & Sons, Inc., 1967), pp. 369–371.

ers indigenous to the area, who are trained and whose employment is a prime objective of the subsidization. The participating firm must also agree not to lay off workers elsewhere and sometimes must hire workers only from the immediate area.

Equally clear is the prospect that government's persistent striving to maintain economic stability while maximizing employment will lead to the increased involvement of government in the processes of price setting and wage determination. The foreseeable step is that proposed in 1968 to Vice President Hubert H. Humphrey (then a candidate for the Presidency) by a task force headed by Prof. Otto Eckstein of Harvard University. It was suggested that an annual conference of employers, union representatives, and government officials should establish "realistic" rates of price increase and wage increase to which they would be expected to subscribe. Such a step is in one form or another accepted practice in other capitalistic-democratic societies.

In summary, government's increased intervention in the labor market has limited and will limit further the traditional freedom of business enterprise. On the other hand, government's increased intervention has expanded the supply of workers available to employers. Under conditions of a labor shortage in a given occupation or geographical area, the governmental training, mobility, and placement programs have increased the number of workers from which a firm can choose the employees it needs. In instances of drastic labor shortages, the governmental programs launched during the 1960s can afford business firms invaluable assurance of meeting their manpower needs.

In the 1970s government may take other actions that will further curb the business firms' freedom as employers. Proposals advanced during the late 1960s suggest that government should increase its regulation of private pension funds, that it should aid (or require) business firms to redefine jobs so that less-skilled workers can be employed and can perform acceptably, and that it should require that business firms give early warning of prospective layoffs and thus facilitate the retraining and replacement of workers.

Business reaction to what has taken place, and what is in the offing, has not reflected substantial concern or opposition—other than opposition to government's increasing involvement in the determination of wages and the setting of prices. There has been no great outcry and, indeed, there has been substantial participation in the several activities that now constitute government's manpower program.[37]

[37] This does not mean that some business groups have not had strong opinions. The private employment offices are bitterly opposed to an expanded U.S. Employment Service, because it represents competition to them. (See F. T. Bow, "The Great Manpower Grab," *The Reader's Digest,* October, 1964.) Yet corporations, such as Litton Industries and IBM, that carry out training contracts on a profit basis naturally are enthusiastic about the new manpower activities. This is also true for trade associations whose members are facing particularly serious skill shortages, such as the Automotive Service Industry Association or the National Tool Die and Precision Machining Association. (Note *Hearings on the Manpower Development and Training Act,* by the House Select Subcommittee on Labor of the Education and Labor Committee, 88th Cong., 1st Sess., 1963, p. 539; also, *Hearings on Amending the Manpower Development and Training Act of 1962,* 89th Cong., 1st Sess., 1965, pp. 207 and 240.)

CHAPTER 11

Business in
a Planned Economy

TYPICALLY, businessmen have held that national planning is incompatible with free enterprise and that a "free economy" is the antithesis of a "planned economy." Planning by business is "good," but planning by government for the whole society is, in the eyes of most businessmen, "bad" (perhaps because government planning has come to be identified with Communist countries).

Is this view adequate to guide public policy in the latter third of the twentieth century? Is national economic planning— governmental determination of what economic actions shall be taken to achieve goals arrived at through the political process— an inevitable consequence of the growth and change of the socio-economic structure during the post-World War II era?[1] What

[1] For fuller analysis of the emergence of national economic planning, the nature of such planning, and arguments for and against such governmental

are the consequences of national economic planning for the individual enterprise? For the traditional American system of free enterprise?

In an effort to answer these and related questions, this chapter pictures the emergence of planning in the 1930s and its extent, the commitment to planning this country made at the close of World War II, and the evolution of planning as a function of government during the years since 1946.

PLANNING BEFORE WORLD WAR II

Prior to World War II, manipulation of the money supply and of interest rates was, in effect, the sole means by which government (actually, the quasi-public Federal Reserve System) took positive action to influence the course of the economy. The Federal Reserve System, relatively independent of the President, "had been the agency of cyclical control, and its most trusted mechanism had been the discount rate."

In 1913 economist Wesley Mitchell had perceptively foreshadowed what was to come. He pointed out that in a "money economy," one based on the exchange of goods with the use of money rather than barter (as had been the custom in the agricultural society prevailing almost to 1900), citizens play two roles. They strive by their individual actions—buying, selling, spending, saving—to "make money" (a term which came into being about 1900!). Simultaneously, and less consciously, they determine by their actions the level of business prosperity that will prevail throughout the nation.

The efforts made in the United States to combat the economic crises of 1907, 1919–1921, and 1929–1933 demonstrated a growing determination not to leave the business prosperity of the nation to the unguided and haphazard actions of individuals.

activity, see J. M. Clark, "Free Enterprise and a Planned Economy," *Economic Institutions and Human Welfare* (New York: Alfred A. Knopf, Inc., 1961), chap. 11; James A. Tobin, "How Planned Is Our Economy?" *National Economic Policy* (New Haven, Conn.: Yale University Press, 1966), chap. 1, pp. 5–14; John Jewkes, "Ordeal by Planning in the Sixties," *The New Ordeal by Planning* (New York: The Macmillan Company, 1968), part 1, pp. 3–44; and Walter Heller, "Advice and Consensus in Economic Policy Making," *New Dimensions of Political Economy* (Cambridge, Mass.: Harvard University Press, 1966), chap. 1, pp. 1–57.

These efforts demonstrated an ability to design institutions that could mitigate the devastations of the business cycle. And they reflected what has become even more apparent during the second third of this century: that the ideals as to the welfare of the whole society have expanded and grown more generous with each generation.

During the first third of the twentieth century, fiscal means were not used to combat the downswings of the business cycle or to upgrade the social welfare. The prevailing doctrine held that expenditures should be kept at a minimum, the budget should be balanced, and the public debt retired—if it had to be incurred at all. As with personal finances, high expenditures, annual deficits, and increasing debts were considered indications of governmental mismanagement or, perhaps, profligacy. As late as 1932, when unemployment was widespread and many families suffered, President Hoover echoed the social welfare ideal of a passing generation; he insisted on expenditure retrenchment and higher taxes. "Nothing is more necessary at this time than balancing the budget," he declared.[2]

Not until the later years of the New Deal (1937–1940) were these hoary fiscal principles first questioned. In 1933 Roosevelt pushed the Economy Act through Congress as a recovery measure. Through 1937 he personally seemed to believe in the annual balanced budget as an ideal, but the demands of these years fashioned New Deal fiscal policies in a pattern that did not accord with traditional principles and evoked substantial and bitter opposition from business.[3] Between 1937 and 1940 many government officials who had considered annual deficits as a necessary evil came to accept the notion that they could be a positive good.[4]

Two contemporaneous happenings wrought this shift in policy. The first was the undertaking during the mid-1930s of an assortment of social welfare programs to relieve widespread unemployment and human distress. The second was the publication

[2] Lewis H. Kimmel, *Federal Budget and Fiscal Policy, 1789–1958* (Washington: The Brookings Institution, 1959), p. 150 and chaps. I and II generally.

[3] For an excellent analysis of the evolution of fiscal policy during the years 1933–1939 see Herbert Stein, *The Fiscal Revolution in America* (Chicago: University of Chicago Press, 1969), chaps. 4–6.

[4] On fiscal policy in the Roosevelt years generally, see Kimmel, *op. cit.*, chap. V.

in 1936 of *The General Theory of Employment, Interest, and Money* by John Maynard Keynes.

Between 1929 and 1940, payments to individuals by federal, state, and local governments more than doubled. This was the consequence of, first, the launching of a series of hastily improvised relief, work relief, public works, and agricultural adjustment programs (1933–1935) and, second, the enactment and development of the social security programs (1936–1940). Each of these programs represented long-term governmental plans for substantial sectors of the society—the destitute, the farm population, and the aged.[5] In the agricultural adjustment programs government eventually forecast the volume of food and fiber required for the nation's needs (including exports) and devised programs that were expected to yield that volume and to assure improved incomes for farm families. In the social security programs, government (with the aid of actuaries drafted from private insurance companies) forecast for a generation ahead the number of aged persons that would be retired and the approximate income required for their sustenance, and devised a system of payroll taxes and benefits that was substantially self-operating.[6]

Keynes' revolutionary ideas came at a time when the rigors of a depression were forcing this country's government—as well as that of his own—to plan unprecedented courses of action. His argument—that the effective demand for goods and services wanted by consumers in a capitalist economy would, under certain circumstances, require supplementation in order to absorb all the goods and services the economy was able to produce—

[5] In *Economic Development in Under Developed Countries, Planning for Economic Development,* an international group of experts appointed by the Secretary General of the United Nations (October, 1963) elaborates on two relevant points illustrated by the evolution of planning in private enterprise and mixed economies and centrally planned economies alike: (1) national planning evolves from the development of sectoral plans, and (2) the human need for the expansion of socially provided income and services has resulted in the development of sectoral plans which eventually are combined with plans for the productive sectors of the economy (pp. 15–30).

[6] Title VI of the Economic Opportunity Act of 1964 requires the preparation of a "Five Year National Poverty Action Plan." This is perhaps the most current manifestation of sectoral planning by the federal government; it comprehends aggregate expenditures of $25 billion in fiscal year 1969 and $44 billion in fiscal year 1974.

came at a moment when this fact was being dramatically illustrated in this country. Keynes proposed that the public sector deliberately raise expenditures above revenues and thereby stimulate demand. He suggested that the government could also restrain booms by deliberately running budgetary surpluses during times of prosperity.

Although the Roosevelt administration incurred relatively large deficits in the mid-1930s, it seems quite obvious that they were not incurred with any clear intent to stimulate the economy through fiscal policy, but were impelled by the need to meet the costs of welfare and other programs deemed necessary.[7] And it is equally questionable whether business leaders who still argued for a balanced budget recognized that governmental planning of significant sectors of the society had already been established. Roosevelt did not publicly endorse Keynesianism during these years, either because the pragmatic FDR would not accept any theory in toto or because he believed that it was not yet feasible politically to endorse budgetary deficits. Indeed, a *Fortune* poll of 1939 found that in a choice between a balanced budget through reduced spending and a deliberately unbalanced budget, 61 percent of the public preferred the first alternative and only 17 percent preferred the second.[8] By 1940, however, the President was willing to refer in his budget message to "the deliberate use of Government funds and Government credit to energize private enterprise. . . ." He also said, "Government must have the wisdom to use its credit to sustain economic activity in periods of economic recession and the courage to withhold it and retire debt in periods of economic prosperity."[9]

[7] Keynes personally urged his policy proposals upon Roosevelt, notably at a meeting in the summer of 1934 and in a famous open letter to the President (The *New York Times*, Dec. 31, 1933).

[8] *Fortune*, March, 1939, p. 135. In 1943 *Fortune* published a poll which asked the public to choose the statement with which they agreed: (1) "There is no difference between government and private debt. In both cases, current budgets should be balanced as soon as possible; otherwise ruin follows." (2) "Provided we have an expanded national income, it is not necessary to fear the expansion of government debt in the way that we fear an unbalanced private or business budget." The response was 86 percent in favor of the first statement and 14 percent in favor of the second. *Fortune*, Oct., 1943, p. 34.

[9] *Budget of the United States*, 1941, pp. vi and vii.

THE COMMITMENT TO
PLANNING, 1946

While it is questionable whether prior to World War II the federal government had accepted responsibility for acting to influence the course of the economy, the postwar developments left no such doubt. By 1946 the Congress and the President had committed the government to plan and take actions that would promote and maintain prosperity.

The main impetus to this commitment (as was noted in the previous chapter) was the fear that unemployment might rise to the levels experienced during the 1930s. According to one public opinion poll, 70 percent of the population expected a "widespread depression" within 10 years.[10] In the 1944 election campaign both candidates responded to these fears: Roosevelt proposed "close to 60 million productive jobs" as a necessary postwar goal, and Dewey agreed that "Government's first job in the peacetime years ahead will be to see that conditions exist which promote widespread job opportunities in private enterprise." [11]

It has been said that "there has been in our generation no other confrontation on so massive a scale over the basic character of the American economy" [12] as the struggle before the Congress over the Employment Act of 1946. The struggle reflected sharp differences over *whether* government should assume the responsibility for guiding the economy and, if so, *how* it should influence the ups and downs in the cycle. In one memorandum circulated within the government during the debates over this act, an outright Keynesian fiscal policy was advocated. Government, it was contended, should "guarantee the stability of purchasing power at high levels. The Government can do this by expanding development and social service programs, and by flexibility in its fiscal program to compensate for fluctuations in the creation of purchasing power by private investment." [13] And the draft of the

[10] *Fortune,* January, 1947, p. 12.

[11] Stephen K. Bailey, *Congress Makes a Law: The Story Behind the Employment Act of 1946* (New York: Columbia University Press, 1950), pp. 42 and 43.

[12] An Economic Symposium, Joint Economic Committee, *Twentieth Anniversary of the Employment Act of 1946,* Feb. 23, 1966, p. 144.

[13] "Postwar Employment," memorandum prepared by Alvin Hansen, Weldon Jones, and others, and submitted to the President on Oct. 9, 1944. See

Full Employment Bill that passed the Senate included a "National Production and Employment Budget" which would systematize and institutionalize a compensatory fiscal policy. Conservatives rejected the very idea of government action.[14] They argued that the best route to prosperity lay in giving free rein to private enterprise and that government should intervene only, if at all, through state and local governments backing up their efforts to care for the unemployed. Most business organizations (with the notable exception of the Committee for Economic Development) took such a position,[15] and businessmen were generally cool to or suspicious of a compensatory fiscal policy. For example, in a 1946 Gallup poll, 71 percent of business and professional men advocated a balanced budget rather than reduced taxes and the resulting imbalance.[16]

The final compromise version of the Employment Act (markedly "watered down" from the original draft bill) passed the Senate unanimously and passed the House by an overwhelming vote, 320 to 84. Congress had officially declared "that it is the continuing policy and responsibility of the Federal Government to use all practicable means . . . to promote maximum employment, production and purchasing power." President Truman, in signing the bill on February 20, 1946, said: "The Employment Act of 1946 is not the end of the road, but rather the beginning. It is a commitment by the Government to the people—a commitment to take any and all of the measures necessary for a healthy economy, one that provides opportunities for those able, willing, and seeking to work. We shall all try to honor that commitment." [17]

U.S. Congress, Senate Subcommittee on Employment and Manpower of the Committee on Labor and Public Welfare, *History of Employment and Manpower Policy in the United States,* vol. 7, pp. 1–27, with this quote from p. 10.

[14] Of S. 380 (a Senate bill preceding the Employment Act), the then president of the National Association of Manufacturers said, "There could be no greater discouragement to business."

[15] The U.S. Chamber of Commerce, one of the largest organizations of business firms, took a somewhat ambiguous stand; the Chamber's president, Eric Johnson, was personally not opposed to the Senate bill (Bailey, *op. cit.,* p. 140), but Alvin Hansen noted that the act was launched "in an atmosphere of widespread suspicion." *Twentieth Anniversary of the Employment Act of 1946, op. cit.,* p. 93.

[16] Gallup poll released Sept. 4, 1946.

[17] Quoted from Council of Economic Advisers, *First Annual Report to the President,* December, 1946, p. 3.

POSTWAR TRENDS
IN PLANNING

When this commitment was made, it could not be foreseen that over the next two decades:

■ The growth in population would lead to the need for quadrupling the capacity of this nation's schools and colleges, for providing training programs for (employed and unemployed) workers, and for substantially extending plans to assist the aged, viz., Medicare.

■ The growth and "eruption" of the cities would make necessary plans for modernizing more than a fourth of all urban housing that stood in 1946, for the reconstruction of major sections of each large city, and for the modernization of transport systems that carry vast numbers of people into, out of, and within sprawling new metropolises.

■ The technological revolution would stimulate vast governmental efforts to plan the utilization of a new source of energy (the atom), the exploration of space, the discovery of the causes and cures of disease, the exploration under the seas, and the training of essential scientists and engineers.

■ The shrinking of the universe, coupled with the persistence of the cold war, would involve this country in two wars in the Pacific, maintain expenditures for national security at unprecedented levels, engage the United States in a race for supremacy in space, and impose a large and unrelenting demand for economic aid and military assistance for the developing countries throughout the world.

■ The growth in this country's national income, coupled with a steadily increasing concern for the quality of life enjoyed by all Americans,[18] would give rise to plans for the elimination of poverty, the protection of the consumer, the improvement of the environment—and would give rise to a revolution in civil rights.

Much of the discussion during the debate on and following the enactment of the Employment Act implied that "maximum em-

[18] Bertram Gross, a prime mover in the enactment of the act and the first secretary of the Council of Economic Advisers, has stated that "we are now on the brink of a great shift to 'quality of life' objectives" which "while including growth with stability, go much further. None of us yet quite knows how much further they will go." *Twentieth Anniversary of the Employment Act of 1946, op. cit.,* p. 76.

ployment, production and purchasing power" [19] would be achieved through the use of the monetary and fiscal tools inherited from the 1930s. But that discussion did not foresee the vast growth of the "business of government" relative to the total national economy. It did not foresee the advances in the science of economics (e.g., the development of national income accounting and the use of economic indicators, econometric models, and input-output tables) which provided mechanisms that greatly facilitated planning for a complex, interrelated society. It did not foresee the acceptance and evolution of planning as an integral and central function of the management of private enterprise as corporations became larger and their investments in plant and equipment greater.[20]

These forces—the widespread acceptance of planning in business, the advances in the science of economics, and particularly the vast growth in the scope and expenditures of government—constitute the backdrop against which the use of monetary and fiscal tools is viewed.

PLANNING AND MONETARY POLICY

Monetary instruments, the oldest means available for influencing the economy, were used more effectively in the 1950s and 1960s than in the 1930s (when they failed to turn the tide of depression) or in the 1940s (when they were largely inoperative because of direct economic controls and because the Federal Reserve was focusing its energies on the support of the government bond mar-

[19] The act directed the government to "use all practicable means consistent with its needs and obligations and other essential considerations of national policy . . . to coordinate and utilize all its plans, functions and resources for the purpose of creating and maintaining . . . conditions under which there will be afforded useful employment opportunities, including self-employment, for those able, willing, and seeking to work, and to promote maximum employment, production and purchasing power."

[20] A 1966 survey on the use of economic projections in long-range business planning, conducted by the National Planning Association's Center for Economic Projections, reveals that 84 percent of the responding firms prepare long-term corporate plans today, as compared with only 19 percent before 1955. Fifty-four percent state that projections of national and industrial economic trends play a major role in their plan formulation. Joel Darmstadter and Morris Cobern, "Economic Projections in Long-range Business Planning," *Looking Ahead*, September, 1967.

ket). The Treasury's dominance over the Federal Reserve came to an end, however, with the famous "Accord" of March 3, 1951, which called for a gradual abandonment of the "pegging" policy; by December, 1952, the Federal Reserve's Open Market Committee was freely selling securities to restrain expansion experienced at that time.[21]

Taking full advantage of its newfound freedom, the Federal Reserve used all its powers throughout the eight years of the Eisenhower administration to contract the money supply and raise interest rates during periods of expansion and to employ the reverse tactic during recessions. Viewed in retrospect, the Board's actions prove that even such an august body can be all too humanly fallible. On numerous occasions both the timing and the degree of action taken by the Federal Reserve came under fire. Thus the Board was criticized for reacting too tardily to curb an inflationary boom (e.g., in 1954–1955) and for tightening money too severely because of its fear of inflation at a time when little danger of it existed (e.g., in 1958–1959).

A more constructive flexibility was demonstrated by the Federal Reserve in the 1960s. At the same time, in the words of two competent observers, "it showed a degree of ingenuity in dealing with problems generated by the juxtaposition of large balance-of-payments deficits and a recalcitrant economy." [22]

In an open economy in which goods and services are freely traded between countries (the kind of economy that we have in the twentieth century), there can arise a domestic situation which calls for monetary actions quite opposite to those required by the international situation. Such conflicting circumstances obtained during the later 1950s and the 1960s, making the Federal Reserve's efforts vastly more difficult. Rising interest rates,

[21] The literature on this subject is prolific. See, for example, James L. Knipe, *The Federal Reserve and the American Dollar: Problems and Policies, 1946–64* (Chapel Hill: University of North Carolina Press, 1965); Henry C. Wallich and Stephen H. Axilrod, "The Postwar Record of Monetary Policy," in Arthur Okun (ed.), *The Battle against Unemployment* (New York: W. W. Norton & Company, Inc., 1965); Otto Eckstein, "Economic Policy in the United States, 1949 to 1961," in E. S. Kirschen and Associates, *Economic Policy in Our Time*, Country Studies (Chicago: Rand McNally & Company, 1964), vol. II.

[22] Wallich and Axilrod, *op. cit.*, p. 191, and pp. 188–191 generally. See also Roy E. Canterbery, "The Federal Reserve versus American Goals," *Economics on a New Frontier* (Belmont, Calif.: Wadsworth Publishing Company, Inc., 1968), chap. 12, pp. 155–171, for contrasting views.

prompted by domestic requirements, jeopardized the increased exports needed to offset the outflow of military and foreign aid expenditures which were largely responsible for United States deficits in international payments.

By and large, the Federal Reserve used its monetary powers to stimulate the economy during the early 1960s and to restrain it during the 1966–1969 period. Throughout these years the Board acted in substantial agreement with the executive branch, though the submissiveness of the pre-Accord days was not revived.[23] Not until late 1965 did the Board of Governors break with the Johnson administration by raising the discount rate. Their action, criticized at the time as unduly and unnecessarily restraining, was proved sound by the inflationary pressure that gained momentum in 1966 and 1967.

The Federal Reserve's role had changed over the postwar period. Indeed, "since the end of World War II, the System has taken on itself a major share of the national worries about employment, production, growth, and prices." [24]

PLANNING AND FISCAL POLICY

Fiscal policy, unlike monetary policy, is not formulated by a single agency and hence is not readily controllable. The President recommends spending and tax policies by means of the budget, but final action is taken by Congress and its committees. Spending decisions are usually based on the desirability of thousands of individual government programs, not on the aggregate impact of expenditures on the economy. Analogously, on the revenue side, the tax structure is designed not only to withdraw funds from taxpayers but also to achieve a number of nonrevenue objectives, such as redistributing income and encouraging certain types of enterprises. Finally, much of the fiscal impact of a given year's expenditures and revenues depends on the functioning of "automatic stabilizers" such as unemployment compensation and the progressive income tax. These act to increase or decrease sums paid by government and to increase or decrease amounts withdrawn by the personal income tax as the national income rises or

[23] See Seymour E. Harris, *Economics of the Kennedy Years and A Look Ahead* (New York: Harper & Row, Publishers, Incorporated, 1964), pp. 28–29 and 121.

[24] Knipe, *op. cit.,* p. 36.

falls. Fiscal policy, in short, can be planned, but cannot be centrally controlled. To discern the meaning of postwar fiscal trends, one must look for the fiscal intent of successive administrations and examine their attempts to fashion national fiscal policy. President Truman's first budget message made it quite clear that he intended to achieve specific economic ends by means of the budget.[25] If he did not always succeed, it was not for lack of trying. In the years immediately following the war, the administration strongly urged, among other anti-inflation measures, a deliberate budgetary surplus. This was to be achieved by avoiding further tax reductions after the one passed in 1945. Congress, however, reflected the national impatience to relax wartime rigors and voted general tax reductions repeatedly. Truman vetoed the bills each time; the first two vetoes stuck (1947), and the third was overridden in an election year (1948).

The administration's subsequent efforts, both in time of recession and in time of expansion, were not given full congressional support, and thus their effectiveness is difficult to assess.

President Eisenhower's first budget message reiterated his wish to "chart a fiscal and economic policy which would reduce the planned deficits and bring the budget into balance." [26] When reductions in defense spending at the end of the Korean War precipitated the 1953–1954 recession and when, similarly, a cut in defense orders contributed to the 1957–1958 downturn, demands for a substantial tax cut to stimulate the economy were voiced not only by academic economists but also by such businessmen as the president of the U.S. Chamber of Commerce, the board chairman of J. P. Morgan & Company, and the chief executive of the Council of State Chambers of Commerce. The President adamantly opposed such a move and ultimately his views prevailed in Congress.[27]

During the expansion of 1958–1960, many Democrats in Congress argued that cyclical recovery and economic growth were

[25] "With the growing responsibility of modern government to foster economic expansion and to promote conditions that assure full and steady employment opportunities, it has become necessary to formulate and determine the Government program in the light of national economic conditions as a whole." *Budget of the United States,* 1947, p. vi.

[26] *Budget of the United States,* 1955, p. M104.

[27] Knipe, *op. cit.,* pp. 107–109; Eckstein, *op. cit.,* pp. 38, 41. Senator Lyndon Johnson, it might be noted, helped to mobilize congressional support against the tax cut. *Congress and the Nation* (Washington: Congressional Quarterly Service, 1965), p. 421.

being retarded by an excessively restrictive fiscal policy. But Mr. Eisenhower was anxious to achieve a balanced budget by 1960. Although he accepted the view that eventually tax reduction would be needed for economic growth, he urged that in the meantime a budgetary surplus was required to fight inflation.[28]

Kennedy and Johnson administrations

Economic growth was a focal issue in the 1960 presidential campaign, since the United States lagged behind most industrialized countries of the world in the rate of economic growth during the decade of the 1950s.[29] President Kennedy moved promptly to return to the compensatory policy of the Truman administration. The budget inherited from Eisenhower was transformed from surplus to deficit as expenditures were increased by several billions of dollars. An extension of corporate income and excise tax rates was requested to keep the resulting deficit down, however. Also, a number of tax "adjustments" and a liberalization of depreciation schedules on plant and equipment were proposed to stimulate business investment. Despite budgeting for a deficit at the beginning of his administration, Mr. Kennedy did not depart philosophically from the long-standing principle of fiscal moderates that deficits might be incurred during recessions as long as surpluses were incurred in prosperous years.[30]

In 1962 Walter Heller and other economists close to the President advanced the argument that a significant, across-the-board tax cut was needed, not for short-run stabilization purposes but for long-run stimulation of economic growth. This should be undertaken, they argued, to release what they called a "fiscal drag" on the economy: as incomes rose, taxpayers "graduated" into higher tax categories, and thus the tax burden became relatively

[28] The British economist Andrew Shonfield says of the 1960–1961 recession, referring to the surplus of 1960, "In this instance the damage done had all the appearance of a self-inflicted wound." He points out that this recession did not occur in Europe. *Modern Capitalism: The Changing Balance of Public and Private Power* (New York: Oxford University Press, 1965), p. 13.

[29] United States annual percentage increase in GNP (with allowance for price changes) was 3.2, while France's was 4.7, Italy's 6.4, Germany's 8.5, and Japan's 10.1. *Statistical Abstract of the United States,* 1969, p. 313.

[30] On Feb. 2, 1961, the President declared, "This Administration is pledged to a federal revenue system that balances the budget over the years of the economic cycle—yielding surpluses for debt retirement in times of high employment that more than offsets the deficits which accompany—and indeed help overcome—low levels of economic activity in poor years."

heavier. To measure the degree of fiscal drag, a concept called the "full employment surplus" had been developed. This was a hypothetical budget surplus that would occur if the economy were operating at an unemployment level of 4 percent. The surplus had become particularly big after 1958, it was calculated, and reduction of the surplus was necessary for faster growth.[31]

Kennedy was reluctant to advocate a big tax cut, both because of an inherited fiscal conservatism and because of concern that such a cut would jeopardize his general tax reform measures then pending before Congress. But he apparently changed his mind, and in the State of the Union message of January, 1963, he officially unveiled his proposal: a net tax reduction in the neighborhood of $10 billion. The unorthodox nature of the policy was reflected by the fact that (1) the tax cut would be taking place during a period of relative economic expansion instead of recession and (2) it would add to a deficit that was already expected. It was a historic step in the evolution of federal fiscal policy.[32]

Passage of the tax cut was delayed until after Kennedy's death and did not become law until February, 1964, after a concerted drive for passage by President Johnson. The measure reduced the total corporate income tax rate from 52 to 48 percent and, when fully operative in 1965, lowered personal income tax rates from the 20 to 91 percent range to the 14 to 70 percent range. The aggregate reduction was $11.5 billion.[33]

Although the Vietnam War provided an additional stimulus, most observers give this tax reduction much credit for the subsequent performance of the economy: GNP jumped 6.5 percent, a gain of $40 billion. In the wake of further tax reductions proposed and obtained by President Johnson in 1965 (plus further

[31] See *Economic Report of the President,* January, 1966, p. 43, for estimates of the surplus.

[32] Theodore C. Sorensen, *Kennedy* (New York: Harper & Row, Publishers, Incorporated, 1965). See pages 425–431 for discussion of the evolution of President Kennedy's thinking on taxes and the economy.

[33] The effect of this tax reduction upon the behavior of individuals and families, upon their spending-saving decisions, is explored in a valuable book by George Katona and Eva Mueller, *Consumer Response to Income Increases* (Washington: The Brookings Institution, 1968). This book offers significant evidence of government's ability to influence aggregate demand by tax reduction. Another work that provides more comprehensive analyses of the working of federal fiscal actions is *Studies in Economic Stabilization* (Washington: The Brookings Institution, 1968), edited by Albert Ando, E. Cary Brown, and Ann F. Friedlander.

intensification of the war), economic performance improved in the following year. In 1966 the growth rate was 6.4 percent, considerably above that of all the countries whose rates were mentioned earlier,[34] except Japan. The rate of growth did not, however, persist in the years 1967 and 1968.

A revolution in attitudes

Federal receipts have quadrupled during the postwar years, and federal expenditures have grown sixfold. State and local government receipts and payments multiplied roughly seven times. Despite this continual expansion, deficits occurred in each successive year since 1961, reflecting not only the growth-oriented fiscal policies of the 1960s, but also a radical shift in attitudes.

In 1939 a *Fortune* public opinion poll indicated that only 17 percent of the public accepted the idea of a deliberate budgetary deficit. After World War II, the same fiscal orthodoxy seemed to persist. As late as 1959 Gallup's interviewers found that a majority of the American people associated an unbalanced budget with inflation, thus presumably siding with President Eisenhower's view that the primary aim of fiscal policy should be avoidance of inflation rather than stimulation of growth.[35]

In 1962, the year in which President Kennedy was changing his mind on the tax question, the public seemed also to be veering away from orthodoxy to acceptance of the "new economics." In late July, 1962, Gallup reported that 72 percent of the public opposed the tax cut and only 19 percent favored it. By September, 1963, however, the change in opinion was obvious: according to Gallup, 60 percent of the public favored the tax cut and only 29 percent opposed it. A radical shift in attitude had occurred.[36]

Opinion in the business community also shifted away from fiscal orthodoxy in the postwar period, perhaps in advance of that of the general public. In 1946, as was noted, 78 percent of the business and professional people interviewed by Gallup favored a balanced budget rather than reduced taxes. In 1949, according to a poll conducted for *Fortune,* only 16 percent of the 25,000 businessmen interviewed advocated raising taxes during a

[34] *Gross National Product—Growth Rates and Trend Data by Region and Country,* Agency for International Development, RC-W-138, April, 1969.
[35] Gallup news release dated Jan. 30, 1959.
[36] Gallup news releases of Aug. 1, 1962, and Sept. 29, 1963.

recession in order to balance the budget. The majority—53 percent—preferred to leave tax levels unchanged and accept the deficit. Some 26 percent went further and said that taxes should be deliberately cut to stimulate investment and purchasing power.[37]

In the early 1960s many business leaders spoke out for a tax reduction, when it was obvious that reduction of taxes would result in a large budgetary deficit. The U.S. Chamber of Commerce abandoned its traditional fiscal orthodoxy and advocated tax reduction to stimulate economic growth. Businessmen were pleased by the stimulative effect of the investment credit and the liberalized depreciation of 1962 and wanted more of the same. When in May, 1961, the Opinion Research Corporation asked 150 business executives, "What steps by the government in Washington do you feel would be most helpful in stimulating the growth of business generally?", the most popular response (cited by 45 percent) was "revision and reduction of taxes." The liberalization of depreciation was mentioned by 19 percent. In contrast, the response "leave business alone" was favored by only 29 percent; "balance the budget" by 19 percent; "crack down on labor" by 13 percent; and "sound money and fiscal policies" by 12 percent.[38]

The revolution in attitudes was strikingly reflected by the opinions stated by two governmental officials in Godkin Lectures at Harvard University. From this forum Lewis Douglas said in 1935, immediately after having resigned as Director of the Budget under President Roosevelt, that "the essence of the system to be substituted [a 'planned eonomy'] is one of complete regulation by the government, eventually developing into State ownership." [39] Walter Heller, in 1966, after he had left the post of chairman of the Council of Economic Advisers, said from this forum that "the promise of modern economic policy in a democracy . . . can be realized only if government, first, carries out its responsibility under the Employment Act of 1946 to create and maintain the conditions for a thriving full-employment economy; second, does so by means that will reconcile rational government

---

[37] *Fortune,* August, 1949, p. 48.

[38] Opinion Research Corporation, *Incentives for Economic Growth,* 1961, p. A-7.

[39] *The Liberal Tradition* (New York: D. Van Nostrand Company, Inc., 1935), p. 15.

behavior in economic matters with decentralized decisions and freedom of economic choice; and, third, puts the products of prosperity and growth to uses that carry out a democratic society's aspirations not only for material betterment but for a rising quality of life and growing equality of opportunity." [40]

POSTWAR PLANNING
IN PERSPECTIVE

Looking back from the vantage point of more than two decades' experience under the Employment Act, it is clear that the commitment President Truman accepted for the federal government in February, 1946, has been increasingly fulfilled—intensively and extensively.

The use by government of monetary and fiscal devices—first, to combat recessions, then to promote postwar economic adjustments, and, finally, to encourage continual economic growth— has been increasingly woven into the processes of government and accepted by the business community and the public. Moreover, government's use of monetary and fiscal devices to promote economic growth has been relatively successful. Despite obvious weaknesses in the ability of governmental planners to forecast the economic future, government has shown during the 1960s how by managing aggregate demand it can bring about the fuller utilization of the private economy, reduce unemployment, and maintain prosperity.

Simultaneously, government has shown a disheartening inability to turn off the increased fiscal flow when such action is needed. The federal government has not been successful in controlling inflation; indeed, this is the Achilles heel on which governmental planning floundered during the late 1960s. But the difficulty lay not in a lack of knowledge as to what actions need be taken; it lay in the reluctance of the legislative arm of government to grant authority to the executive branch to act when action was needed.

The evolution of government's function as planner is eloquently pictured in the 23 successive economic reports published since the Council of Economic Advisers was created in 1946. The interpretation of the mandate given by the Employment Act has necessarily varied over the two decades during which five Presi-

[40] Heller, *op. cit.*, p. 58.

dents and eight chairmen of the Council have held office. With degrees of emphasis that varied from Eisenhower-Burns to Kennedy-Heller, monetary and fiscal tools were persistently applied to promote the expansion of private production and thus the maximization of employment and standards of living. Monetary and fiscal tools were supplemented, as the circumstances of war and postwar adjustment required, by controls and, during the years after 1960, by legislation designed to stimulate investment in plant and equipment (e.g., depreciation allowances, an investment credit against taxes) and legislation to stimulate the training and job placement of low-skilled workers.

But the most striking characteristic of this evolution of government's function as planner has been the fundamental enlargement of the social objectives that government strove to attain. Even during the Eisenhower administration, when the Council was least aggressive, there was recognition that "the area of explicit Federal concern" had been enlarged irrevocably. The *Annual Report of the Council of Economic Advisers,* 1961, emphasized that this was "without diminishing the scope of private, state and local responsibility." [41] Economic planning has evolved from an advisory-hortatory function, focused primarily on monetary and fiscal actions, to a positive guidance and coordination of various activities of the society that were deemed to be in the public interest.

When the federal government strives to achieve goals as varied as those that now constitute its function and when (as preceding chapters have shown) it subsidizes large segments of the private sector, regulates an increasing portion of all enterprises, expends 7 percent of GNP through contracts with private enterprises, substantially supports most research and development, strives to exercise an increasingly pervasive guiding hand over increases in prices and wages and over the development of manpower for employment in commerce and industry, it must formulate, rationally and deliberately, policies to guide and coordinate these manifold activities. This is planning and this planning touches every family and every enterprise in myriad ways.

---

[41] The broadened federal concern was further recognized by the Eisenhower administration when it published the *Goals for Americans: The Report of the President's Commission on National Goals* (Englewood Cliffs, N.J.: Prentice-Hall, Inc., 1960) which implied still further extension of "the Federal concern."

Businessmen have come to accept (if not to embrace) planning, but they resent and fear efforts by government to influence their managerial decisions. Their freedom of enterprise is not limited by "plans" but by their enforcement.

Government's enforcement of plans commenced in 1962 with enunciation of the wage-price guidelines. The guidelines were first offered as a suggestion to influence the behavior of business-men and union officials. (See Chapter 9.) In subsequent years, however, they became an edict rather than a plea.[42] After the steel price incident in 1962, business executives increasingly found it desirable, if not mandatory, to "clear" with the Council of Economic Advisers before making price increases effective (a practice abandoned after the Nixon administration came to power). Plagued by the adverse balance of payments, government appealed to industry and to banks to restrict voluntarily investments and lending overseas. During succeeding years, these appeals, too, gained an increasing degree of coerciveness.[43] A "suggestion" by Gardner Ackley, then chairman of the Council of Economic Advisers, that businessmen should consider the public interest when formulating their plans for capital expenditures was interpreted by many businessmen as a precursor of one more emerging control.

PLANNING AND FREEDOM

The record of the postwar years makes it obvious that the old notion, once commonly held by businessmen, that planning by government is "bad" is obsolete. When nearly a third of the gross national product passes through the treasuries of federal, state, and local governments, when government credit and guarantees and government support for research and development exert a far-reaching influence over the functioning of the economy, and when government operating activities affect directly many enterprises and many families, obviously it is in the interest of every businessman that what government does should be planned care-

[42] Arthur F. Burns, "Wages and Prices by Formula?" *Harvard Business Review*, March–April, 1965.

[43] For effective discussion of the relation of governmental planning to its expansion of governmental scope see Gunnar Myrdal, *Beyond the Welfare State* (New Haven, Conn.: Yale University Press, 1960), particularly chap. 5, "Planning in the Welfare State."

fully, in full recognition of its extensive impact.[44] The view that government should not plan is wholly inadequate to guide public policy in the latter third of the twentieth century.

Indeed, developments in other democratic-capitalistic societies [45] suggest that planning in this country may involve increasing intervention by government in the direction of individual business enterprise. Despite preliminary efforts to "enforce" plans, the absence of substantial constraints on the freedom of enterprise of most firms has left the businessman emotionally free to accept the fruits of a guided economy. As early as 1955, 74 percent of a sample of proprietors and managers agreed that it was the responsibility of the federal government "to see that the country is prosperous"; only 15 percent said that the government

[44] The feasibility of "Ending Investment Controls," as promised by Richard Nixon during the presidential campaign of 1968, was questioned in an editorial in the *Wall Street Journal* (Oct. 17, 1968). This question by a conservative business journal suggests a degree of acceptance or the inevitability of such controls.

[45] In France business leaders discuss with officials of the Commissariat du Plan the investment to be made in particular industries and geographic areas. These plans are then implemented by an effective process of promotional activities, including tax concessions and governmental loans to individual firms willing to cooperate, and through what is called a "quasi-contract" according to which financial assistance is given the contracting firm in return for agreed-upon behavior by way of investment projects, production programs, and research.

With the exception of West Germany, where the term "planning" remains somewhat an anathema as in the United States, most other West European governments manage their economies to a similar extent. Sweden, for example, employs an investment loan fund into which business firms are induced by tax concessions to set aside up to 40 percent of their profits during prosperous times. Whenever the government determines that a stimulus is needed to achieve target levels of production, the Labor Market Board authorizes the use of the investment reserves for specified purposes, e.g., for the construction of plants in the relatively undeveloped north of Sweden, at times specified by the government. Compliance is not compulsory; the firm is tempted into participation by generous tax inducements. Britain has traditionally employed noninterventionist instruments of economic control. But British leaders have looked with envy upon French planning during the 1960s, as the French economy has grown and the British economy has limped from one crisis to the next. The British government has introduced a succession of innovations in its "incomes" policy, including the requirement of advance notice of wage-price increases, that reflect acceptance of the necessity of intervention. A notable example was the introduction by the Labour government in the mid-1960s of a "Selective Employment Tax" to restructure the economy and throw off economic stagnation. All employers were taxed 25

could not "do much about this." [46] Today the proportion is likely much larger.[47] Business economists no longer dispute, as they did in the 1920s, whether government can affect the economy; they now argue over the appropriate means and over the degree of influence. Moreover, business leaders increasingly recognize that the planning for their own enterprises can be more successful if the economy is more predictable—and predictability is established when the business cycle is moderated and economic growth maintained.

The future evolution of planning in the United States seems clear. It will become more comprehensive in scope and more interventionist in character (in relation to the individual firm). The process of planning will not be based on a formal annual plan, but will proceed by steps as government first explores the wants of the society and then prepares its plans to satisfy these wants. The persistent extension of planning [48]—that is assured by the desire for continued economic growth and sustained prosperity and by the quest for an improved quality of life for all citizens—means that the individual business firm will be guided more by governmental regulations, subsidies, and con-

shillings per week for each employee; manufacturers, who, it was hoped, could be stimulated to expand by this device, received a tax refund of more than the amount of the tax, i.e., 32s 6d per employee per week; other enterprises did not receive this refund. In short, this instrument of economic planning attempted to stimulate the productivity of individual companies and industries through a generalized means.

See Shonfield, *op. cit.*, chaps. VI and VIII for a general discussion of economic planning in Great Britain, and chaps. VII and VIII on French planning. Also, John Sheahan, *Promotion and Control of Industry in Post-war France* (Cambridge, Mass.: Harvard University Press, 1963), and Neil W. Chamberlain, *Private and Public Planning* (New York: McGraw-Hill Book Company, 1965).

[46] Opinion Research Corporation, *How the Eisenhower Administration Rates with the Voters*, 1955, p. A-44.

[47] The "partnership for prosperity," to use one of President Johnson's phrases, has become a powerful force influencing business to accept and approve governmental intervention.

[48] Both Shonfield (*op. cit.*, p. 122) and Myrdal (*op. cit.*, pp. 78–82) suggest that once government intervenes to accomplish particular objectives—improving the health of its citizens or increasing employment—it is forced to correct the distortions thus produced by more extensive planning and coordination. See also Gerald Serkin, "Guidelines of the Visible Hand," *The Visible Hand: The Fundamentals of Economic Planning* (New York: McGraw-Hill Book Company, 1968), chap. 8.

tracts in the making of its decisions as to product, distribution methods, financing, employment, and even pricing. Such persistent extension of planning also means that the distribution of an increasing proportion of the services on which citizens rely (particularly health, education, and welfare services, including housing) will be allocated by governmental decision and not by the market.

PART 4

Consequences in Roles and in Power

*THE agonies of the late 1960s—threatening
division among our people, riots in the ghettos and
on the campus, the spread of drug usage, rising crime
rates, and persisting and deepening racial tension—
demonstrate vividly that a society with generally
comfortable or high personal incomes, generally profitable and expanding business enterprises, and a gross
national product at peak levels is not the end-all of
American objectives. As change wracks this society,
the aspirations, goals, and values of those families and
individuals that make up the American society change.
These changes pose demands on all parts of the society,
but on no part of an industrialized society more than
on the institution of business. Hence the succeeding
chapters picture the changing values of the society
and their impact on business enterprise—the new
responsibilities it is expected to bear, the new role
it is expected to play, and the lessened power it is
likely to exercise.*

CHAPTER 12

The Impact on Business
as a Society Updates Its Values

*P*ERSISTENT, irresistible change is the transcendental fact of life with which businessmen must learn to cope and which they must learn to shape, as this country moves into the Humane Society of the last third of the twentieth century.[1] Forces impelling that change were outlined in the first chapter of this book. Subsequent chapters have depicted the adaptations made within the politico-economy of this country since World War II and have identified the inflexible institutions that obstruct or prevent them.

These adaptations have shaped and expanded a grants economy. extended public regulation, and established many new nonprofit institutions. They have reduced dependence on the market

---

[1] President Nixon told the nation's governors on Labor Day of 1969, "The central race in the world today is neither an arms race nor a space race. It is a race between man and change. . . ."

economy and its incentives, increased the directional power of political institutions, and focused this country's politico-economy more on the well-being of all and less on the profitability of individual enterprises.

THE FRUSTRATING PRESENT

But change is ongoing, and despite the obvious betterment of the human lot that had taken place [2] in the late 1960s, this country experienced at that time more frustration, unrest, even rebellion than at any previous time within the memory of living men.

The students had rebelled on scores of campuses and the blacks had rioted in scores of cities. As this country entered the 1970s, racial tension was high and conflicting groups were polarized—the young and their elders; those demanding an end to an unpopular war and those supporting existing war policies; those proposing a greater effort to mitigate the lot of the poor, the hungry, and the disadvantaged and those holding that the individual must stand on his own two feet. The prevalence of crime and the use of drugs were alarming. An uneasy and uncertain peace prevailed. In a number of cities young priests voiced their dissatisfaction with the policies of the hierarchy of the Catholic Church. And an organization of uniformed military personnel— "G.I.'s United"—openly criticized the commands under which they served on a dozen or more military bases. Truly, as in Charles Dickens' *A Tale of Two Cities*, "it was the best of times, it was the worst of times, it was the age of wisdom, it was the age

---

[2] On the basis of census statistics, two perceptive observers—Ben J. Wattenberg and Richard M. Scammon, director of the U.S. Bureau of the Census, 1961–1965—concluded in their book *This U.S.A.* (Garden City, N.Y.: Doubleday & Company, Inc., 1965) that Americans in 1967 were healthier, better housed, better fed, better educated, and even more religious than at any time in the past. Poverty, they pointed out, was steadily being reduced, family ties were growing stronger, the birthrate was under control, drug addiction and crime were less than half of what they were a century earlier, and the cities, they claimed, were neither declining nor dying. In the light of what has happened subsequently, only the last contention is suspect when matched against cold statistical fact. If one were to pursue their analysis with the aid of the 1970 census, it is almost sure that all or most of these measures would show further betterment of the human lot. The 1970 census data will assuredly show that nearly 15 million people are no longer in poverty and that in terms of income, education, employment, and amenities, the gap between whites and nonwhites has been substantially narrowed.

of foolishness . . . it was the spring of hope, it was the winter of despair. . . ."

The condition in 1969 was a dangerous one, and it was not confined to students, Negroes, hippies, followers of George Wallace, and intellectuals. "The man in the street," as John Gardner perceptively pointed out, "feels powerless and useless in a vast complex society," suffers "from loss of a sense of belonging, 'of connection,' of meaning and identity, feels that the society has actively deprived him of his identity and turned him into a number, a computer card." [3]

Why should this frustration, unrest, and unprecedented violence mar our lives, when we possess the resources to achieve social objectives and have made much progress in improving the ways by which our politico-economy harnesses those resources, including an expanding technological capacity?

ADAPTING VALUES TO A NEW CONTEXT

Part of the answer is that as a people we have clung, in the face of persistent change, to old ways and old concepts.[4] We have lacked the social and political maturity that would enable us to break with obsolete ideas and handicapping institutions (e.g., forms of local government, building codes, union featherbedding practices, the AMAs persistent efforts to limit the number of doctors, legal precepts as to private property, the responsibilities of business enterprise for profit, and fixations as to the roles of business and of government).[5] We have failed to take advantage of

[3] The Godkin Lectures, Harvard University, Lecture II as broadcast by WGBH-TV, Boston, Mass., Mar. 26, 1969.

[4] In mid-1969, President Nixon's nominations of Warren Burger and C. J. Haynsworth, Jr., for seats on the Supreme Court were supported by some on the grounds that Burger was a "strict constructionist" and that Haynsworth could interpret the Constitution "as it was intended to be." In the face of industrial, scientific, and social change can the Constitution be interpreted "strictly" or as "was intended"?

[5] Other handicapping institutions that come to mind are:

Government: The maze of 80,000 local governments to contend, squabble, and cope with; the antiquated nation-state concept still hanging around our necks despite its obvious inapplicability to present-day conditions. *Education:* Growing obsession with escalating diplomas; diminishing lack of purpose and, consequently, relevance. *Transportation:* Boxing ourselves in—like the sorcerer's apprentice—and building our own handicaps by pushing too

our growing wealth and bountiful scientific advances. And, consequently, we have not developed a consensus as to how we shall preserve values that are traditional to America. This crisis of values is the root cause of the insecurity, frustration, resentment, and unrest that have been painfully prevalent.

Robert Frost's poem "The Black Cottage" [6] speaks of how the values established for this infant nation by the Declaration of Independence will be weighed time and time again.

> That's a hard mystery of Jefferson's.
> What did he mean? Of course the easy way
> Is to decide it simply isn't true.
> It may not be. I heard a fellow say so.
> But never mind, the Welshman got it planted
> Where it will trouble us a thousand years.
> Each age will have to reconsider it.

And so it has been. Each age has had to reconsider basic American values in the light of changed circumstances. The turbulence of the 1960s is largely attributable to the simple fact that the pace and magnitude of change during the postwar decades have been so much greater than in any earlier era. And yet, in view of the rapidly increasing rates of change observed in preceding decades, the rates of change observed in the 1960s may well be but part of a trend of ever-more-rapid acceleration.

Looking at the nature of the discontent that has been reported —the demands of the students, the Negroes, the disadvantaged, the less-developed nations, and the rest—there is a certain logic, a harking back to first principles, and a substantial moral content which cannot be waved aside. While many specific demands show ignorance of history, impatience with established practices, unwillingness to make concessions to what is administratively feasible, and a poor sense of timing, still they are not easy to rebut because from one point of view these demands make sense. Perhaps the success of the Forsyte Saga as a TV presentation, its meaning to the young particularly, is evidence that viewers see in its message about the changing nature of property an analogy to our own age. Clearly, these expressions of discontent need analy-

indiscriminately for the development of the automobile and the highway network, killing off the railroads and sealing off the inner city in the process.

[6] Quoted by Henry M. Wriston in his essay "The Individual" in *Goals for Americans: The Report of the President's Commission on National Goals* (Englewood Cliffs, N.J.: Prentice-Hall, Inc., 1960), p. 38.

sis and, if we are indeed to arrive at a consensus, the protests must be examined and considered; mere confrontation is not enough.

If businessmen are to have a part in shaping the politico-economy within which they will operate in the decades ahead, they need to recognize the reconsideration of values that is going on —as well as the meaning of this reconsideration in terms of the additional responsibility they must assume or the functions they will lose—and to help build the consensus that is being approached. Consider, for example, these values—and how each involves the businessman.

Freedom

While freedom is the value Americans have traditionally cherished most, abridgments of freedom persist doggedly. Vestiges of religious prejudice, racial discrimination, and conventions as to the role of women limit the freedom of many. There are people who enjoy precious little real freedom because of poverty, low earning power, or ill health. Others' freedom is limited by pension provisions which chain them to an enterprise or by employer or union seniority provisions which limit their opportunities to advance. And, increasingly, people fear enslavement under the new technology even as they enjoy its beneficence.

We conceive now of freedom as comprehending the right of the workingman to organize and the obligation of employers to bargain with their unions; the right of Negroes to equal educational opportunities, equal employment opportunities, and the choice of where to live; and the rights of all to maintain some identity—more than a number—in the large institutions in which they work, study, or live. We conceive of freedom, too, as comprehending access to health care facilities and to the public park and swimming pool where the cooped-up inhabitants of box-sized apartments may tan their skins in the sun.

The recent past makes clear that demands for greater freedom —in the sense of greater equality, the protection of personal identity in large organizations, and expanding opportunity for every individual—will persist and increase in the 1970s and beyond. And the demand will be made not alone upon government, but upon employers, unions, landlords, bankers, small loan company executives, and others throughout the society.

Simultaneously, to ensure that the individual will enjoy the fruits of an advancing science rather than be enslaved and demeaned by it, there will be a growing demand for protection against the automation that displaces workers; the radiation, new drugs, synthetic foods and pesticides that threaten life; and the computer that tends to erase or at least to diminish personal identity.

The technological progress of recent decades is apparent everywhere. It can be seen in the food we eat (packaged, frozen, and radiated); in the clothes we wear (Dacron, Fortrel, and Corfam are examples); in the automobiles we drive (their speed, quietness, braking capacity, and greater safety); in the games we play (note the steel and aluminum tennis rackets); in the drugs we take (the use of lithium for the relief of mental depression, for example); in the pesticides that increase agricultural productivity and human comfort (DDT, for example); and in the use of nuclear materials for the cure of human ills and for the generation of electric power.

Neither the hazards nor the expansion of regulation has lessened the appetite of Americans for scientific advance. Many Americans confidently look forward to the prospect that our scientists will find ways to control pollution; solve the urban mass transit problem; control crime; find the cures for the major threats to good health; vastly improve the processes, techniques, and materials of education; and even control the weather. Moreover, a goodly number of Americans have come to expect that each successive advance in science will reveal ways to advance still further in many fields—that if we will but put enough money and effort into the attempt, we can and should solve any major problem of civilization.

But the experience of the post-World War II decades has shown that if this invaluable national asset—our knowledge and capacity for discoveries—is to increase the freedom of Americans from a scarcity of goods, from ill health, from a polluted environment, and from the threats of unemployment and depersonalization, government will have to assume a steadily increasing responsibility for regulating the application of the new technologies.

Material well-being

Some of our founding fathers came to this land in search of riches, even if many of them sought political and religious freedom. Throughout succeeding decades, Americans have persistently striven to apply their energies toward utilizing the rich resources this land makes available to raise the standard of living. As individuals we have persistently tried to provide well for our families. A prime function of this country's politico-economy has always been to provide an ever-growing volume of goods and services for an increasing proportion of all families.

As the national wealth has reached unforeseen levels, not only has the prevailing concept of an adequate standard of living broadened, but also the national conscience has been pricked by marked disparities in the distribution of income. Two developments of the 1960s rubbed salt in this abrasion on the national conscience. The civil rights revolution illuminated the low incomes of those denied the opportunity for improvement because of the color of their skin. The rediscovery of poverty in this land of plenty prompted doubt as to whether it need be that "the poor we will have with us always."

Redefinition of goals to make this traditional value of material well-being valid in an affluent society has provoked debate and division that revolves around

■ What government should do (or not do) to ensure continuing economic growth. If the volume of goods and services available to satisfy the wants of individuals could be increased to provide an average annual family income of as much as $12,000 (in 1958 dollars) by increased intervention by the government and by concentrating more power in the federal executive branch, would the cost be worth the gain?

■ How far government should go to achieve further reduction of unemployment, let us say to not more than 3 percent of the total labor force

■ Whether government should use the tools that are at its disposal to promote a more equitable distribution of income and relatively stable prices. If wage and price controls are necessary to achieve these ends, is the imposition of such controls truly acceptable?

Equality of opportunity

For the poor, the foreign born, and those belonging to religious and racial minorities, the opportunity for good schooling, the chance to get and keep a job, and the chance to get ahead by dint of one's effort and merit are still drastically limited. Children of the poor do not have the same chance for education (and thus for the improvement of their own condition) as do children of better-off parents. Foreign-born children and adults are not always "melted" into jobs and neighborhoods on equal terms. So it is in varying degrees, in various places, for Jews, American Indians, Negroes, Puerto Ricans, and Mexican-Americans. Studies of social mobility—i.e., of the level of education, of job, of income, and of social status achieved by the son as compared with the father—demonstrate that opportunity "to get ahead," while expanding, is still limited.[7]

These inequalities have been highlighted by urbanization, television, and the civil rights rebellion. Their increased visibility has brought about acceptance of the twin—and traditional— ideas that it is the obligation of the individual to "keep on growing" and the obligation of the society to increase to the fullest the opportunities for every man, woman, and child.

To meet its obligation, society is gradually expanding access to its schools not only for those from 6 to 18 years of age but also for (1) those infants 3 to 5 years of age whose families are least able to provide them with surroundings that encourage their growth; (2) adults who have completed their formal schooling years before but now require education to qualify for a new job, to advance in their present job, or just to keep up with the rapidly changing world about them; (3) erstwhile "dropouts" who are irrevocably lost within the existing system but could be held and developed by better schools and better teaching; and (4) those capable of learning more but who have been denied access to higher education by their inability to meet the costs.

Much of the obligation to provide conditions that will enable each individual to develop his talents to the fullest falls on employers. Increasingly, they will be expected to employ, train, and promote many individuals customarily passed over; to restructure jobs within their plants and offices to enable each individual to work his way up; and to facilitate the individual's self-development by providing extensive general education as well as job training for all employees.

Providing such opportunities will add costs that employers will be expected to bear in return for the privilege of employing fellow human beings. This added burden will be accepted by em-

[7] See particularly U.S. Department of Health, Education, and Welfare, "Social Mobility: How much opportunity is there?" *Toward a Social Report,* January, 1969, chap. II.

ployers as they increasingly recognize the need (their own as well as society's) for specialized talent—artists and plumbers, engineers and mechanics, physicians and hairdressers, scientists and chefs, and many others. To develop talent requires more and better schools. In a rapidly evolving technological society, the schools can start each individual on his way, but the individual must be regularly aided by his employer to expand his own understanding and skills as his job and the world about him change.

The dignity of the individual

Whatever Jefferson's glorious words meant in 1776, in 1976 they will mean that each institution of our society—the government, the business enterprise, the church, and the family—will be expected to assume increasing responsibility for motivating every individual to develop his talents to the fullest. The dignity of the individual in terms of the Humane Society will mean that the individual must not be frustrated by social conventions that deny him and his family the right to live in any neighborhood, to send his children to any school, to belong to any club, to swim in any pool, and to rise to any job for which he can qualify. And the obligation of abolishing practices and conventions that limit the opportunity of Negroes, young people, women, Mexican-Americans, and others falls on all citizens alike.

For many individuals the chance for self-fulfillment—in retirement, during working days, or in childhood—requires the assurance of health care. The pace of advance in health sciences offers great promise of that assurance. But its fulfillment will require control of the spiraling costs of medical care and drastic change in the relation between those who provide medical care—the doctors, nurses, hospitals, and others—and those who need medical care. And the political struggles that have revolved around health care and related programs—Medicare, Medicaid, proposals for the enactment of health insurance, and the establishment of controls over the sale of drugs and over the processes by which industries have polluted the air and the water—reflect the economic and social pains involved in assuring many individuals the health care that for them is the prerequisite to self-fulfillment.

Privacy

The early Greeks established for Western civilization the notion that each individual should be free of the curiosity of others and the surveillance of institutionalized authority—be it government, employer, church, or family. Privacy remains—perhaps to a greater degree than any other fundamental value—an undefined and unclear concept, even while it is zealously claimed.

In the urban society of the 1970s privacy is a very different thing than it was in the rural society of the 1870s. It was one thing in a simple world in which business records were kept with a quill pen, and it is a very different thing in the world of the computer and the credit card. Privacy is one thing in a small enterprise where the boss and his employees have a daily, face-to-face relationship; it is another thing in the world of the aptitude and personality test and television surveillance of the workplace. It is one thing for the consumer who makes buying choices on the basis of some knowledge of the goods for which he pays and a very different thing for the consumer whose decisions are influenced by subliminal advertising. It is one thing for the citizen whose home is his castle and another thing for the citizen whose telephone may be wiretapped or whose bedroom may be bugged.

Privacy, these illustrations evidence, is not a philosophical notion today, but a value being shaped by what employers, government, newspapers and television, and still other modern-day institutions do day by day.

Environmental well-being

The brownstone mansions in New York City, the southern planter's colonial home, the flowerpot alongside the ramshackle hut of a West Virginia miner or a Mexican-American's shack in the Southwest, all reflect, each in its own way, a traditional quest for pleasant surroundings. The gradual development of parks and city planning and the heightening of the crusade against slums illustrate this same fundamental value.

But the high birthrates of the late 1940s, substantial migration to the cities, and the rigidities that stifle urban reconstruction (municipal zoning laws, building codes, and the practices of the building trades unions) pose the dismal prospect that the homes and cities within which many Americans live will get a lot worse before they are improved.

Conditions have in some ways been improved during recent years; in other ways, and in some cities, they have markedly worsened. With increasing governmental aid, more houses have been built and some slums have been cleared. But the volume of new housing never sufficed to meet the needs of new families; of migrants moving in; and of those families whose homes had become obsolete, dilapidated, and even uninhabitable.[8] And the redesign and reconstruction of the cities themselves—many of them as obsolete for life in the 1970s as is the Model T Ford for transportation today—to cope with urban transport problems, today's employment mix, and the recreational requirements of a society with more youth, more aged, and more leisure is simply not being done.

Advancing the arts

Americans have always held "that the arts can give all of us . . . much of what is best in human life and enjoyment; and that a nation which does not put this at the disposal of those who have the liking and the capacity for it, is failing in a most important duty." [9] But we place a large value on the prevalence and progress of the arts in the American society because they tend to elevate the sensibility and perception in people to the highest level and they stimulate imagination.[10] These qualities we cannot do without.

The cultivation of creative work in the arts and the making of the arts more accessible to more Americans is difficult to pinpoint. There has been no cultural boom where direct attendance at live performances was involved. Still such names as Marian Anderson, Robert Frost, Helen Hayes, Arthur Miller, Martha Graham, José Greco, Van Cliburn, Risë Stevens, and Leontyne Price—their reputations and their general popularity—testify to creative progress. And widespread ownership of television sets (despite the limitations of this medium); the familiarity of children in the slums with Rumpelstiltskin, Peter Pan, and still

---

[8] A total of 27.7 million new housing units will be needed during the 1970s according to an estimate of Anthony Downs in *Agenda for the Nation* (Washington: The Brookings Institution, 1968). The prospect of meeting that need seems bleak when we recognize that we have succeeded in building as much as 1.6 million units a year in only three years since the end of World War II; during the late 1960s, only 1.3 million units per year were built.

[9] Lord Bridges in his 1958 Romanes Lecture, quoted in W. J. Baumol and W. G. Bowen, *Performing Arts: The Economic Dilemma* (New York: The Twentieth Century Fund, 1966), p. 370. The President's Commission on National Goals (*op. cit.*) expressed this idea in these words, ". . . the success of the United States as a civilized society will be largely judged by the creative activities of its citizens in art, architecture, literature, music, and the sciences."

[10] Herbert Read, "The Necessity of Art," *Saturday Review*, Dec. 6, 1969.

other greats of literature; and the "paperback revolution" constitute some evidence of the greater availability of the best in literature, music, and art (along with much that is not great). "New
technologies have not only widened the access to art, but also
permitted new forms of artistic expression, from films to new
kinds of sculpture and music." [11]

Increased leisure and increased incomes are sure to foster a
greater demand for access to the arts in the remaining third of
the twentieth century—and a progressively more discriminating
evaluation of the arts. But the economy of the arts is not a prom-
ising one. This country's symphony orchestras, ballet companies,
operas, museums, and theaters operate at large deficits.[12] Relatively, there are fewer patrons when many more are needed; the
fine arts, as contrasted with the mass-produced art used on TV
and sold in the drugstores and supermarkets, have not developed
an economy of their own that promises to be self-sustaining. New
sources of subsidy need to be found if new generations of artists
are to be reared and in turn succeeded by others and if existing
institutions are to survive.

BARRIERS IN THE WAY

Alfred North Whitehead wrote some years ago that "those societies which cannot combine reverence for their symbols [I suggest
that you read "values" for "symbols"] with freedom for their revision must ultimately decay." He summed up in those words
what is involved in making traditional values meaningful in a society markedly altered by change.

If we are to surmount the barriers that make the updating of
values difficult, we must redefine the roles of the individual, the
family, the business enterprise, the government, the university,
the hospital, and other institutions. We must reshape long-held
beliefs as to the reverence due the patriarch (parent, executive,
official, and teacher); the inviolability of hierarchy as an organizing principle; the unworthiness of those who do not live by such

[11] *Toward a Social Report, op. cit.,* p. 75.

[12] Baumol and Bowen (*op. cit.,* p. 396) demonstrate that, except for Broadway, all performing arts groups in the United States operate at a deficit,
varying (in 1964) from 15 percent for the regional theaters to 46 percent for
all 25 major orchestras. Merely to keep this "income gap" from growing
larger, "ticket prices would have to rise by more than 70 percent by 1975,"
according to the authors' conservative estimate.

long-standing conventions as the virtue of work, self-dependence, chastity, and marital fidelity; and the inflexibility of our attitudes toward different races and religions. We must abandon or update such prevailing practices as the dependence of the cities on the property tax and the inflexibility of their building codes and zoning provisions; the hiring, upgrading, training, and pensioning practices of employers; the admission, seniority, and featherbedding practices of unions; and prevailing notions or inertia that discourage population planning. The painful process of adapting or renouncing these and other built-in institutions, beliefs, and practices is a price of entry—admittedly high—to a truly Humane Society.

THE ROLE OF THE ENTERPRISE

Here we are primarily concerned with redefining the role of business enterprise as this country moves on from the Post-Industrial (or Service) Society to the Humane Society. Business enterprise will be expected in the future to produce the bulk—and an expanding and improved bulk—of all the goods and services required by Americans. But during the late 1960s business enterprises were also being asked to assume new responsibilities, to take on unaccustomed tasks.

Specifically, they were being asked to:

■ Seek out and employ the hard-core unemployed, many of whom do not meet minimum standards customarily used in selecting those to be hired—the physically handicapped, the mentally retarded, members of minority groups, and others among the "disadvantaged"

■ Engage in educational activities ranging from "adopting" a high school to providing basic education for undereducated workers

■ Finance construction of low-income housing in ghetto areas, sometimes at less than normal rates of return, and assist in launching business ventures to be operated by members of minority groups

■ Establish enterprises in economically underdeveloped areas, e.g., in the ghettos and in Appalachia

■ Overcome harmful effects resulting from business behavior —the pollution of the air and water caused by industrial wastes, the unemployment resulting from automation, the transportation snags caused by the location of plants and offices

■ Participate with the leaders of formerly submerged groups (e.g., Negroes) in determining the needs and interests of the community and the nation and in finding ways of meeting them

■ Support financially, and by providing leadership, the struggle to resolve the problems of civic operas, theaters, orchestras, museums, and libraries [13]

These activities were not all equally new to business. Business firms had employed handicapped workers and had taken timid first steps to limit their pollution of the air and the water a decade or even two decades earlier. Many, especially among the larger business enterprises, had long participated in efforts to meet the social problems of the communities in which they were located. They had contributed money (approximately $800 million a year), facilities, or time to such noncommercial institutions as schools, universities, hospitals, community chests, charitable agencies, and such cultural institutions as the municipal theater, opera, orchestra, or educational television station.[14]

NEW MEASURES OF BUSINESS DUTY

No longer was it sufficient for the business enterprise to be a good citizen—to keep its sidewalks clean and its lawn mowed, to contribute as other citizens do to community enterprises from the Boy Scouts to the local college and symphony orchestra, and to encourage its executives to lead the annual community chest and Red Cross drives. Business enterprises were essentially told that they were expected to utilize their financial and manpower resources, with no prospect or limited prospect of profit, to carry

[13] For example, Richard Barr, a Broadway producer and president of the Cultural League of New York, said in a speech in New York City on May 1, 1969, that businessmen were failing to participate meaningfully in the country's cultural development and that the businessman has a large obligation to the total culture "that he has failed to meet."

[14] The magnitude of this financial support is suggested by General Motors Corporation's 1968 Annual Report. It states (p. 18) that the corporation's "contributions to charitable and similar organizations" and its "financial aid to education in that year" totaled $13.4 million. This sum was about equal to the aggregate grants of the Carnegie Corporation, the third largest private philanthropic foundation in the United States.

on activities that had traditionally been the responsibility of government, of such nonprofit institutions as the university or the church, or of the family.

Irwin Miller, chairman and chief executive officer of the Cummins Engine Company, pointed up the issue when he defined "the present internal threat confronting the United States" in these words:

> It is the product of population growth
> —times urban congestion,
> —times ghetto poverty,
> —times racial issues,
> —times seriously uneven education,
> —times transportation deficiencies,
> —times inflation and a debased currency,
> —times air and water pollution,
> —and all of these times a growing aversion to taxes and a serious national difference of opinion as to the place and role of government. . . . It is clear that current programs to attack urban decay, school crowding, racial discrimination, lack of job opportunities, air and water pollution, and transportation congestion are simply not keeping us even. In each of these we suffer, month by month, a visible deterioration.

And Mr. Miller concluded that while government should play the role of "systems manager" in harnessing a national attack upon these and other problems, business must accept an increased and large responsibility for resolving them.[15]

Peter Drucker stated the issue forthrightly when he wrote that [16] "the new demand is . . . a demand that business and businessmen make concern for society central to the conduct of business itself. It is a demand that the quality of life become the business of business. The traditional approach asks: How can we arrange the making of cars (or of shoes) so as not to impinge on social values and beliefs, on individuals and their freedom, and on the good society altogether? The new demand is for business to *make* social values and beliefs, create freedom for the individual, and altogether produce the good society."

---

[15] Address before the Annual Congress of American Industry, sponsored by the National Association of Manufacturers, New York, Dec. 5, 1968.

[16] "Business and the Quality of Life," in Peter Drucker (ed.), *Preparing Tomorrow's Business Leaders Today* (Englewood Cliffs, N.J.: Prentice-Hall, Inc., 1969), p. 77.

CONFLICTING VIEWPOINTS

The persistence of this demand that business assume some responsibility for the quality of life and business' accumulating experience with such ventures have given rise to conflicting viewpoints as to what and how much business enterprises should do in shouldering such responsibilities.

Many men in government and some in business hold with Richard Nixon that "the modern corporation is not simply an economic unit. It has become a social unit, an action unit, and its skills are needed where the action is." [17] Others subscribe to the view voiced by Donald C. Burnham, chairman of the Westinghouse Electric Corporation, that "A corporation cannot justify using the stockholders' money to solve social problems on the slender excuse that this would produce a better climate for profits. Happily this justification is not needed. The principal reason industry is ready and eager to work on social problems is that these areas offer great opportunity for growth and profit, as well as for betterment of our society." [18]

Not all businessmen are as sanguine as to the prospect of profit in many of the responsibilities thrust upon them, and the consequential conflict underscores a question not yet resolved: What is the social responsibility of business?

[17] Address before the Annual Congress of American Industry, sponsored by the National Association of Manufacturers, New York, Dec. 8, 1967.

[18] *Saturday Review*, Jan. 13, 1968, p. 60.

CHAPTER *13*

The Evolving Mix of Private and Public Enterprise

*T*HERE are obvious reasons why business is being expected to assume larger social responsibilities. But first let us be clear as to what is meant. By "social responsibility" is not meant simply responsibility for coping with such problems as unemployment or the lack of decent housing in the slums. In producing and distributing essential goods and services and in developing new products and new services, business has always borne large and important responsibilities upon which society is dependent. But business has been called upon of late to assume responsibilities additional to those included within its traditional role. Why?

Society's goals are larger

One obvious reason is that human wants have expanded. During the postwar years, the federal government, pressed by widespread concern about the quality of life, has assumed responsibility for numerous new and ambitious social goals: maximizing employment opportunities for all who want to work, providing higher education for all who can benefit, assuring adequate health care for the elderly and the needy, rebuilding the cities, overcoming environmental pollution, and continually stimulating economic growth.

Accomplishment of these goals requires the collaboration of the private, public, and nonprofit sectors of the economy. Business will be expected to provide many or most of the jobs; universities will be expected to offer the facilities required for the higher education of substantially greater numbers; hospitals will be the principal instrument through which more and more adequate health care will be provided. But, despite this distribution of the total responsibility, it is the government that must bear in increasing measure the brunt of this vast effort. Technological changes, population growth, and urbanization have increased tremendously the traditional responsibilities of all levels of government in a society in which schools, hospitals, urban renewal projects, welfare services, police protection, transportation networks, methods of waste disposal, and other services have proved inadequate, outmoded, and inefficient.

Government needs help

Government's existing staffs and facilities have been insufficient, in many instances, to cope with these burgeoning responsibilities. Governmental leaders have often lacked firm knowledge about social developments with which plans and policies could be formulated. Hence, government has sought with increasing frequency to enlist the capabilities of private enterprise—business enterprises, universities, hospitals, and many other agencies, both nonprofit and profit making.

To federal, state, and local governments, the business system offers a convenient mechanism for providing jobs that can solve poverty problems in a way that welfare handouts never will. It also offers a convenient mechanism for supplying the technical competence, motivation, and innovative power required to help launch new enterprises, to construct needed housing in the ghettos, and to accept responsibility for mitigating most of the problems of air and water pollution and of the woefully inadequate inner-city transport.

In addition, and importantly, business possesses capabilities which can significantly supplement those of government. It can contribute the zeal created by the prospect of profit. A few enterprises can contribute the ingenuity and creativity that can produce new solutions. Some enterprises possess skills in job training, in housing design and finance, in systems analysis and engineering, and in other fields which make their contribution especially useful. Still other enterprises—a minority—possess a capacity for organization that they are capable of transferring to the complex milieu of the urban center.

Business caused the problems

Business has been asked to bear the responsibility for the cost of solving a number of current social problems because, it is argued, business created them in the first place. Consequences of business behavior place on business the responsibility for combating the social problems created by its actions.

Introduction of automation and other forms of technological change in industry and in commercial establishments has given rise to some of the present unemployment of unskilled and semi-skilled persons. This unemployment is aggravated by the influx to urban slums of farm workers displaced by technological developments generated by industry. Urban congestion and transportation jams are, in some measure, a result of business decisions as to the location of plants and offices; in some instances, location in already crowded downtown areas has intensified congestion while in other instances, movement to the suburbs has speeded the central city decay.

Air and water pollution provide examples of business culpability that have been most generally recognized—by business executives as well as the general public. Industrial wastes have destroyed rivers and streams. Industrial pollution of the air has created smog and related problems in a number of cities. The widespread effects on animal and plant life, human health, and weather are only beginning to be recognized.

Federal, state, and local governments have made some efforts to limit business practices which result in pollution, and businesses have taken some voluntary steps, but more needs to be done if we are to enjoy a respectable environment. In large part, the need is for research to correct the harmful effects of pollution and find alternative ways to produce steam and to generate heat, to dispose of waste, to purify the air fouled by the automobile exhaust, and to control the "aftereffects" of detergents and pesticides. Both government and business are engaged in such efforts, and neither can hope to succeed alone.

By conforming to the prejudices that have limited the educational opportunities and the job opportunities available to Negroes (in many instances to the least-skilled and lowest-paid level) business has added to the causes that have fostered unrest. Business unresponsiveness to irresistible social change leads not to the maintenance of the status quo but to deep trouble for all, including business.

Businessmen have increasingly recognized their responsibility for coping with these problems. Their recognition reflects, in part, a conviction that unless businessmen voluntarily shoulder their responsibilities, government will impose regulations that will force them to do so.

Business, too, is humane

In addition to this clear-eyed recognition, business has shouldered some social problems simply because—no matter what its critics may say—"it, too, has a heart." The "human rights revolution," which has made urgent the search for solutions to problems of human needs, has been as apparent to businessmen as to other thoughtful citizens.

Poverty, slums, racial discrimination, unemployment, unequal educational opportunities, and inadequate health and welfare services are nothing new in this country's history. But our growing affluence has increased the gap between the needs of the least fortunate and the rest of our society. And improved communications have brought about greater awareness among those least fortunate and made their problems seem intolerable.

In many communities, businessmen have been at the helm of those institutions—the community chest, the "committee of one hundred," the churches, the civic clubs, or the Chamber of Commerce—that have striven to do something about these problems.[1] Some believe with Donald C. Burnham of Westinghouse

[1] The organization in 1967 of the Urban Coalition, in which business, labor, the churches, government, and the minority groups banded together to diagnose and to solve the ills of urban centers, constituted a recent illustration of an effort by business to aid in the solution of the most pressing social problems.

that a social problem such as the problem of America's jobless youth is "a national problem that belongs not just to government, nor to education, nor to charities." [2]

But an increasing number of businessmen candidly explain their assumption of costly and unprecedented social responsibilities in such terms as, "If we don't, there will be no society in which to pursue the profit of free enterprise."

A CENTRAL ISSUE

But can responsibility for the resolution of social problems be entrusted to enterprises that are simultaneously responsible for producing a profit for their owners?

Daniel J. Haughton, chairman of the board, Lockheed Aircraft Corporation, has said: "I know that industry sometimes gets criticized for trying to make a profit out of solving social problems. I confess I can't understand this attitude. Nobody objects to paying for automobiles, or television sets, or machine tools . . . these are things society wants. Now it wants something else—clear air and streams, preservation of natural resources, cleaning up the slums, renovating the cities, employing the hard-core, reducing poverty, and so on. Are these things worth paying for? I think they are. . . ." [3]

Other businessmen imply that business cannot stand by unaffected while these social problems remain unsolved and that businessmen must find a way of making a profit from their participation in the handling of these problems. A few businessmen avow, and a larger number follow, a different course. Essentially, they say, business enterprises are assisting, and must assist, with the solution of social problems—probably with little or no profit —even while satisfying the requirement that they earn *from other activities* an adequate return on their owners' investment. [4]

[2] In explaining to all employees why Westinghouse accepted a contract to run a Job Corps camp, Mr. Burnham cited Westinghouse's experience in training its own employees as the particular skill it brought to this project, indicated that the project would produce "a small profit," but emphasized business' obligation to help with national, social, and economic problems as a principal reason his corporation sought this contract with the government.

[3] Quoted by Hobart Rowen in an article entitled "Government Must Lead in Combating Social Ills," *Washington Post*, May 12, 1968.

[4] Arthur M. Louis, reporting on a survey of the opinions of 300 chief executives from among the 500 largest industrial corporations and the 50 largest

It has been argued that the mixture of social and profit-making objectives is untenable. Essentially, three points are made. The first is that solutions for most of or all these problems are simply not economic; i.e., the investment of sums to achieve these ends cannot be expected to yield an appropriate return in dollars. To that point of view Theodore Sorensen has countered that enlightened self-interest is not the only rationale for assumption of social responsibilities, that there are higher obligations and broader motivations than economic benefits that should and do guide the business enterprise.[5]

The second point is that most individuals who are oriented toward the making of a profit are incapable of thinking simultaneously in terms of social objectives. Irwin Miller had this in mind when he suggested that businessmen, like other powerful groups in history ("the Loyalists in early New England, the French aristocracy in the eighteenth century, feudal lords in the late Middle Ages, Southern slave owners in the nineteenth century, the Spanish monarchy in the twentieth century"), are incapable of distinguishing the welfare of the whole society from the particular state of affairs that is best for them.[6] The validity of his viewpoint is illustrated by the following example. When asked to aid in financing a science building at a women's college, an official whose corporation gives substantial sums for the support of higher education refused, explaining that his company did not employ women in technical and scientific positions. In short, this executive could answer this request for financial aid only in terms of the need and practice of the corporation by which he was employed. Yet obviously there are businessmen like Mr. Miller (e.g., leaders in the Urban Coalition, the Committee for Economic Development, and other businessmen's organizations) who are capable of thinking broadly of the interests of the society as a whole even while guiding the destinies of a private enterprise.

Spokesmen for business have contended that "corporate giving

banks, insurance companies, retailers, transportation companies, and utilities, writes (*Fortune,* September, 1969) that typical corporate leaders believe that "Business can and should do more about employing and training the hard-core unemployed, and about other social and environmental problems, such as supporting education and combating air and water pollution."

[5] *Saturday Review,* May 14, 1966, p. 24.

[6] "Business Has a War to Win," *Harvard Business Review,* March–April, 1969, pp. 4–10.

should not . . . be governed mainly by philanthropic principles but rather by the principles of prudent corporate management . . . gifts are justifiable mainly because there are good reasons for such expenditures in its pursuit of a company's business objectives. The business objectives of corporations must not, of course, be narrowly limited to profit maximization alone." [7] But, accepting that viewpoint, the question remains: Can businessmen, necessarily and desirably oriented toward the production of a profit for the owners of the business, be entrusted with responsibility for the resolution of social problems? The answer is, recent experience suggests, that they can—at least for some social problems. They can be expected to assume responsibility for those problems in which they can clearly see a relation to the objectives of their own enterprise.

The third point is that there are some activities which the American people do not want supplied at a profit (education and hospital care are the prime examples). Numerous "schools" that sprang up after World War II to educate or train returning soldiers who were entitled to GI educational benefits illustrated that when the school had to choose between making a profit and ensuring the caliber of the education provided, the GI often was shortchanged. The general disfavor in which "proprietary hospitals" are held by the health care industry offers another illustration. And there are those who hold that objective scientific research cannot be carried out under the aegis of profit-making enterprise and that the drugs some men and women must have if they are to live should not be made and sold for a profit.

This last point of view simply highlights the growth of a variety of human wants that are being satisfied outside the market economy. It does not preclude business participation in the satisfaction of such wants under nonbusiness direction.

BUSINESS AND THE QUALITY OF LIFE

Two facts have become increasingly clear. The first is that the social problems that plague this country require for their solution the ablest men and women the country has. The second is that

---

[7] Richard Eells, "A Philosophy for Corporate Giving," *The Conference Board Record*, January, 1968, p. 16. See also Alfred C. Neal, "A More Rational Basis for Nonprofit Activities," *ibid.*, pp. 5–7.

business possesses not only much of the human talent, but also the flow of income, the know-how, and the organizational capability required.[8] Existence, on the one hand, of unemployment, poor housing, discrimination, inadequate health care, pollution, and the insolvency of many cultural institutions and recognition, on the other hand, of the large resources business possesses poses the question: Can this country's business system be adapted to aid with these national problems? Can the genius of businessmen be focused on social objectives? Can profit-making enterprises be enlisted in the accomplishment of social functions which offer little or no prospect of profit?

Answers to these questions are being hammered out. Gradually, business has been assuming four levels of additional social responsibility, and experimenting with a fifth.

The well-being of its own employees

Almost imperceptibly over the decades since the Depression of the 1930s, business enterprise has assumed increasing responsibility for the well-being of its own employees. In part, this has been in response to the pressure of organized workers; in part, to increasing recognition throughout the society of the insecurity of the wageworker in an industrialized society; and in part, because of the convenience of the payroll as an instrument for achieving social objectives in a society in which most people are employed by others. Each broadening of business responsibility has meant, in effect, a transfer of responsibility from the individual and his family or from the government.

Much of this broadening of business' responsibility for the well-being of its employees has been brought about by legislation (establishing minimum wages, limiting hours of work, and introducing social security). Other aspects were the result of competitive pressures (e.g., the provision of hospitalization and health care insurance or the subsidization of employee cafeterias).

The signs indicate that business will assume still broader responsibility for its employees and their families. Unemployment in the urban ghettos and their general deterioration suggest that

---

[8] J. Wilson Newman, chairman, finance committee, Dun & Bradstreet, Inc., has made more specific "the know-how, and the organizational capability" business can contribute. He suggests, in a paper entitled "Relevant Values in A Changing Society" (privately circulated), that businessmen can "supply realism needed for balance . . . supply incentive techniques for motivation . . . supply decisiveness for action."

business may assume responsibility for transporting workers to places of employment, particularly when plants are moved out of slums to the suburbs. The leveling up of skill requirements, the displacement of workers as a consequence of automation, and the necessity for many or most workers to acquire new skills after a lifetime of work suggest that employers may assume responsibility not only for training and retraining for jobs in their plants but also for educating and training workers for subsequent careers with other employers.[9] Increasing concern with the need of lower-income workers for the assurance of medical care whenever required forecasts that *all* employers may be expected to provide for the health care of their employees.[10]

Corporate philanthropy

Business enterprises have gradually come to be expected, in similar fashion, to contribute to the quality of life in the communities in which they are located. This was reflected in the contribution policies of many enterprises three or four decades ago; they accepted, as did other citizens of the community, a share of the responsibility for supporting the community chest, the Boy Scouts, the local hospitals, and other agencies.

Prior to World War II corporate contributions for charitable, educational, health, welfare, and similar purposes averaged less than one-half of 1 percent of net income before taxes. After World War II corporate giving was broadened in purpose and increased in amount (although it remained stationary at slightly above 1 percent of net income before taxes). And whereas corporate giving had been made in largest part for welfare purposes, much of the increased giving since World War II has been for education, community health services, the easing of racial tensions (including the provision of capital for enterprises owned by Negroes and other minorities) and for cultural activities such as community orchestras, theaters, and museums.[11]

[9] See, for extension of this viewpoint, Howard C. Harder, "The Corporation: An Educational Institution," in Peter Drucker (ed.), *Preparing Tomorrow's Business Leaders Today* (Englewood Cliffs, N.J.: Prentice-Hall, Inc., 1969), pp. 95–102.

[10] Governor Nelson A. Rockefeller of New York proposed in late 1968 that federal and state legislation be enacted requiring employers to assume responsibility for hospital-centered health care benefits for employees.

[11] That the concept of corporate giving is not yet accepted by all corporate stockholders is indicated by the introduction of resolutions by stockholders of the Ford Motor Company (annual meeting, Apr. 4, 1969) to limit, and by

Maintaining socially desirable policies

During the 1960s business enterprises have been pressed to adopt policies nearer to the cutting edge of social advance. One of the first of such policies had to do with nondiscriminatory hiring and advancement of Negroes. When this policy was first advanced, in the 1930s, several corporations held that they could not adopt a policy in conflict with the mores and practices of a community in which a plant was located; three decades later it is clear that all business enterprises are expected to apply such a policy regardless of local prejudices, and that by doing so they can actually exert beneficial influence.

Secondly, business enterprise has gradually come to be expected to assume an increased responsibility for assuring that its actions will not endanger either its neighbors or its customers. The nationwide expectation that business enterprises shall not pollute the environment points up this responsibility, as does the automobile manufacturers' concern with the safety of automobile users and the limitation of gasoline exhaust emissions. The experience of the cigarette manufacturers, along with the actions of newspaper publishers and television and radio station operators in refusing to accept cigarette advertising, affords still another illustration.

A third policy, less widely adopted by business enterprises as yet, has to do with the lending of their weight to the establishment of equal opportunity housing in the communities in which their plants are located. The International Business Machines Corporation set a notable example when it established new plants in Lexington, Kentucky, and Manassas, Virginia. IBM informed local real estate offices and banks, through which it was assisting hundreds of employees to locate in these communities, that it would deal with no local enterprise that did not assist in providing access to available homes to employees without regard to color. IBM is credited with having exercised a major influence on the establishment of nondiscriminatory housing policies in these Southern communities.

stockholders of the E. I. du Pont de Nemours and Company (annual meeting, Apr. 14, 1969) to prohibit, contributions for charitable, educational, and similar purposes. Both proposals were defeated. Reintroduced at the Ford Motor Company Annual Meeting the following year (May 14, 1970), the resolution was defeated again.

Focusing creativity on social problems

The creative development, promotion, and distribution of new products and new services may fairly be regarded as the principal contribution of business to social advance throughout the history of this country. Usually, however, most businessmen have treated the problems of hospital operation, the improvement of primary and secondary education, the housing of low-income families, or the improvement of intraurban transportation as beyond their ken, areas of unlikely profit, or governmental concern. Particularly, they have avoided the application of their creative capabilities to the analysis of the core activities involved in each of these problems—the betterment of patient care in the hospital; the improvement of teaching in the schools; or the appraisal of the family size, shelter, needs, and incomes of poor families.

Of late, an increasing number of illustrations can be cited showing that business is willing to focus its creative abilities on these fields. The Westinghouse Electric Corporation devoted a page in its 1968 Annual Report to the opportunities for profit in "Attacking Public Problems." It cited its explorations of the housing, transportation, education, and health care fields. TRW Inc. has advertised its efforts to apply the capabilities of systems analysis developed in the aerospace industry to problems of hospital operation, urban redevelopment, crime prevention, and mass transportation. The International Paper Company has devoted its creative capabilities to the medical care field and to the use of paper products in hospital operations (everything from nurses' uniforms to sheets and pillow cases). The IBM Corporation and the General Learning Corporation (owned jointly by the General Electric Company and Time, Inc.) have focused the attention of their staffs on the learning and teaching processes, with the prospect of significant contributions to the schools.

Experimenting with new nonprofit responsibilities

Each of the foregoing levels of responsibility for the quality of life is within traditional concepts of the role of business enterprise and assumes that business can accept each responsibility and continue to operate at a profit. But in the late 1960s frequent suggestions were made that business should undertake a variety of relatively new activities in which the prospect of any profit (or at least the normally expected level) was not foreseeable.

The most frequently suggested and most generally accepted activity is that of seeking out and employing individuals who by all conventional standards possess neither the skill and work habits nor, in some instances, a reputation for integrity.

The National Alliance of Businessmen, organized in 1967 in response to a request from the President of the United States, obtained during the years 1968–1969 pledges from business leaders in 125 cities to employ unemployed and minimally qualified persons from the ghettos of these cities (see Chapter 10, page 226). The National Association of Manufacturers and the U.S. Chamber of Commerce organized separate programs to assist businessmen in the training of unemployed workers who did not meet prevailing employment standards and in organizing their communities to cope with unemployment and other problems. The automobile manufacturers set a notable example by recruiting from the ghetto areas of Detroit workers who would previously have been deemed unqualified and by establishing training programs to equip them to hold jobs. Other business firms established plants in slum areas to provide jobs. Aerojet-General, for example, established a tent-making plant in the riot-torn Watts district of Los Angeles; Westinghouse established a new plant in a slum area of Pittsburgh; Avco established a printing plant in the Roxbury area of Boston; and Fairchild Hiller aided the establishment of a plant in Washington, D.C., to make pallets, ammunition boxes, and other items.

Employment of the hard-core unemployed involves unusual risks and large additional costs for training these workers in order to raise them from a submarginal to a productive level. In some instances it involves providing employment for which there is no substantial economic need. In those instances in which corporations established plants to provide employment in the ghettos, there was little or no prospect of earning a return comparable to that expected on capital invested in other plants; indeed, in most instances it was contemplated that ownership of the plant would eventually be turned over to local black owners.

Some business firms have invested time and funds in efforts to overcome the critical shortage of housing for low-income families in a number of cities. The life insurance companies, as a group, pledged $1 billion for loans for the construction of housing and for the establishment of new businesses in the urban slums. In other instances, with the aid of governmental underwriting, private builders and some employers not engaged in the housing industry have put capital, time, and effort into the provision of needed housing with little or no prospect of earning a profit. A third activity in which a number of firms have engaged has been the support of "Black Capitalism." Industrial firms (Xerox in Rochester) and banks (several banks collaborating in New York City) have aided Negroes to establish their own businesses, usually in the ghetto areas. In Chicago, Swift and Company helped Negroes establish ice cream parlors. Safeway helped Negroes establish cooperative supermarkets in several cities. The John Hancock Insurance Company has made available lawyers, accountants, and other specialists to black entrepreneurs.

Still other business firms have helped improve the school in slum areas. Kaiser Industries worked with teachers and parents in a depressed neighborhood in Oakland to develop a work-study program. Michigan Bell Telephone Company and Chrysler adopted ghetto high schools in Detroit. General Electric developed for two Cincinnati high schools a new curriculum for training electrical appliance repairmen and promised jobs to those who completed the course.[12]

A review of 67 annual reports of major corporations (a majority with sales in excess of $500 million) revealed specific claims in 47 cases. Most often the corporation reported that it was employing and training minority group members; this was usually coupled with a statement that the corporation was actively participating in the program of the National Alliance of Businessmen. Reports of the utilities and the steel companies described efforts to overcome environmental pollution. Other reports described corporate efforts to improve housing, to aid in bettering the public schools, or generally to aid with "urban affairs." [13]

[12] Numerous additional examples could be cited. See Thomas J. Diviney, "Survey on Corporate Urban Programs," *Report of the National Conference on Corporate Urban Programs,* National Industrial Conference Board, Jan. 10, 1968.

[13] Edward B. Hinman, president, International Paper Company, after describing a number of activities his company was carrying on to meet "its social obligations as a corporate citizen," told his corporation's stockholders attending its 1969 annual meeting: "I hope I have indicated to you that we are fully aware of our social responsibilities and are working effectively to meet them." This is an explicit acceptance of new responsibilities and a reflection of the fact that the company's stockholders expect the enterprise to meet these responsibilities.

The costs and why they are accepted

The undertaking of such activities—with little or no prospect of profit—even while morally commendable, runs headlong into the hard fact that business enterprises exist to make a profit. The cost of these several activities varies markedly. It is likely that the nonprofit responsibilities with which business has recently been experimenting cost no more than corporate contributions for tax exempt purposes, that is, about 1 percent of net income before taxes. The maintenance of socially desirable policies may add no identifiable costs. The better provision for the corporations' own employees (depending upon the labor intensiveness of the industry) and for the elimination of pollution may add very substantial costs. The focusing of creativity on social problems may yield, in the long run, substantial profit.

Conventional economic theory (even if thread-worn) holds that the economy consists of numerous owner-operated, one-product firms, competing with one another for the trade of reasonably well-informed customers and for short-run profits. That set of circumstances bears little resemblance to the real economy of the late twentieth century in which many large, manager- (not owner-) operated, multiproduct corporations, which are able to influence both demand and supply to a greater degree than was earlier recognized, compete for growth in volume and in net worth and for *long-run* satisfactory profits. Such firms—or an increasing number of them—undertake some nonprofit activities in the belief that, in the long run, these redound to the benefit of the corporation. The benefits they foresee include a more favorable image in the minds of consumers, more amicable employee relations, and the possible discovery of opportunities for profit making. Hence, the prospect is good that business will continue to bear these responsibilities and that government will succeed in forcing the acceptance of the more costly responsibilities—the increasingly generous provision for employees and the elimination of "external" effects of business operation, such as pollution.

AN EVOLVING STRUCTURE

It has been customary for businessmen to assume that a transfer of responsibilities was occurring but that government was assuming the additional responsibilities through intervening in the business realm or by regulating business operations. "We are headed toward socialism," has been a frequently heard plaint at trade association conventions. Yet that cry neither describes what government has been doing to promote economic growth, to minimize unemployment, and to maintain economic stability, nor suggests what business has been doing in collaboration with government in such diverse fields as education, health, insurance, transportation, housing, or consumer protection. Nor does this oft-heard cry contribute to straight thinking; more reasoned judgments are required.

Clearly, business has been moving in a different direction.[14] Some business firms, as the examples cited in previous pages demonstrate, have assumed greater responsibility for the well-being of their employees; for the enforcement of advanced social policies; and for the development of needed new products and services to facilitate the performance of public functions in the fields of education, health, housing, and transportation. The evidence strongly suggests that it is only a portion of the larger business firms—and particularly those that have more influence over the prices they charge—that have accepted such responsibilities.

It is clear that as human wants continue to expand in the era of a more humane society, the mechanisms that have been markedly expanded during the post-World War II decades will be used in fuller measure to utilize the capabilities of business, a variety of hybrid government-business agencies, the universities, and other nonprofit institutions in carrying out public functions. We are witnessing the evolution of the mixed economy. That evolution will be expedited by three structural developments

---

[14] A 1968 survey of 1,033 companies (conducted by the National Industrial Conference Board) showed that 76 percent had "recognizable public affairs programs." The function of the public affairs executive, as described by an industrial machinery manufacturer, was "to make management aware of the fact, direction and consequence of sociological change and to develop concepts and programs so the corporation will be able to manage this change." (*The Record,* March, 1969.)

In order to "improve and increase corporate performance in relation to social goals," the Committee for Economic Development's Lawrence Kegan, then Director of Special Studies, proposed in 1969 the establishment of a separate division of public business in corporations "where the size of the public business involved is large enough."

that are contributing to the efficiency with which this nation's human and organizational resources are put to work on the society's problems:

The expanding role and responsibility of the federal government

During the postwar decades the federal government has assumed an ever-increasing responsibility for the rendering of services to citizens—directly or via the provision of financial aid and "supervision" to state and local governments. The construction of roads, the operation of schools and colleges, the provision of public health services, the construction of housing, and the assurance of income security are the principal areas of expanded effort. In addition, and importantly, the federal government has gradually assumed a larger responsibility for managing the American economy—a responsibility formerly (and still in major part) left largely to the "unseen hand" working through the marketplace.

Especially during the 1960s, government has made much progress toward the more sophisticated use of fiscal policy in managing the national economy. Simultaneously, government's use of monetary policy has evolved from an astigmatic focus on interest rates and credit conditions to comprehend an increasing concern with the quantity of money and the rate at which this supply is growing.[15] Particularly, this decade has seen marked advance in the economic understanding of the American people and their political leaders. It has also seen the rise of a popular demand that government see to it that the economy function better to serve the individual. Accordingly, government has refined and greatly extended its regulatory processes to protect the worker, the traveler, the shopper, the consumer, and others. It has developed a system of inducements—which we have dubbed the

[15] Arthur M. Okun in *The Political Economy of Prosperity* (Washington, D.C.: The Brookings Institution, 1970) envisions continual governmental effort to promote a balance between overall supply and demand without inflation and without monetary restraint, by use of the presidential budget focused on the full employment surplus and coupled with a "flight plan" developed by the Federal Reserve Board in the light of the President's fiscal program, spelling out in quantitative terms "the path of money, bank credit and other liquid assets, and the course of interest rates and credit conditions" it will strive to achieve through its guidance of monetary factors. See also Otto Eckstein, "The Economics of the 60's," *The Public Interest*, Spring, 1970, pp. 86–97.

grants economy—to involve business and nonprofit enterprise in the achievement of a variety of social goals—e.g., the reduction of unemployment, the improvement of housing, the betterment of the schools, and the provision of health care.

It is not likely that the issue for the future will be the threadworn one of "socialism" or "getting the government out of business." Rather, the debates between business leaders and government officials will focus on methods of regulating the quality and prices of products and services, on attitudes toward competition, on ways of inducing business action (e.g., by contract, grant, or tax incentive), on the rate and purpose of capital investment, and on proper rates of return on capital invested.[16]

Yet the ability of any national administration to utilize the more sophisticated tools at its command—fiscal, monetary, regulatory, and grants—is still markedly handicapped by the creaking character of our political machinery. Effective fiscal and monetary actions in response to the ebb and flow of demand are delayed or prevented by the frequent inability of the Congress to act promptly, by its unwillingness to delegate to the President the authority to make changes in tax rates (subject to early review by the Congress), and by the occasionally counterbalancing effects of expenditure and tax actions by state and local governments. Despite its imperfections, government has evolved a substantially advanced system for influencing the course of the economy, a system that substitutes a substantial measure of governmental direction for automatic direction by the market.

Government will increasingly function as both the "market creator" and the "system manager" of a very extensive system comprehending most of or all this country's business enterprises, its nongovernmental, nonprofit agencies as well as the state and local governments.[17] It creates markets indirectly through monetary and fiscal policies, and directly through subsidies and still other devices (such as rent supplements and Medicare payments).

[16] Eric Roll, *The World after Keynes* (New York: Frederick A. Praeger, Inc., 1968), p. 48.

[17] This development is materializing even while there is much talk of the decentralization of authority to state, local, and neighborhood public agencies and the sharing of revenue from the federal income tax with state and local governments. The collapse of space and the concentration of talent in the federal government promises that the increased authority and income made available to other levels of government will be exercised within a system in which the federal government functions as manager.

It directs the total or partial energies of the units of this national system to the satisfaction of an expanding variety of human wants that cannot or have not been met through the market economy.

The expanding role of mixed and nonprofit enterprises in performing public functions

An assortment of mixed public-private enterprises have been established in space communication (Comsat), air transport (the financing of the supersonic transport SST), export trade ("overseas private investment corporation" proposed by President Nixon in May, 1969), the collaborative regulation of food manufacture by private food manufacturers and the Food and Drug Administration, health insurance (handling of Medicare claims by the Blue Cross), and housing (Federal National Mortgage Association).

Nongovernmental, nonprofit agencies have demonstrated that in terms of talent and motivation they are better equipped than the profit-making business enterprise for an expanding variety of activities. These agencies—the universities, the hospitals, the research institutions, and a broad assortment of others—have embraced the opportunities afforded them to expand and alter their functions in order to assist with the performance of public functions. The need for their capabilities in carrying on activities for which business is less qualified (or unqualified), or for which government is unequipped, assures their growth and even greater utilization.

Strengthening, despite resistance, of the voices of once submerged minority groups

The revolution of the 1960s is a revolution against the cynicism of the politically impotent masses in the cities and on the campuses, against the control of ideas by the few who direct the media of communications, against the power exerted single-mindedly by selfish lobbyists, and against the deference accorded to some who contribute little or nothing at all to the goals of the Humane Society but who are the holders of corporate economic power.

The revolution of the 1960s has revealed a widespread demand that in many institutions—corporations, universities, public school systems, hospitals, local poverty agencies, the Catholic

Church, and even the U.S. Army—the individuals that depend on them have a greater voice in their guidance. Simultaneously, scientific advance and increasing specialization have endowed the specialist with substantial power to influence the policies not only of the institution of which he is a part but of the society itself. These developments constitute a substantial constraint on the exercise by the federal government of its expanded authority and a powerful force in shifting the locus of power within the American political economy.

SHIFTS OF POWER

The power to effect social change is, as Bertrand Russell has pointed out, fundamental to an understanding of human affairs in the same sense in which energy is the fundamental concept of physics.[18] The locus of that power has shifted as we have come to recognize as a people that our lives are not determined by inexorable natural laws, that they need not be determined by either concentrated economic power or concentrated political power, and that they can be determined by the values we believe in and aspire to.

Fifteen years ago, C. Wright Mills provoked controversy by attributing to the "corporate rich, the political directorate and the military" the power to effect social change.[19] Some criticized Mills' view on the grounds that a social upper class of business owners and corporate managers dominates the significant decisions made by the "political directorate" and the "military." Other critics found fault with Mills' reasoning on the grounds that the groups he had singled out were not so interrelated as to constitute a concentration of power. They contended that labor, farmers, small businessmen, and various professional groups (e.g., physicians) hold significant power and can and do prevent *ex cathedra* decisions.[20]

[18] *Power: A New Social Analysis* (New York: W.W. Norton, 1938), p. 12.

[19] *The Power Elite* (Oxford University Press, 1956).

[20] The controversy as to who has the power to effect or deter social change continues. Several writers, following Mills' lead, concluded that there is a national upper class of rich businessmen and their descendants whose members control corporations, foundations, the largest of the mass media, major opinion-forming associations, and—through campaign financing and their presence in key cabinet and advisory positions—the executive branch of the federal government. See, for example, E. D. Baltzell, *Philadelphia Gentle-*

Throughout the era of the Industrial Society business claimed, and had, great power to foster or to deter social change. It still has that power today, since corporate decisions on the specific ways of injecting capital into the national economy have far-reaching—often determining—effects on the final social direction. But business' power is considerably lessened by the fact that its control of capital application—once the exclusive domain of business—is now exercised jointly by corporations and government in many areas. As the role and authority of the federal government has grown, the power of business has diminished. Business has never been able to exercise as great an influence over the federal government as over state and local governments, except for its relations with the purchasing officers and the regulatory agencies where no competing groups (e.g., labor or the blacks) contend for power.

With the growth of government, the mixed enterprises, and the nonprofit institutions, the relative ability of business to influence social change by virtue of its control over the flow of income and the provision of employment has diminished. Business still controls the bulk of the national income, but a very large proportion of that flow of income is inflexibly committed to the ongoing requirements of these enterprises—the payroll, the inventory, capital expansion, and the return to owners. Most of business' increasing contributions for charitable, educational, and related purposes go to support traditional institutions and activities; only a minor fraction can be utilized to effect social change. Much of the income that business devotes to the influencing of elections is counterbalanced by the substantial resources of labor and the strident voices of the blacks and the poor. Business still provides the bulk of all jobs; but the location, the continuity, and the character of an increasing proportion of

men (New York: The Free Press, 1958) and *The Protestant Establishment: Aristocracy and Caste in America* (New York: Random House, Inc., 1964); G. Wm. Domhoff, *Who Rules America?* (Englewood Cliffs, N.J.: Prentice-Hall, Inc., 1967); J. Monsen and M. Cannon, *The Makers of Public Policy: American Power Groups and Their Ideology* (New York: McGraw-Hill Book Company, 1965). For more recent views on the locus of power in the American society, see Grant McConnell, *Private Power and American Democracy* (New York: Alfred A. Knopf, Inc., 1966); Theodore J. Lowi, *The End of Liberalism* (New York: W. W. Norton & Company, Inc., 1969); Arnold M. Rose, *The Power Structure* (Oxford University Press, 1967); and particularly A. A. Berle, *Power* (New York: Harcourt, Brace & World, Inc., 1969).

those jobs are dependent upon contracts for defense, space exploration, and other public purposes. During the 1960s a major proportion of all additional jobs came into being in government and in the nonprofit health and education agencies while the total employment in all manufacturing enterprises remained substantially static.[21] Business still is the prime creator of wealth and of economic growth, even though that function is increasingly underwritten and guided by government. But as the wants of the society for new knowledge and for schools, health centers, housing, day-care centers, better urban transportation, and the like have markedly expanded, and as these wants have been satisfied by a growing government, the leadership role of business has diminished.

A still more fundamental cause of the decline of business' power and influence is found in Adolf Berle's third law of power: power, he contends, "is invariably based on a system of ideas or philosophy." [22] As long as this country was guided by the ideas or philosophy that prevailed while this country was building its industrial strength, business' influence was large or dominant. But that set of ideas has gradually been replaced by a philosophy that attaches higher value to social and environmental goals than to the growth and profitability of a business enterprise. Business is not generally identified with these social and environmental goals; rather, it is often interpreted as opposing them. The public reaction is suggested by the tendency of an increasing—even if indeterminate—proportion of college graduates to avoid employment in large corporate enterprise; by the current movements, led by the President of the United States, popularly branded as "consumerism" and "environmentalism"; and by suspicion sometimes voiced by representatives of labor, minority groups, and spokesmen for government that businessmen have participated in social programs either to slow them down or destroy them, or else to exact an undue profit.

Business' loss of power has unfortunate social consequences. Many of the men possessing driving energy have been attracted to business careers by the relatively large rewards available for those who succeed there. The shift in the locus of power away from business leadership has meant that a regrettably large num-

[21] U.S. Department of Labor, *Statistics of Manpower, A Supplement to the Manpower Report of the President,* March, 1969, p. 49.

[22] A. A. Berle, *op. cit.,* p. 37.

ber of men with good minds and great energy are unavailable for the resolution of the primary problems of contemporary society. Those minds are designing advertising or packages for detergents rather than drafting plans for relief of racial tensions. It has meant also that the ablest and broadest-gauged leaders of American business have been increasingly frustrated.

The lesson to be learned from this shift of power has been described as the Iron Law of Responsibility, i.e., "Those who do not take responsibility for their power, ultimately shall lose it." [23] If society is to have the benefit of the large reservoir of human intelligence that is found in the business system, if business leaders are to have a part in the reshaping of the political economy that is taking place, and if business leadership is to have the self-fulfilling satisfaction of contributing to the resolution of this country's social ills, businessmen must free themselves of outmoded ideological dogmas.

Businessmen, generally, must recognize and better understand the social and technological change that is taking place. There are business leaders who see and understand this change and its implications for the American business system quite clearly; the need is for greatly expanding their number. Unless more—many more—businessmen can come to understand the ongoing change, they cannot influence the evolution of the more Humane Society which must come—and is coming.

Businessmen, generally, must recognize the nature and the logic of the evolving partnership with government that is integral to the emerging Humane Society. More businessmen need to recognize that the function of the politico-economy of which they are a part has never been the mere satisfaction of material wants. They need to recognize the broader goals of the society and the broader responsibilities business enterprise is expected to bear, and they must appreciate the new opportunities for service and for profit that are built into this new partnership.

Businessmen, if they are to have an influence equal to that of other segments of the society—labor, racial minorities, and the scientific community—must find ways of formulating and advancing views that reflect a real awareness of social needs and the contribution that business can and is prepared to make.[24] Business

[23] Keith Davis, "Understanding the Social Responsibility Puzzle," *Business Horizons,* Winter, 1967.

[24] J. T. Hackett (vice president—finance, Cummins Engine Company) presented a confirming view in "Corporate Citizenship, The Resolution of a Di-

influence has been limited by the simple fact that such representatives of the business point of view as the U.S. Chamber of Commerce, the National Association of Manufacturers, the Committee for Economic Development, the National Federation of Independent Businessmen, and scores of others have voiced a chorus of views reflecting different ideologies. Differences will and should persist. But if businessmen generally see and understand the change that envelops them and the logic of the business-government partnership, their differences will be reduced and their influence in shaping the politico-economy that serves this society will be the greater.

The advent of the Humane Society holds greatest promise in those very areas that have been traditionally regarded as the exclusive responsibility of government and which are now clearly identified as a joint responsibility of the economic and the political forces within the country. By creating the institutional framework capable of transforming ancient foes—business and government—into partners, we have already moved toward tackling the problems of housing, education, health care, and poverty. By perfecting this framework, we can make them allies in the great endeavor of solving the ills that plague us. This is a heady prospect.

lemma," *Business Horizons,* Oct., 1969, pp. 69–74, when he wrote:

"Our society is changing rapidly, there are demands for a more equitable distribution of the nation's wealth, there is insistence on more attention to the quality of life in our country, there is a demand that the individual be given equal status with the institution, and there is a widespread movement to re-evaluate the purposes and objectives of our society.

"The corporation must participate, it must examine its objectives and purposes, it must raise fundamental questions about its function and role in society, and it must respond to new and varied demands. Otherwise, once again, society will create new legislation and new regulatory authorities, and force compliance, as it did in the 1930's and once again business executives will deny themselves the opportunity to help shape the role of the corporation to meet the needs for which it was created."

Index

Ackley, Gardner, 197, 257
Aerojet-General Corp., 290
Aerospace Corp., 108 *n.*, 137, 140, 145
Aerospace industry, 60, 64, 117
  expenditures, table, 75
Aerospace Research Application Center (ARAC), 103 *n.*
Affluence (*see* Wealth)
AFL–CIO, 7, 209 *n.*, 211
African American Institute, 83, 139
Agency for International Development (AID), 54–56, 78, 137, 138
Agriculture:
  aid to, 19, 193, 242
  and science, 102–103, 114, 119
Agriculture, Department of (USDA), 58, 114, 119
AID (*see* Agency for International Development)
Air Force, 86 *n.*, 117, 144 *n.*, 145
Air pollution (*see* Pollution)
Aliber, Robert Z., 208 *n.*
Allied Chemical Corp., 55 *n.*
American Bankers Association, 225 *n.*
American Civil Liberties Union, 15–16
American Field Service, 138
American Institute for Free Labor Development, 139
American Institute of Planners, 137
American Medical Association, 7, 11 *n.*, 265
American Psychological Association, 91 *n.*, 138
American Stock Exchange, 144, 166

American Telephone and Telegraph Co. (AT&T), 160 *n.*, 188
Analytic Services, Inc., 137
Ando, Albert, 252 *n.*
Antitrust policies, 129, 158, 183–186
Apollo program, 80, 82, 87 *n.*
Appleby, Paul H., 33
Applied Physics Laboratory, 136
Area Redevelopment Administration (ARA), 225
Argonne National Laboratory, 137
Armed Services Procurement Regulation (ASPR), 85 *n.*, 88 *n.*, 94
Arts, 273–274, 276
  economy of, 274
Associated Universities, Inc., 136, 140
Atomic Energy Commission (AEC), 59, 77, 89, 99, 101, 103, 105 *n.*, 119, 159, 161, 162
Automation, 213, 220, 232, 268, 281, 287
Automobile industry:
  competition, 170, 172, 173
  mass transit and, 52, 265 *n.*
  pollution, 123, 176
  regulation, 170, 172 *n.*, 173
  safety, 170, 171
  (*See also* Highway safety; Standards)
Automobile Manufacturers Association, 172
Automotive Service Industry Association, 238 *n.*
AVCO Corp., 83 *n.*, 290
Aviation industry:
  regulation, 158